A Fresh Look at Formative Assessment

in Mathematics Teaching

Edited by Edward A. Silver
and Valerie L. Mills

NCTM® | NATIONAL COUNCIL OF
TEACHERS OF MATHEMATICS

Library of Congress Cataloging-in-Publication Data

Names: Silver, Edward A., 1948—editor. | Mills, Valerie L., editor.
Title: A fresh look at formative assessment in mathematics teaching / edited by Edward A. Silver,
    Valerie L. Mills.
Description: Reston : The National Council of Teachers of Mathematics, Inc., [2018] | Includes
    bibliographical references.
Identifiers: LCCN 2018001692 (print) | LCCN 2018007254 (ebook) | ISBN 9781680540192 (ebook) |
    ISBN 9781680540185 (pbk.)
Subjects: LCSH: Mathematics teachers—Training of. | Mathematics—Study and teaching—
    Evaluation. | Educational evaluation.
Classification: LCC QA10.5 (ebook) | LCC QA10.5 .F74 2018 (print) | DDC 510.71/2—dc23
LC record available at https://lccn.loc.gov/2018001692

The National Council of Teachers of Mathematics supports and advocates for the
highest-quality mathematics teaching and learning for each and every student.

Printed in the United States of America

Contents

Foreword

This is an important book and represents a milestone in our understanding of effective formative assessment. Different disciplines have each developed their own unique modes of understanding involving actions, tools, specialized vocabulary and genres, and representations of knowledge. As a result, formative assessment will look different in its implementation depending on the discipline. What this book does is squarely place formative assessment within the discipline of mathematics in ways that are completely accessible to practitioners and those whose work is to support them. It clearly illustrates the importance of discipline-specific formative assessment and takes us from a generic set of "techniques"—often implemented in superficial ways—to a robust vision of formative assessment grounded in deep disciplinary knowledge. After reading the book no one will be in any doubt about the role of formative assessment in effective mathematics teaching and learning, what it looks like in practice, and how teachers can be assisted to develop knowledge and skills needed for successful implementation.

The book explores formative assessment through several extant research-based mathematical frameworks: classroom discussion and discourse; cognitively guided instruction; culturally relevant pedagogy; learning progressions; mathematical tasks framework; and response to intervention. The common thread among the chapters is that the purpose of formative assessment is to inform learning, not to measure it or sum it up; it is assessment that focuses on learning as it is taking place, not at the end of a sequence of learning; and is intended to move learning forward from its current status. The frameworks offer valuable insights into how formative assessment can occur as an organic part of ongoing, everyday classroom activity, not as external adjunct to teaching and learning.

Each of the frameworks represents how evidence of learning can be elicited so that teachers can make decisions about how to advance that learning from its current status, the hallmark of formative assessment. Significant in the treatment of eliciting and interpreting evidence is the idea of formative assessment as the means to recognize students' initial, emerging, or partial mathematical understandings during the course of their learning. Formative assessment is too often understood (or rather, misunderstood) as a means to determine if students "got" or "didn't get it" and, in the case of the latter, the pedagogical response is to "reteach." If we are to be concerned about the mathematical learning of each student, we cannot resort to "reteaching." Instead, students need to be supported to take next steps in learning through pedagogical action that is matched to the edge of their current understanding, so they can progress to a more developed or more sophisticated understanding. And it is the job of formative assessment to help teachers understand the edge of learning, wherever it may be, of individual students. When teachers think of formative assessment as "got it, didn't get it, reteach" they are attempting to fit a square peg into a round hole, losing much, if not all, of the power of formative assessment for student learning.

Teachers' capacity to act on evidence to advance learning toward desired goals is crucially dependent on their disciplinary knowledge. It is this knowledge that informs their interpretive skills in the classroom. This combination of knowledge and skill is supported in each of the frameworks, putting students' mathematical thinking at teachers' finger tips. While many books tell teachers that they should be doing this, and they should be doing that, this book's unique contribution to our understanding of discipline-based formative assessment is that it provides concrete and vibrant examples of students' mathematical thinking, interpretive commentary, and suggestions for next steps in learning based on evidence. If educators were not already convinced about the importance of disciplinary knowledge to formative assessment, after reading this book they surely will be!

Effective formative assessment requires teachers to have the skills to access information about student learning, orchestrate a variety of complex judgments in the course of a lesson, often in real-time, and take appropriate and immediate actions in response to evidence. When teachers have these high-level skills, formative assessment becomes seamless in teaching and learning. While it may look seamless in the hands of a skilled practitioner, the execution of formative assessment demands flexible planning so that teachers can respond to individual students' thinking, as well as the inclusion of strategies to ensure that students understand the goals they are pursuing and the criteria that will be applied in assessing their learning. Once again, this planning, as the examples in the book make clear, requires disciplinary knowledge of students' thinking.

The book does not leave us in the lurch about how teachers, both in preservice and in-service contexts, can be supported to acquire the knowledge and skills necessary to be effective. Suggestions range from collaborative groups to analyze students' work or to design effective tasks as both learning events and opportunities for formative assessment, to design of similar tasks that are culturally responsive, to video analysis of practice, to lesson planning, implementation and reflection. Crucially, these approaches recognize that there is no single way to become skilled formative assessment practitioners, and that initial and continuing professional learning are the keys to success.

The concluding chapter in the book raises a very important issue with respect to formative assessment: the student role in the process. Successfully engaging students in formative assessment is an indication of higher levels of expertise. Teachers who are expert practitioners in formative assessment share the responsibility for moving learning forward with their students; learning is recognized as a social process and becomes a joint responsibility. While the book is not silent how students can be involved, this is an area that merits more exploration. It seems that there will need to be further contributions in a second edition of this landmark book that explore in more detail the active role that students can take in support of their own learning.

This is a very welcome book that can serve as a model for other disciplines. If they can emulate its achievements, this will be a still more welcome outcome.

Margaret Heritage

Preface

This book is specifically designed for educators who wish to improve mathematics teaching and learning. In particular, it is designed to provide mathematics teacher educators and professional development specialists with examples of where and how formative assessment can be integrated into a variety of professional learning efforts on a range of topics (e.g., classroom discourse, Cognitively Guided Instruction, etc.) to support its effective use as a critical component of daily instructional decision-making. The book will be a resource for those who facilitate efforts to promote high quality mathematics teaching by suggesting the value of a regular focus on the set of teaching practices associated with formative assessment. The chapters in this volume illustrate how formative assessment is deeply connected to many other instructional frameworks, tools, and approaches with which mathematics teachers and teacher educators are familiar, such as Cognitively Guided Instruction (CGI) and the Mathematical Tasks Framework.

This book emerged from an initiative of the National Council of the Supervisors of Mathematics (NCSM) and the Association of Mathematics Teacher Educators (AMTE) that was launched in 2013 to promote an intentional and systematic approach to implementing formative assessment in U.S. mathematics classrooms. Toward this goal a joint task force was appointed whose first activity was the development of a formative assessment position paper that was adopted by both organizations.

With support from the National Science Foundation in the form of a grant to the University of Michigan, we developed a national survey and then in October 2014, held a working meeting to explore possible connections between formative assessment and popular research-based instructional frameworks, tools, and approaches. If connections could be identified, we wondered if and how the role of formative assessment might be made an explicit focus of study in teacher education or professional development when one of these popular instructional frameworks, tools, or approaches is being addressed. Working meeting invitations were sent to experienced users of five different instructional frameworks, tools, or approaches (FTAs) widely used in mathematics teacher education and/or professional development: Cognitively Guided Instruction, Classroom Discussion/Discourse Tools, Culturally Responsive Pedagogy, the Mathematical Tasks Framework, and Response to Intervention. Meeting participants were ask to consider closely key features of the formative assessment process and the strategies that support the formative assessment process as described in the joint NCSM/AMTE position paper in relationship to the framework, tool, or approach for which they had particular expertise. For example, we asked participants to identify important opportunities to collect evidence of student thinking that are highlighted within their FTA. We also ask them to consider the ways in which formative assessment strategies might be linked to their FTA or if there were notable disconnections.

As the meeting progressed and it became clear that our experts were identifying strong connections, we then asked them to consider the opportunities and challenges that might be associated with integrating attention to an FTA and formative assessment rather than treating each separately.

From both the conversations held at this meeting of leaders and an emerging consensus from several subsequent conference panel discussions, the idea to create this book was born. These discussions helped to convince us that the work of mathematics teacher educators and professional development specialists could be enhanced if they a) recognized the connections between formative assessment and many of the mathematics FTA and b) had access to compelling examples of where and how professional learning about formative assessment could be integrated with the professional learning of other instructional approaches—CGI, Discourse, RTI, and so forth. Such integration would make it possible to help teachers see how important ideas in teaching connect to each other. We see formative assessment as playing an essential role in fostering this coherence, and this book rests on that foundation. The examples provided in this book are different from the typical current approach in which formative assessment is treated as a separate professional development effort. The book should provide much needed support for building greater coherence across teacher education and professional development initiatives in our field, suggesting ways that formative assessment—the practice of eliciting and using evidence of student thinking to guide instruction—can provide a unifying thread.

A foreword by Margaret Heritage, a world-renowned expert on formative assessment, opens this book. The remainder is organized into three main sections. In the first section, two chapters lay out the foundations. The opening chapter explores our evolving understanding of the formative assessment process over the last twenty years and the challenges that have impeded its widespread implementation. It also explicates some of the evidence base for the importance of these instructional practices in supporting students' learning of mathematics. The second chapter presents the findings from the survey of NCSM and AMTE members mentioned above, as well as some details about the follow-up meeting briefly described above.

The second section contains six chapters, each discussing an influential instructional framework, tool, or approach that is well-known to educators: Classroom Discourse and Discussion Tools, Cognitively Guided Instruction, Culturally Responsive Pedagogy, Mathematical Learning Trajectories, the Mathematical Tasks Framework, and Response-to-Intervention (RTI). In each chapter, the authors—who are experts in the use of the instructional framework, tool, or approach discussed in the chapter—provide detailed descriptions and examples of ways in which the formative assessment process is an essential embedded element in mathematics classrooms.

The third section contains four chapters that consider major cross-cutting themes and lessons drawn from the earlier chapters. The first chapter in this section examines the connections between formative assessment and the eight Mathematics Teaching Practices named in the National Council of Teachers of Mathematic's (NCTM). The next chapter looks carefully at educational equity and its linkages to formative assessment and the chapters in the second section of the book. A third chapter considers the proposition that focusing on formative assessment might cohere and thereby improve the effectiveness of the professional learning experiences of teachers. The final chapter in this section, and in the book, proposes a few topics that might constitute useful next steps in efforts to promote formative assessment in mathematics classrooms.

We are very much indebted to all the authors who have contributed to this book, and we appreciate their patience and willingness to share their expertise. We also want to thank Eleanore Tapscott, NCTM Publications Director, for her support and encouragement. Finally, this book would not have been possible without the insights and hard work of our four partners on the NCSM/AMTE Formative Assessment Task Force: Wanda Audrict, Megan Burton, Marjorie Petit, and Marilyn Strutchens. Not only did they author or co-author a number of the chapters in this volume, but their consistent contributions to the work of the Joint Task Force and the development of the ideas that undergird this book were numerous and invaluable to our progress.

Edward A. Silver

Valerie L. Mills

Acknowledgments

The preparation of this book was supported in part by the National Science Foundation under Grant No. DRL-1439366, *Improving Students' Mathematical Proficiency through Formative Assessment: Responding to an Urgent Need in the Common Core Era.* Any opinions, findings, conclusions or recommendations expressed here are those of the principal investigator, project staff, and chapter authors and do not necessarily reflect the views of the National Science Foundation.

Section 1

Focusing on Formative Assessment: What, Why, and How?

Chapter 1
Our Evolving Understanding of Formative Assessment and the Challenges of Widespread Implementation

Chapter 2
Why Focus on Formative Assessment in Relation to Mathematics Instructional Frameworks, Tools, and Approaches?

The two chapters contained in Section 1 provide the conceptual and empirical foundations of this book as it emerged from a joint initiative of the National Council of the Supervisors of Mathematics (NCSM) and the Association of Mathematics Teacher Educators (AMTE), which was launched in 2013 to promote an intentional and systematic approach to implementing formative assessment in U.S. mathematics classrooms. Toward this goal, a joint task force was appointed that, among its many activities, developed a formative assessment position paper that was adopted by both organizations. Elements of that position statement, supporting evidence, and related information are taken up in the first chapter. Chapter 1 thus provides the foundational conceptualization of formative assessment in mathematics teaching that is taken up throughout the rest of this book.

In Chapter 2, the authors provide a brief summary of the findings of a national survey of mathematics teacher educators and teacher professional development specialists, regarding their beliefs about the importance of formative assessment and the extent to which they emphasize formative assessment in their work with preservice or in-service teachers of mathematics. This chapter also provides a summary of the work of a group of experts in mathematics teacher education who met to consider how formative assessment relates to other prominent frameworks, tools, and approaches to making mathematics teaching more effective. Chapter 2 provides an empirical foundation for this book and the rationale for including the chapters contained in Section 2.

Chapter 1

Our Evolving Understanding of Formative Assessment and the Challenges of Widespread Implementation

Valerie L. Mills, Marilyn E. Strutchens, and Marjorie Petit

The power of formative assessment for learning, when well done, is firmly established in the research.

Black and Wiliam, 1998

I know of no other school improvement innovation [referring to formative assessment practices] *that can claim effects of this nature or size.*

R. Stiggins, 2002

It's really not surprising that formative assessment works so well. What is surprising is how few U.S. teachers use the process.

J. Popham, 2013

These three quotations from well-respected educational researchers, when juxtaposed, leave us scratching our heads and wondering *why*? Why has formative assessment not been used more regularly in the decades since Paul Black and Dylan Wiliam published *Inside the Black Box* (1998)? How is it possible that an instructional innovation with such potential to improve student learning has not been more widely adopted? For those interested in accessing the potential of the formative assessment process, these are vital questions worth exploring. Therefore, we open *A Fresh Look at Formative Assessment in Mathematics Teaching* with a brief look back—first, to review formative assessment's research base, and then to consider why formative assessment may not have been widely adopted. This discussion can then serve as both foundation and motivation for a *new* approach to understanding and implementing formative assessment for mathematics education researchers and practitioners alike.

The Case in Support of Formative Assessment

In the 20 years since Black and Wiliam first published their meta-analysis of the effects of formative assessment practices on learning, *Inside the Black Box* (1998), the topic has received much attention. As a measure of this attention, a non-specific *Google Scholar* search for "formative assessment" on June 8, 2017, yielded nearly 600,000 results, along with a list of 16 related searches such as formative assessment tools, formative assessment strategies, and so forth. This active research stream focused on formative assessment has generally affirmed the findings of effect sizes ranging from 0.40 to 0.70, which were first suggested by Black and Wiliam in 1989. For example, we have additional large meta-analysis studies from Ehrenberg's et al. (2001) and Hattie (2009). Ehrenberg's et al. (2001) found that the impact of formative assessment on student achievement is four to five times greater than reduction of class size. Hattie's (2009) work synthesized approximately 800 meta-analyses covering a wide range of educational programs, policies, and innovations on academic achievement. He found formative assessment and the related strategies of self-assessment and feedback to be ranked in the top 10 of the 138 interventions examined with effect sizes of 0.90, 1.44, and 0.73, respectively. Further, the literature suggests that not only are the gains associated with formative assessment use larger than most instructional innovation strategies (Hattie, 2009), this process has also been found to be particularly helpful for students who have previously struggled (Wiliam, 1989), and appears to produce learning that is sustained over extended periods of time (Wiliam, 2005). Finally, these findings are consistent across developed countries (i.e., the United States, Canada, England, Israel, and Portugal), across age brackets, and across content areas. Indeed, the evidence base associated with formative assessment's potential to support significant growth in student learning is compelling.

This robust research base has led to a growing consensus across educational communities that formative assessment is a powerful instructional tool worthy of every teacher's attention and an important element of effective instruction. Evidence for this consensus can be seen with the inclusion of formative assessment in three of the most influential contemporary frameworks for mathematics teaching. First, NCTM's 2014 publication *Principles to Actions: Ensuring Mathematical Success for All* lists "Elicit and use evidence of student thinking" as one of eight named research-informed Mathematics Teaching Practices. The authors write, "Effective teaching of mathematics uses evidence of student thinking to assess progress toward mathematical understanding and to adjust instruction continually in ways that support and extend learning" (NCTM, 2014, p. 10). Second, Schoenfeld (2015) includes formative assessment as one of only five essential dimensions of mathematics classroom practice in his mathematics education framework, *Teaching for Robust Understanding* (TRU). Regarding this dimension, the framework notes that we are likely to develop powerful student thinkers based on "The extent to which classroom activities elicit student thinking and subsequent interactions respond to those ideas, building on productive beginnings and addressing emerging misunderstandings. Powerful instruction 'meets students where they are' and gives them opportunities to deepen their understandings" (p. 163). A third influential framework for effective teaching is Deborah Loewenberg Ball's 19 High-Leverage Practices (Ball & Forzani, 2010). This framework digs deeply into the work of teaching to elucidate component skills needed to facilitate learning. In this schema, formative assessment components are teased apart for close examination, including the following:

- Eliciting and interpreting individual students' thinking
- Coordinating and adjusting instruction during a lesson
- Checking student understanding during—and at the conclusion—of lessons

- Interpreting the results of student work, including routine assignments, quizzes, tests, projects, and standardized assessments
- Providing oral and written feedback to students

Each of these frameworks represents an attempt to synthesize the knowledge and practices needed to promote learning for each and every student. Whether it is one of eight, five, or 19 practices, formative assessment is well represented in each.

Formative assessment research since 1998 has not only supported the Black and Wiliam findings but it has also added important detail and depth to our understanding of the process and the instructional strategies that contribute to that process. This maturing understanding of formative assessment is illustrated in the work of the Formative Assessment for Students and Teachers (FAST) State Collaborative on Assessment and Student Standards (SCASS). The FAST SCASS is a working referent group for educators employed primarily by the various state-level education departments from across the country. This special interest group is organized under the Council of Chief State School Officers (CCSSO) for the purpose of providing guidance and resources to state-level policy makers on formative assessment. When the group initially formed in 2006, they created a working definition for formative assessment. The group, led by Margaret Heritage, adopted an updated definition designed to reflect their evolved understanding of the process and the associated instructional strategies in 2017. It is instructive to compare the two definitions found side by side in Table 1.1 below, attending to the ways in which the two descriptions of formative assessment are alike and different. The similarities and differences described below, particularly the differences, exemplify the ways in which our thinking about this instructional innovation has grown and matured over the past 15 or 20 years.

Table 1.1. Similarities and differences between FAST SCASS 2006 definition and FAST SCASS 2017 definitions of formative assessment

FAST SCASS 2006 Definition	FAST SCASS 2017 Definition
Formative assessment is a process used by teachers and students during instruction that provides feedback to adjust ongoing teaching and learning to improve students' achievement of intended instructional outcomes.	Formative assessment is a planned, ongoing process used by all students and teachers during learning and teaching to improve student understanding of intended disciplinary learning outcomes, supporting students becoming more self-directed learners. Effective use of the formative assessment process requires students and teachers to integrate the following practices: • Clarifying learning targets within a broader progression of learning; • Eliciting and analyzing evidence of student understanding; • Engaging in self-assessment, self-reflection, and peer assessment; • Providing actionable feedback; and • Using evidence and feedback to move learning forward by adjusting either learning strategies or next instructional steps.

While both definitions carefully describe formative assessment as a *process*, compared side-by-side, one notices that in the updated version the description of the *process* gains detail becoming a *planned ongoing process*. Further the subjects of the process shift from *teachers and students* to *all students and teachers*, emphasizing the role that students play in the process. The role of students in the process gets an additional lift as the "when we employ" formative assessment evolves from "during *instruction*" to "during *teaching and learning*." This change is again intended to signal that students as well as teachers play a role in the process. Readers will also notice that the learning targets of formative assessment are broadened from *intended instructional outcomes* to become *improve student understanding of intended disciplinary learning outcomes, supporting students becoming more self-directed learners*. This change alerts us to both the critical role of individual subject areas within the process, and the opportunities formative assessment affords learners to cultivate skills we associate with life-long learners. Finally, the revised definition assigns a list of explicit strategies to the process description that adds clarity and depth to the reader's understanding of the formative assessment process. While each adjustment is relatively small, the changes and additions substantively add to our thinking about who, what, when, and how the process is intended to be implemented.

The addition of explicit strategies to better describe the formative assessment process has been part of the effort to understand and advance formative assessment from the beginning of this educational storyline. Four years after the U.S. publication of *Inside the Black Box (1998)*, these researchers, with others, published *Working Inside the Black Box*. These authors summarized findings from the study they designed to unpack the components of this process. This work identified and described four component strategies: Questioning, Feedback through Grading, Peer and Self-Assessment, and Formative Use of Summative Assessments. Three years later, Leahy et al. (2005) in *Minute by Minute* described the following five formative assessment tools that added greater detail to our understanding of the strategies that fuel this instructional process:

- clarifying and sharing learning intentions and criteria for success;
- engineering effective classroom discussions, questions, and learning tasks
- providing feedback that moves learners forward;
- activating students as the owners of their learning; and
- activating students as resources for one another.

In the years that followed the Leahy et al. list, other groups have offered either more detailed or focused lists of strategies, or both, to better support users at varying grade-levels in their efforts to understand and implement this productive instructional process. These lists have been further developed as the basis for a wide variety of books and resources with illustrations and suggestions for using the strategies in classrooms to support teachers working to move formative assessment into the components of their practice.

Based on confirming research gathered over the past twenty years, a maturing explication of formative assessment, and a growing catalog of resources to support users in implementing the process, the education community has signaled its confidence in this process and its important place in our understanding of teaching practices that are likely to support greater learning for each and every student.

Challenges and Barriers to Implementation

Having briefly explored the evolving research and practice supporting the significance of formative assessment as an effective practice, we turn our attention to the last of the opening quotations for this chapter and the question it prompts: Why has formative assessment not been taken up more consistently in the decades since the publication of *Inside the Black Box*? Further, which challenges or barriers might we hypothesize have hampered implementation thus far, but could be addressed going forward? One place to begin this discussion is to wonder if our early, less articulate descriptions of the process may have undermined teachers' understanding of the formative assessment process and their ability to translate it into their day-to-day practice. We find some evidence for this in studies that have questioned the magnitude and range of effect sizes described above. Several researchers have challenged the accuracy of the estimated effect sizes for student achievement gains based on concerns about the original studies used to develop these projections (Wininger & Norman, 2005; Dunn & Mulvenon, 2009; Apthorp et al., 2016; and Briggs et al., 2012). Many of these concerns are connected to variability in the way that different researchers/studies chose to define formative assessment and their sometimes small sample sizes (Wininger & Norman, 2005).

From the point of view of the practitioner, anecdotal evidence suggests that early, less complete descriptions of formative assessment have contributed to at least two prevalent misconceptions. First, it seems that many educators, including teachers, principals, policymakers, and other leaders have had difficulty distinguishing between summative assessments and the formative assessment process. Confounding these two processes is the word *assessment* that appears in both. The challenge has been to help educators broaden their current understanding of assessment as *events* (chapter tests, quizzes, large-scale assessments) that occur *outside* day-to-day lessons to also include assessment as a *process* that takes place *inside* the daily stream of teaching and learning for the purpose of adjusting instruction. For many this conflated thinking about formative and summative assessment has meant that to adopt formative assessment practices is to layer additional assessment events into the school calendar, rather than incorporating a process of eliciting and using evidence of learning to adjust instruction into daily practice. The additional assessments, erroneously labeled formative, take many forms such as benchmark assessments or pre-tests administered prior to teaching but not used to adjust initial instruction. Assessments used in this way cannot deliver the promised growth enabled by the formative assessment process that is intended to occur within the daily stream of planning and instruction.

A second common misconception occurs when educators understand that formative assessment is intended to be embedded in instruction, but use only one or two of the individual strategies. In this situation, strategies that could be productive are left to stand alone rather than being connected to a completed process. For example, many teachers use exit tickets to gather evidence of student understanding, or carefully post daily student learning goals, or ask students to critique one another's work, but these practices are not then used to advance learning as part of the process. That is, exit tickets are used to efficiently collect evidence of student's current learning, but are rarely summarized and then used to adjust instruction. Similarly, while student learning goals are posted, they may not connect to the day's instructional tasks, and students are not given the time or support needed to analyze their work in relation to the learning goals. Although individual strategies can be useful, each constitutes only a portion of the process that includes identifying learning goals, eliciting and collecting evidence of learning around the goal, and then *critically*, using the evidence to adjust the instruction and engage students in ways that advance learning toward the goal *during instruction* (Heritage, 2008). Individual strategies that contribute to the overall process are important elements within the process, but alone, they may not be sufficient to advance learning.

Prevalent misuses and misunderstandings about formative assessment as a process suggest that there is still a great deal of work to be done. Despite the maturing descriptions, additional resources, and growing consensus, the education community has yet to fully grasp and effectively use this powerful instructional practice. Clearly the field is working to advance understanding for practitioners and researchers alike, but this work has not been sufficient, and the need still exists to help greater proportions of the education community to understand and use formative assessment productively.

A New Look at Formative Assessment

In January of 2013, a small group of practitioners and researchers from the National Council of Supervisors of Mathematics (NCSM) and the Association of Mathematics Teacher Educators (AMTE) came together to begin exploring the questions raised in the sections above and to wonder if a joint NCSM/AMTE effort might be developed to promote greater understanding and use of the formative assessment process. The group wondered why current research and professional learning efforts have not been more successful, despite maturing descriptions of the process and additional resources. The group also wondered if there was a different way into the formative assessment conversation that might be productive for practitioners and researchers alike. That is, how might the treatment of the formative assessment process in preservice and in-service learning be adjusted to better enable teachers to use these practices as intended? Based on the robust research base suggesting the importance of this instructional process, and the need for additional work, given the challenges associated with implementing these practices, the group agreed that a joint NCSM/AMTE task force should be formed. To ground this work, the task force began by clarifying, for our audience and ourselves, what is meant by formative assessment and included descriptions of the five component strategies outlined by Leahy et al. (2005) in the publication of a joint NCSM/AMTE position paper, *Improving Student Achievement in Mathematics Through Formative Assessment in Instruction.*

Beyond the grounding of task force efforts with the development and publication of the joint position paper, the task force also launched efforts in two other directions. The first was to commission a small group of practitioners and researchers led by Jeane Joyner and Mari Muri to develop a collection of formative assessment professional learning modules. These modules are designed for preservice and in-service leaders working with those who are new or inexperienced with formative assessment practices as they relate to mathematics teaching and learning. The *Jump-Start Formative Assessment* professional learning resources are now available to NCSM and AMTE members and can be accessed from the respective association websites.

The second effort of the joint task force was far less well defined and rested on an insight that emerged early-on as members explored causes and opportunities to impact the current state of formative assessment in America. This insight was prompted as the group began to speculate on possible connections between the formative assessment process and other well-researched approaches in mathematics education. What followed this early discussion was an exciting, enlightening, and ultimately productive journey. The journey grew to include practitioners and researchers from across the country and to produce evidence suggesting that formative assessment plays a far more significant role in mathematics teaching and learning than was previously understood or explicitly described. The chapters that follow describe the rich results of this exploration including—

- a study developed and implemented to better understand how leaders in the field currently use or do not use the relationship between formative assessment and other mathematics frameworks, tools, and approaches;

- a working meeting with experienced users to initially explore formative assessment connections to each of five different instructional frameworks, tools, or approaches;

- thorough analysis and description of formative assessment connections in six widely used mathematics instructional resources written by practitioner and researcher teams deeply experienced with the resource;

- discussion of additional connections to NCTM's Effective Instructional Practices and issues of equitable achievement, and finally; and

- discussion of the important implications for changes in how we organize professional learning for formative assessment.

In closing, consider a final quotation from Paul Black and Dylan Wiliam. Their words foreshadow both our evolving understanding of the complexity associated with implementing formative assessment effectively and the work of the NCSM/AMTE task force to make explicit the role of formative assessment within many of mathematics education's supporting instructional frameworks, tools, and approaches.

> The evolution of effective teaching. The research studies . . . show very clearly that effective programs of formative assessment involve far more than the addition of a few observations and tests to an existing program. They require careful scrutiny of all the main components of a teaching plan. Indeed, it is clear that *instruction and formative assessment are indivisible.* (Black & Wiliam, 1998)

References

Apthorp, H., Klute, M., Petrites, T., Harlacher, J., Real, M., & Society for Research on Educational Effectiveness. (2016). *Valuing a More Rigorous Review of Formative Assessment's Effectiveness.* Paper presented at The Society for Research on Educational Effectiveness Conference, Washington, DC.

Ball, D. L., & Forzani, F. M. (2010). Teaching skillful teaching. *Educational Leadership 68*(4), 40–45.

Black, P., & Wiliam, D. (1998). Inside the black box: Raising standards through classroom assessment. *Phi Delta Kappan, 80*(2), 139–148.

Briggs, D.C., Ruiz-Primo, M. A., Furtak, E., Shepard, L., & Yin, Y. (2012). Meta-analytic methodology and inferences about the efficacy of formative assessment. *Educational Measurement: Issues and Practice Winter, 31*(4), 13–17.

Dunn, K. E., & Mulvenon, S. W. (2009). A critical review of research on formative assessment: The limited scientific evidence of the impact of formative assessment in education. *Practical Assessment, Research & Evaluation, 14*(7), 1–11.

Ehrenberg, R. G., Brewer, D. J., Gamoran, A., & Williams, J. D. (2001). Class size and student achievement. *Psychological Science in the Public Interest, 2*(1), 1–30.

Hattie, J. (2008). *Visible learning: A Synthesis of over 800 meta-analyses relating to achievement.* New York: Routledge.

Heritage, M. (2008). *Learning progressions: Supporting instruction and formative assessment.* Washington DC: Council of Chief State School Officers.

Leahy, S., Lyon, C., Thompson, M., & Wiliam, D. (2005). Classroom assessment: Minute by minute, day by day. *Educational Leadership, 63*(3), 19–24.

National Council of Teachers of Mathematics (NCTM). (2014). *Principles to actions: Ensuring mathematical success for all.* Reston, VA: NCTM.

Schoenfeld, A. H. (2015). Thoughts on scale. *ZDM: The International Journal on Mathematics Education, 47*(1), 161–169.

Wininger, S. R., & Norman, A. D. (2005). Teacher candidates' exposure to formative assessment in educational psychology textbooks: A content analysis. *Educational Assessment 10*(1), 19–37. doi:10.1207/s15326977ea1001_2

Chapter 2

Why Focus on Formative Assessment in Relation to Mathematics Instructional Frameworks, Tools, and Approaches?

Edward A. Silver, Megan Burton, and Wanda Audrict

In Chapter 1, the authors identified a set of instructional practices that are commonly called formative assessment—eliciting and using evidence of student thinking and learning to guide classroom instruction and student learning—and they provided a rationale for focusing on formative assessment practice as a key component of efforts to improve the teaching and learning of mathematics. In this chapter, we offer our rationale for treating formative assessment in ways that highlight how it is embedded within and intertwined with important instructional frameworks, tools, and approaches. These frameworks, tools, and approaches are widely used in mathematics teacher education and professional learning settings, and include Classroom Discussion and Discourse, Cognitively Guided Instruction (CGI), Culturally Relevant Pedagogy, Learning Progressions, Mathematical Tasks Framework, and Response to Intervention (RTI).

Why discuss formative assessment in relation to other frameworks? Formative assessment is typically treated as if it were a distinct topic separate from other approaches suggested to improve mathematics instruction. Anecdotal evidence is readily available suggesting that teachers might be exposed to CGI or learning progressions, for example, without ever seeing an explicit link to formative assessment, even though both frameworks are designed to provide important evidence of student thinking. In complementary fashion, we have observed that teachers are often exposed to professional development on formative assessment without ever linking it to other ideas that are central to effective mathematics instruction, such as the use of cognitively demanding tasks or the importance of classroom discussion of mathematical ideas. As a consequence of such disconnected treatments of approaches to improving mathematics teaching, we think it likely that teachers may come to view formative assessment as "one more thing to do," in a teaching regime that most think is already packed with too many things to do!

Our anecdote-based hunch about this phenomenon has been supported by empirical data derived from a survey of mathematics teacher educators and professional development providers. In this chapter, we share selected findings from that survey to support the atypical approach we take in this book to the treatment of formative assessment in mathematics classrooms and share ideas gleaned from a working meeting of leaders in these various frameworks, tools, and approaches. These findings and ideas set the stage for the chapters that follow.

Who Was Surveyed?

In November 2013, members of the Association of Mathematics Teacher Educators (AMTE) and the National Council of Supervisors of Mathematics (NCSM) were invited to complete an online survey. The 25-item survey elicited information about some aspects of the respondents' practices in either the preparation or continuing education of teachers of mathematics, or both. Some questions inquired about respondents' general practices and perspectives, and some focused on their practices and perspectives regarding formative assessment. Roughly 600 responses were analyzed from a set of respondents that was fairly representative of the wide range of those who work with preservice or in-service teachers of mathematics.

Figure 2.1 displays a tally of the number of respondents who indicated each of the employment categories. Roughly one-third of respondents were employed in a college/university setting, and about one-half reported working in pre-K–grade 12 at a state, regional, district, or school level; the remaining respondents were employed in other roles as independent consultants or as employees in education-related businesses.

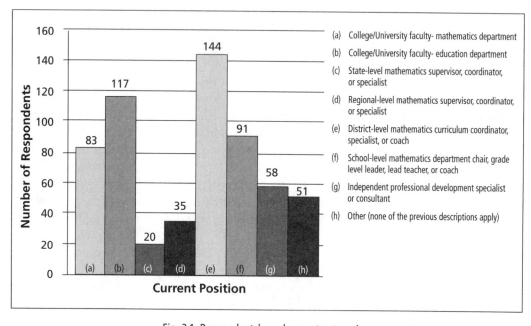

Fig. 2.1. Respondents' employment categories

Respondents who worked with preservice or in-service teachers were distributed across the grade span. The number of respondents working with either preservice or in-service teachers, or both, at each grade level category is shown in figure 2.2. More than 80 percent of the respondents reportedly worked in multiple-grade bands. More than half responded that they worked with teachers in all four levels evaluated.

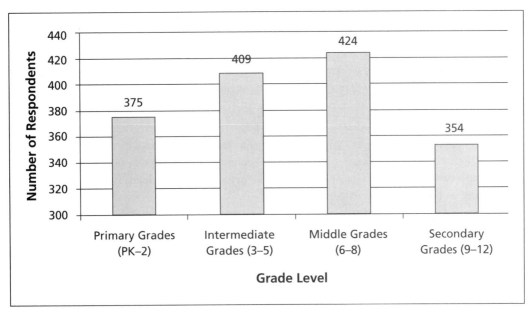

Fig. 2.2. Grade level of teachers with whom respondents worked

Some other descriptive information about survey respondents includes the following:

- About 90 percent of the respondents reported working with in-service teachers, and about one-half worked with preservice teachers. Roughly one in three reported working with both in-service and preservice teachers.

- About 70 percent of respondents stated that they work with elementary teachers (Pre-K–grade 5), almost 80 percent with secondary teachers (6–12), and about one-half reported working with both elementary and secondary teachers of mathematics.

- More than 75 percent of respondents work with both content and methods instruction, with 15 percent focusing only on methods and 5 percent focusing on only content. However, this wording might be unclear to those who are not in a traditional university setting.

Survey Findings: Formative Assessment Views

One goal of the survey was to determine if mathematics teacher educators perceived formative assessment as an important topic and if they addressed formative assessment in their work with teachers of mathematics. Survey respondents overwhelmingly endorsed the importance of formative assessment in work with teachers of mathematics and reported a high level of attention to the topic in their work with teachers. Here is a summary of the major findings:

- Almost all respondents indicated that attention to **formative assessment is important** in efforts to improve the teaching and learning of mathematics.

- Among respondents who judged formative assessment to be an important topic, **89 percent reported treating formative assessment as a moderately important topic or as a major focus of attention** in their work with teachers. However, because this is clearly the focus of the survey, respondent bias to the focus of the survey may account for part of the claimed priority placed on assessment by respondents.

- Those who work only with in-service teachers or with both in-service and preservice teachers tended to view formative assessment as a moderately or extremely important topic more frequently than those who work exclusively with preservice teachers (about 90 percent versus about 75 percent).

- Those who focus on content without pedagogy reported less attention to assessment (about 54 percent reporting moderate or major focus on assessment). Approximately 91 percent of those focusing on pedagogy alone reported moderate or major focus on assessment, which is almost equal to the 92 percent of respondents who reported focusing on both content and pedagogy.

Nearly 70 percent of respondents indicated that the discussions about the adoption of **Common Core State Standards for Mathematics (CCSSM) has increased the importance of attention to formative assessment**, and about 60 percent of respondents indicated that the adoption of CCSSM led them to pay more attention to formative assessment in their work with teachers (see fig. 2.3). The **influence of CCSSM was more evident in responses from those working with teachers or students in Pre-K–12 settings** than for those working in college or university settings with preservice teachers.

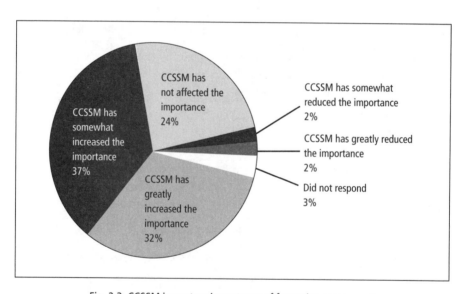

Fig. 2.3. CCSSM impact on importance of formative assessment

Survey Findings: Instructional Frameworks, Tools, and Approaches

Frequency of Use in Work with Teachers of Mathematics

Another goal of the survey was to determine whether and to what extent mathematics teacher educators used the following instructional frameworks, tools, and approaches in their work with teachers: classroom discussion and discourse tools (CDT), cognitively guided instruction (CGI), culturally relevant pedagogy (CRP), the instructional triangle (IT), Japanese-inspired lesson s tudy (JLS), the mathematical task framework (MTF), professional learning communities (PLC), and response to intervention (RTI).

Table 2.1 displays a summary of the responses regarding frequency of use of each instructional, framework, tool, or approach as a moderately important or major topic in work with teachers. A large percentage of respondents indicated use of the two most general FTAs, Classroom Discussion Tools and Professional Learning Communities. The least frequently used across all the respondents were Japanese-inspired Lesson Study, Culturally Relevant Pedagogy, and the Instructional Triangle.

Table 2.1. Frequency of use of each framework, tool, or approach (n = 599)

FTA Used	Percent of respondents who treated the FTA as a moderately important or major topic
Classroom Discussion and Discourse Tools	65%
Cognitively Guided Instruction	35%
Culturally Relevant Pedagogy	16%
Instructional Triangle	12%
Japanese-inspired Lesson Study	18%
Mathematical Tasks Framework	32%
Professional Learning Communities	57%
Response to Intervention	35%

Some other observations about the data displayed in Table 2.1 include the following:

- Respondents indicated **varied frequency of use of the instructional frameworks, tools, and approaches** as moderately important or major topics in their work with teachers, with more than half of respondents indicating treating classroom discussion and discourse tools or professional learning communities in this way in their work. About one-third of respondents reported using CGI, RTI, or the MTF in this way in their work. Fewer than one in five respondents reported using JLS, CRP, or the instructional triangle in this way in their work.

- **Variation in use of some frameworks, tools, and approaches was associated with the population of teachers with whom respondents worked**. For example, RTI was highly used by respondents employed in pre-K–grade 12 settings and used far less by those working in college/university settings; CGI was used by respondents working with pre-K–grade 5 teachers far more often by those working with grade 6–12 teachers; and PLC was frequently used by those working with in-service teachers but rarely used by respondents who work exclusively with preservice teachers.

- About 75 percent of respondents **indicated using more than one framework, tool, or approach** as a moderately important or major topic in their work with teachers of mathematics; more than 50 percent indicated treating two, three, or four frameworks, tools, and approaches as moderately important or major topics in their work.

Frequency of Explicitly Relating to Formative Assessment

As companions to the questions about general use of each of the eight frameworks, tools, and approaches, the survey also contained questions that probed the extent to which respondents made an *explicit, focused connection to formative assessment* in relation to each. Respondents chose from the following answer choices: (a) not at all, (b) occasionally, (c) sometimes, (d) frequently, or (e) almost always. Table 2.2 shows the percentage of respondents who not only used the framework, tool, or approach seriously (i.e., they treated it as either moderately important or as a major focus of attention in their work) but also indicated that they sometimes, frequently, or almost always made an explicit connection to formative assessment.

The data displayed in Table 2.2 indicate a range of attention to formative assessment across the frameworks, tools, and approaches from about 0.6 to nearly 0.9. Those with the higher proportions are likely the ones for which teacher educators and professional development specialists have developed ways to exploit the connection to formative assessment. On the other hand, those with the lower proportions could be targets of opportunity to promote greater connection to formative assessment.

Table 2.2. Proportion of serious users of each framework, tool, or approach who explicitly connect to formative assessment

FTA Used	Proportion of serious users of a framework, tool or approach who explicitly connect it to formative assessment
Classroom Discussion and Discourse Tools	.88
Cognitively Guided Instruction	.74
Culturally Relevant Pedagogy	.66
Instructional Triangle	.64
Japanese-inspired Lesson Study	.74
Mathematical Tasks Framework	.61
Professional Learning Communities	.83
Response to Intervention	.83

Some other observations about the data displayed in Table 2.2 include:

- With one exception, a **majority of respondents** who indicated using a given framework, tool or approach in a serious manner (i.e., treating it as a moderately important topic or major focus of attention) also indicated frequently or almost always making an explicit connection to formative assessment.

- The **proportion of respondents making an explicit connection to formative assessment from among those who used a given framework, tool or approach in a serious manner varied** from a high of .81 for RTI to a low of .61 for MTF.

- Nearly **four of every five serious users of CDT, PLC, and RTI indicated making explicit connection to formative assessment**, and about two of every three serious users of the other frameworks did so.

Responses to the survey suggested that respondents viewed formative assessment as an important topic in their work with preservice or in-service teachers of mathematics. Also, the survey responses indicated that respondents frequently used many of the FTAs in their work with teachers. Yet, the survey findings also suggested that the respondents did not always make an explicit link to formative assessment in their work with teachers.

To examine in more depth and detail if and how formative assessment might be represented within the frameworks, tools, and approaches. Therefore, a working meeting of widely recognized expert practitioners was convened to examine explicitly if the experts recognize the presence of formative assessment in their framework, tool or approach.

The Working Meeting: Who Attended and What Happened?

With support from the National Science Foundation in the form of a grant to the University of Michigan, we held a working meeting in October 2014 to explore whether and how formative assessment might be made a more explicit focus in the teacher education or professional development work of mathematics educators. In particular, we invited experienced users of each of five different instructional frameworks, tools or approaches widely used in mathematics teacher education and/or professional development: cognitively guided instruction, classroom discussion/discourse tools, culturally responsive pedagogy, the mathematical tasks framework, and response to intervention.

The meeting participants focused on how to provide greater coherence to mathematics teacher preparation and professional development by explicitly attending to formative assessment in relation to the dominant framework, tool or approach used in their work. The experts gathered not only to identify key aspects of formative assessment practice embedded within their framework, tool, or approach but also to explore how the connection might be made more explicit to preservice teachers of mathematics in the work of teacher educators and to in-service teachers of mathematics in the work of professional development specialists.

Meeting participants generally seemed to recognize elements of formative assessment in their frameworks, the overall connection and need to be explicit about it seemed less universally shared at the outset. As the meeting progressed, a sharper vision developed regarding why and how such an explicit connection should be undertaken. Participants moved from seeing formative assessment as an implicit component to recognizing the need to be explicit. Overall feedback reflected that formative assessment is an integral part of each framework, tool or approach, but as teacher educators and professional development leaders, this needs to be more explicitly stated in our work so preservice and in-service teachers see the connection that is so central from our perspective.

This book is a direct result of the work of the task force and the findings at the meeting of leaders of the frameworks, tools, and approaches. It is designed to provide mathematics teacher educators, professional development specialists, and curriculum leaders examples of where and how formative assessment can be integrated into a variety of professional learning efforts to support the effective use of formative assessment as a critical component of daily instructional decision-making. In addition, we will suggest ways in which this approach has the potential to cohere professional learning activities that might otherwise be seen as a series of disparate topics—CGI, CDT, RTI, and so on.

Our stance is based on our judgment that teachers are being pulled in too many seemingly disparate directions and that there is a need for greater and more transparent coherence. Just as *Principles to Actions* encourages teachers to examine how curriculum topics connect to each other and across grades to bring coherence to student learning, those who provide initial and continuing education for mathematics teachers also need to consider the same. It is critical to assist teachers to see how important ideas in teaching connect to each other. We see formative assessment as playing an essential role in fostering this coherence.

Acknowledgments

The analysis of survey data and the working group meeting reported in this chapter were supported in part by the National Science Foundation under Grant No. DRL-1439366, *Improving Students' Mathematical Proficiency through Formative Assessment: Responding to an Urgent Need in the Common Core Era.* Valuable contributions to the work that forms the basis for this chapter were provided by Anne Skibitcky, Jillian Mortimer, and Paul Kwame Yankson. Any opinions, findings, conclusions, or recommendations expressed here are those of the PI and project staff and do not necessarily reflect the views of the National Science Foundation.

Section 2

Frameworks, Tools, and Approaches to Improve Mathematics Teaching and Learning

Chapter 3
Using Classroom Discourse as a Tool for Formative Assessment

Chapter 4
Cognitively Guided Instruction and Formative Assessment

Chapter 5
Distinguishing Features of Culturally Responsive Pedagogy Related to Formative Assessment in Mathematics Instruction

Chapter 6
Using Learning Trajectories to Elicit, Interpret, and Respond to Student Thinking

Chapter 7
The Mathematical Tasks Framework and Formative Assessment

Chapter 8
Using Formative Assessment to Guide the Effective Implementation of Response to Intervention (RTI)

The six chapters contained in Section 2 each discuss an influential instructional framework, tool, or approach that is well-known to mathematics teachers and teacher educators: Classroom Discourse and Discussion Tools (CDT), Cognitively Guided Instruction (CGI), Culturally Responsive Pedagogy (CRP), Mathematical Learning Trajectories, the Mathematical Tasks Framework (MTF), and Response to Intervention (RTI). The authors of each chapter are recognized expert users of the instructional framework, tool, or approach discussed therein. In each chapter, the authors explicate essential elements of the particular instructional framework, tool, or approach; describe in detail how the formative assessment process is an essential embedded element, and provide illustrative examples drawn from mathematics classrooms.

Taken together, these six chapters provide evidence for a fundamental premise undergirding this book: namely, that formative assessment should be seen as an essential component of all efforts to improve mathematics teaching and learning.

◖ Chapter 3

Using Classroom Discourse as a
Tool for Formative Assessment

Michelle Cirillo and Jennifer M. Langer-Osuna

In a classroom where pupils use talk to learn about their mathematical ideas, feedback about their learning becomes part of the ongoing discourse. . . . Feedback is only formative (that is, helpful to learning), if the information fed back to the learner is used by the learner in improving their learning.

Clare Lee, Language for Learning Mathematics, *2006, p. 56*

Like most beginning teachers, when Mr. Steven first began teaching he relied heavily on his textbook. On one particular day, Mr. Steven's students had just completed a geometry worksheet that was included with his curriculum resources (see Fig. 3.1). After giving his students the four minutes that he allowed them to complete the first part, Mr. Steven began to go over the answers.

Mr. Steven:	*Okay, number one a, what did you get for letter a, Jenna?*
Jenna:	*Um, for number one I got angle A.*
Mr. Steven:	*Angle A? Yeah, Mike?*
Mike:	*For a I got angle BAE.*
Mr. Steven:	*Okay good when there's more than one angle there you have to say the whole thing—BAE. Seth—one b?*
Seth:	*Uh, for b I got AC and AD.*
Mr. Steven:	*Okay AC and AD. Any others? Nina?*
Nina:	*AC, AD, and AB and AE.*
Mr. Steven:	*Okay right you should have all four of those. Carlos, what did you get for one c?*
Carlos:	*Um, BAD?*
Mr. Steven:	*Yes, BAD is one of them, but it says to name all of them. Marco?*

The Tools of Geometry

(1)

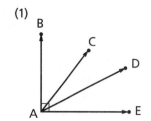

Complete the following using the diagram to the left.
a. Name the right angle.
b. Name all of the rays.
c. Name all of the angles that include side $\overrightarrow{AD}$.
d. Name the pairs of angles that are complementary.
e. Name the vertex of all of the angles.

(2)

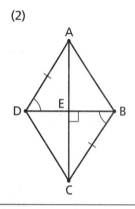

Complete the following using the diagram to the left.
a. Name the line segments that are marked congruent.
b. Name the angles that are marked congruent.
c. Name all of the right triangles.
d. Name the hypotenuse of each right triangle.

Fig. 3.1. Mr. Steven's geometry worksheet

Marco:	*Also EAD?*
Mr. Steven:	*Okay BAD and EAD. One more. Megan?*
Megan:	*I got BAD, CAD, and DAE.*
Mr. Steven:	*Good, BAD, CAD, and DAE. Alright, four d, name the pairs of angles that are complementary. Emma?*
Emma:	*[pause] Uh, okay one minute.*
Mr. Steven:	*[laughs] I don't have a minute. Julia?*
Julia:	*Um, CAD and DAE.*
Mr. Steven:	*CAD and DAE? Study up on what complementary means. Yang, what did you get for four d?*
Yang:	*I got, um, angle BAC and CAE and then, um, BAD and DAE.*
Mr. Steven:	*Okay good job. And finally, e, what's the vertex of all of the angles? Everyone should have gotten this one. Let's hear it.*
Students:	*A.*
Mr. Steven:	*Okay good. Let's move on to number two then . . .*

From this small excerpt, it seems that Mr. Steven is focused on two things: time and correct answers. When asked to reflect on a video clip of this lesson from three years earlier, Mr. Steven said:

Oh my gosh, that's bad! Okay, so what I can say for myself is that back then I felt pressure to get through the material. Before I had the discourse professional development (PD), I didn't realize that I could actually accomplish more by slowing down and focusing on including my students' thinking into the discourse. When I first started teaching I really did just think about teaching to desks in the room, and it didn't actually matter who was in them. As a new teacher, I was mainly focused on time and getting through the material. So I didn't pay attention to students as individuals and try to meet them where they are. Now I understand that it doesn't matter how *I* think about the material. It's my job to understand how *my students* are thinking about the ideas and help advance their mathematical understanding. Seeking information about students' progress with the mathematical ideas now guides my practice. And I do that through discourse.

Here, Mr. Steven discussed his discourse shifting from being teacher-centered to more student-centered. A key point in his reflection is that he realized that it is important for him to focus on student thinking. He was able to make these changes, he said, due to engaging in professional development focused on classroom discourse, but also through experience. He learned that the discourse pattern he was using is the "default" discourse pattern in all kinds of classrooms (Cazden, 1988, p. 53) and is called recitation or I-R-E, where a teacher *Initiates* a question, a student *Responds*, and the teacher *Evaluates* the student response (Mehan, 1979). Mr. Steven learned that I-R-E is not all bad, but that it should not be used exclusively. In contrast, it is best if students have opportunities to also participate in more open, student-centered discourse (see Cirillo, 2013) for more on the benefits of discussion in math class). Student-centered discourse allows students to engage in the discourse and to develop and use mathematical language. It also provides useful feedback to the learners and the teacher. You will read more about Mr. Steven's changes later in this chapter. His change in views toward student-centered discourse aligns well with findings in the research literature and policy recommendations about how students learn math.

Discourse in School Mathematics

The National Council of Teachers of Mathematics' recommendations and policy documents have maintained a long-standing focus on discourse and communication. Beginning with the Mathematics as Communication Standards in *Curriculum and Evaluation Standards for School Mathematics* (National Council of Teachers of Mathematics, 1989), the authors argued that when students write and talk about their thinking, they not only clarify their own ideas but they also give teachers valuable information from which to make instructional decisions. In NCTM's *Professional Standards for Teaching Mathematics* (1991), the Teacher's Role in Discourse included "listening to students ideas" and "monitoring students' participation in discussions and deciding when and how to encourage each student to participate" (p. 35). Continuing this emphasis, in the *Principles and Standards for School Mathematics* (NCTM, 2000), as part of the Communication Standard, the authors claimed that reflection and communication are intertwined processes in mathematics learning and, citing Lampert (1990), argued that when ideas are worked out in public, not only do students benefit but teachers can also monitor their learning. Finally, in the executive summary of their most recent policy document, *Principles to Actions*, NCTM (2014) emphasizes teaching as the "nonnegotiable core that ensures that all students learn mathematics at high levels" (p. 1) and addresses what it frames as obstacles to effective teaching, including too much focus on learning procedures without any connection to the underlying mathematical meaning. Classroom discussions are an ideal context for focusing on mathematical meaning making and offering teachers access to students' meaning-making processes. Indeed, a core practice in *Principles to Action* is "facilitate meaningful mathematical discourse." This teaching practice states: "Effective teaching of mathematics facilitates discourse among students to build shared understanding of mathematical ideas by analyzing and comparing student approaches and arguments" (NCTM Executive Summary, p. 3). Discourse, they argued, should be a purposeful exchange that can advance the mathematical learning of the entire class.

Within the communication standards published over the last nearly 40 years, we see that one can easily find connections to using discourse as a tool for formative assessment. In addition, and certainly not disconnected, there is a growing body of research literature on the importance of classroom discourse, the role of the teacher in discourse, what productive discourse looks like, and so on. Within this literature, we find explicit claims that discourse can and should be used as a tool for formative assessment. For example, Lee (2006) argued that when teachers use discourse to support student learning, they themselves become part of the discourse, and assessment for learning becomes totally embedded in the day-to-day classroom activity. Teachers come to know their students well, and as a result, they plan to meet their individual learning needs and preferences. Chapin, O'Connor, and Anderson (2013) argued that asking students to talk about their mathematical ideas can bring to the surface their gaps in understanding. Consequently, they claimed, this kind of talk allows teachers to hear students' misconceptions and identify what students do and do not understand. The teachers' role during student-centered discussions is crucial. Teachers work hard to: monitor what students are doing and understanding; observe who is and is not engaged; determine who needs more time or different supports to stay in the discussion; decide what to do to assess the success of the discussion; and determine the next steps to continue to build understanding (Kazemi & Hintz, 2014). In contrast, I-R-E can generally limit students' opportunities to learn and provides very little information to the teacher about what students know and can do (Arbaugh, 2010).

Classroom discourse also serves as a formative assessment tool to uncover issues of equity. Classroom discussions are key sites for students' development of identities as mathematics learners; through discussions, students are regularly positioned as authors and evaluators of mathematical ideas within a sense-making classroom community making it more likely that they develop a sense of themselves as doers of mathematics (Langer-Osuna & Esmonde, 2016). In this chapter, we focus on leveraging discourse as a powerful tool for formative assessment in mathematics classrooms.

Purposeful, Productive, and Powerful Discourse

In our work with teachers, we sometimes hear teachers talk about wanting *more discourse*. What we interpret that to mean is that teachers want to have more *student-centered discourse*, where the students are contributing to the class discussion in meaningful ways. However, we should not just wish for *more* discourse, but rather discourse that is purposeful, productive, and powerful.

Herbel-Eisenmann, Cirillo, and colleagues have written about the three *Ps* of classroom discourse. For example, in Herbel-Eisenmann and Cirillo's (2009) *Promoting Purposeful Discourse*, the teacher-researchers, who carefully studied their discourse through action research, wrote about becoming more *purposeful* about their discourse after engaging with the professional literature.

Purposeful discourse is discourse that is intentional, planful, and thoughtfully considered in service of improving the quality of teaching and, consequently, student learning.

When teachers are purposeful about discourse, they set goals, such as: "I want my students to be more precise with their language." Lesson planning reaches beyond the selection of tasks and activities and considers questions, prompts, and responses to anticipated student thinking. When teachers facilitate purposeful discourse, they are intentional about aspects of practice that are both apparent (e.g., using Wait Time) as well as not so apparent (e.g., using discourse to position a particular student as competent). Being purposeful about discourse can occur not only in the planning stages but also during lesson enactment and post-lesson reflection. Purposeful discourse takes into account both mathematical and social goals.

In their professional development curriculum, Herbel-Eisenmann, Cirillo, Steele, Otten, and Johnson (2017) suggested that teachers work towards facilitating discourse that is not only *Purposeful*, but also *Productive*, and *Powerful*.

Productive discourse "refers to discourse that provides students with opportunities to make meaningful mathematical contributions toward particular mathematical learning goals." (p. 142)

Powerful discourse is discourse that "positions students as people who are capable of making sense of mathematics and that supports students' developing identities in terms of status, smartness, and competence in mathematics class." (See Cirillo et al. [2014], p. 142, for more information.)

Here when we write about discourse we define it broadly as any spoken, written, or gestural communication that marks membership in a community of learners. Ideally, classroom discourse is *Purposeful*, *Productive*, and *Powerful*.

Discourse and Formative Assessment

Discourse, purposefully facilitated so that it is both productive and powerful, can serve as formative assessment in classrooms. In the article, "Classroom Assessment: Minute by Minute, Day by Day," Leahy and colleagues (Leahy, Lyon, Thompson, & Wiliam, 2005) wrote: "The teacher who consciously uses assessment to support learning takes in this information, analyzes it, and makes instructional decisions that address the understandings and misunderstandings that these assessments reveal" (p. 19). Replacing the word "assessment" with "discourse," we argue here that—

The teacher who consciously uses discourse to support learning takes in this information, analyzes it, and makes instructional decisions that address the understandings and misunderstandings that the discourse [or student contributions] reveal.

We find the diagram from Rose and Arline's (2008) book, *Uncovering Student Thinking in Mathematics* to relate well to these ideas (see fig. 3.2). Like Leahy and colleagues, Rose and Arline argued that the process of diagnosing students' understandings and misunderstandings and making instructional decisions based on that information is the key to increasing students' mathematical knowledge. Discourse is a tool for doing this important work.

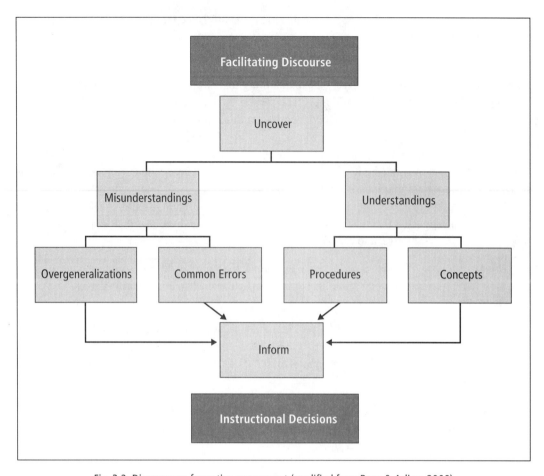

Fig. 3.2. Discourse as formative assessment (modified from Rose & Arline, 2009)

Describing two types of assessment, Leahy et al. (2005) contrasted assessment *of* learning with assessment *for* learning, claiming that assessment *for* learning can and should occur all the time. Here, we connect Leahy et al.'s five strategies of formative assessment, which they claimed were equally powerful for teachers of all content areas and all grade levels, to mathematics classroom discourse. The five strategies are: (1) clarifying and sharing learning intentions and criteria for success; (2) engineering effective classroom discussions, questions, and learning tasks; (3) providing feedback that moves learners forward; (4) activating students as owners of their own learning; and (5) activating students as instructional resources for one another (p. 20). Table 3.1 summarizes these ideas and provides samples of what discourse might sound like when using these moves.

Clarifying and sharing learning intentions and criteria for success. One critical aspect of formative assessment (i.e., discourse) is clarifying and sharing one's learning intentions and how successful discourse is evaluated. Teachers can do so by communicating what the norms and expectations are for student participation in classroom discourse. For example, teachers can communicate to their students that they believe that *all* students are capable of making sense of mathematics and that their ideas are valued (Kazemi & Hintz, 2014). This connects to the idea of facilitating discourse that is powerful. Many of the discourse resources cited at the end of this chapter provide guidance about how to establish norms or "ground rules" for discourse. For example, Chapin and colleagues (2013) suggested that it is the teacher's job to make sure of three things: that every student is listening to what others say; that every student can hear what others say; and that every student may participate by speaking out at some point. Teachers might also choose to establish norms that are not only social, but also mathematical, such as: You must always provide a justification with your answer. Last, teachers have the responsibility of launching tasks in ways that support students' understanding of the task and what they are supposed to be doing during group work. (See Jackson, Shahan, Gibbons, & Cobb, 2012 for more detail.)

Engineering effective classroom discussions, questions, and learning tasks. Teachers can not only engineer but also plan for effective classroom discussions, questions, and learning tasks. The importance of a good task for effective discourse cannot be overstated. If we want our students to have interesting discussions, we have to give them something interesting to discuss. After setting the learning goals, teachers not only select tasks, but can also consider the kinds of questions that are likely to be asked and plan some of their own questions in advance. There are many resources, including some that are cited at the end of this chapter, that can support teachers in orchestrating good discussions (e.g., Smith & Stein's [2011] *5 Practices for Orchestrating Productive Mathematical Discussion*). In addition, with the emphasis on discourse over the past more than 40 years, the field has started to name and describe particular "talk" or "discourse" moves that can be used from moment to moment (see, e.g., Chapin et al., 2013 and Herbel-Eisenmann et al., 2017).

Providing feedback that moves learners forward. A benefit of using discourse as a resource for formative assessment is that teachers can provide feedback to their students in the moment to move their learning forward. Rather than rescuing students when they are stuck, teachers must balance having high expectations for students and providing in-the-moment feedback that keeps them in the productive struggle zone. To do so, teachers are strategic about what to tell and and when to ask questions to help students make progress. Teachers can explore correct and incorrect strategies. Doing so can support students in order to see other correct strategies and avoid pitfalls.It can even help struggling students get back on track. During group work, teachers can monitor the groups to provide feedback, assess how students are doing with the task, and plan for the discussion. Keep in mind that to be effective, feedback needs to cause thinking. Comments such as "Good job" do not do that (Leahy et al., 2005). Discourse that is productive moves learners forward.

Activating students as owners of their own learning. Setting up classroom norms that support powerful discourse is critical to activating students as owners of their own learning. When students know what is expected of them in terms of discourse, students understand that they hold shared responsibility for their own learning. Inviting students to share ideas, positioning students as having the right to evaluate the reasonableness of one another's mathematical ideas, and positioning students as authors of mathematical ideas helps to activate students as owners of their learning. Doing so can change students' beliefs about their learning capacities, causing a "growth mindset" rather than a fixed one (Dweck, 2006). It is important that teachers see their students as capable of improving when given the right help and support (Lee, 2006).

Activating students as instructional resources for one another. Supporting students to see themselves as instructional resources for one another is critical. When students give feedback to one another, students who receive and provide the feedback both benefit (Leahy et al., 2005). This can happen when teachers have students do a Think-Pair-Share activity or work in small groups. Providing students with Accountable Talk Stems (see Michaels, O'Connor, & Res-

27

nick, 2008 for more information on accountable talk) can give them phrases and sentences that will support them as they engage in discourse and respectfully agree or disagree with their peers or assert their own ideas. Having posters on the classroom walls with stems such as these can help students participate and draw on one another as resources:

- "I disagree with . . . and I agree with . . . because . . ."
- "At first I thought . . . but now I think . . . because . . ."
- "I don't understand what . . . meant when s/he said . . ."
- "Now I understand . . . because . . ."

Students can learn to use these stems not only in whole-class discussions, but also in small group discussions. Doing so can help teachers make strategic use of group work.

Table 3.1 illuminates connections between formative assessment strategies, classroom discourse, and teacher moves.

Table 3.1. Connections between formative assessment strategies, discourse, and teacher moves

Strategies for Supporting Formative Assessment	Connections between Formative Assessment Strategy and Discourse	Sample Teacher Moves (What does it sound like?)
Clarifying and sharing learning intentions and criteria for success	• Teachers communicate that all students are sense makers and that their ideas are valued (Kazemi & Hintz, 2014). • Teachers establish classroom norms for productive and powerful discourse. • Teachers launch tasks in ways that support students' understanding of the task (Jackson et al., 2012).	• Okay mathematicians, in this class we are going to communicate our reasoning. • Please keep in mind that everyone in the group is responsible for articulating the group's strategy. • In this class, we ask questions when we do not understand something. • Who thinks they can explain what the problem is asking? • Which words are most important and why?
Engineering effective classroom discussions, questions, and learning tasks	• Teachers use strategies for facilitating rich discussions (e.g., The Five Practices or Number Talks). • Teachers consider the kinds of questions that they are asking carefully, and they plan some questions and prompts in advance. • Teachers understand the relationship between good tasks and good discourse.	• Okay, now we're going to hear from a few groups, and I would like you to think about how each group's strategy is similar to and different from yours. • Who would like to defend their answer? • Can anyone explain why she multiplied? • Did anyone solve it differently? • Now here is a really important question: What's the connection between this term in the expression and the graph?

Table 3.1. Continued

Strategies for Supporting Formative Assessment	Connections between Formative Assessment Strategy and Discourse	Sample Teacher Moves (What does it sound like?)
Providing feedback that moves learners forward	• Teachers are strategic about when to tell. • Rather than rescuing their students when they are stuck, teachers have high expectations for how students should work with their groups. • Teachers sometimes explore incorrect answers. • Teachers monitor the room as their students are working. • Teachers use what they learned during monitoring to plan for productive discussions.	• So what you discovered was that when you divided the circumference of your circles by the diameter, you always got a number that's a little more than 3. You did a great job discovering that. Now I need to tell you that this number has a special name in mathematics. We call it pi. • Okay, in a few minutes we're going to come together as a class, and I want your group to come up and talk about your dilemma. • Okay, so you said you got 50, and this other group got 60. Does anyone see what's going on here? Why the two different answers? • Okay, so Jenna just asked a really important question. Jenna was wondering if there is a way to. . . . Does anyone have any thoughts on that?
Activating students as the owners of their learning	• Teachers invite students to share their ideas. • Teachers position students as having the right to evaluate the reasonableness of one another's mathematical ideas. • Teachers position students as authors of mathematical ideas. • Teachers facilitate a growth mind-set through discourse.	• Okay, we haven't heard from anyone on this side of the room yet, what did you all think? • Is this a reasonable answer? How do you know? • Does anyone want to revise his or her answer? • How do you know that your answer is right? • It's okay if you don't understand it yet, keep working on it. • What can we learn from this? • What strategy are you going to try next? • Now that you understand this, what is your plan to improve your work? • What did you learn from making that mistake?

Table 3.1. Continued

Strategies for Supporting Formative Assessment	Connections between Formative Assessment Strategy and Discourse	Sample Teacher Moves (What does it sound like?)

Activating students as resources for one another	• Teachers have students talk to one another in math class.
	
	• Teachers make strategic use of group work.
	
	• Teachers use the Think-Pair-Share strategy to give students an opportunity to think individually and to give all students opportunities to discuss their ideas.
	
	• Teachers provide students with accountable talk stems (Michaels et al., 2007).
		• Okay, now I want you to first think on your own, and then I want you to talk through your idea with your partner.
		
		• Keep in mind that on the side wall, we have posters with accountable talk stems. I want to hear you using these as I walk around.
		  • "I disagree with . . . , and I agree with . . . because . . . "
		  • "____ said . . . , which gave me an idea . . ."
		  • "Now I agree with ____ because . . ."

Supporting Students through Formative Assessment during Discourse: The Case of Mr. Steven

We met Mr. Steven in the opening section of this chapter. We read about how his views regarding the importance of discourse and student thinking shifted through participation in discourse-focused professional development. Here, we look into his geometry classroom again, three years after the class session discussed earlier. This time, students were asked to sketch a diagram that satisfies several conditions (see fig. 3.3). Mr. Steven had asked Lin, Jenna, Rochelle, and Donny to put the work on the board. Here, Mr. Steven is ready to facilitate a whole-class discussion around their work (see fig. 3.4). You will want to keep the five strategies described above in mind as you read this case.

Coordinating Geometric Notation and Diagrams

Sketch a single diagram that satisfies the following conditions. Mark your diagram.

- $\angle$ FGH is an obtuse angle
- $\angle$ HGJ is a supplement of $\angle$ FGH
- $\overline{FG} \cong \overline{GK}$ and $\overline{FG} \perp \overline{GK}$
- A segment connects F and K.

Name an isosceles right triangle in your drawing. _____

Name an acute angle in your drawing. _____

Fig. 3.3. Mr. Steven's task three years later

Mr. Steven: *Okay, Lin, stay up at the board so we can hear about your diagram and make sure to connect to the conditions from the task. Okay, everyone, so for now, we're just going to go over a few of the diagrams first, and then we'll discuss the two questions that come next.*

Lin: *All right, well first, it said that FGH had to be obtuse, so I drew that* [points to board]. *Then it said that angle HGJ was a supplement to FGH, so that's here* [gestures]. *Okay, so then you said FG and GK had to be congruent, so I drew GK and made the marks. And then I connected F and K.*

Mr. Steven: *Okay, did everyone understand what Lin just said? Does anyone have any questions for Lin? Yes, Tamara?*

Tamara: *Well, did you see the part about FG being perpendicular to GK? Because I don't think you said that, and it doesn't seem like that's in your drawing.*

Lin: *FG perpendicular to GK? Oh shoot. Nope, I guess I missed that. Okay, so I can fix that* [erases and redraws segment GK perpendicular to segment FG]. *Is that right now?*

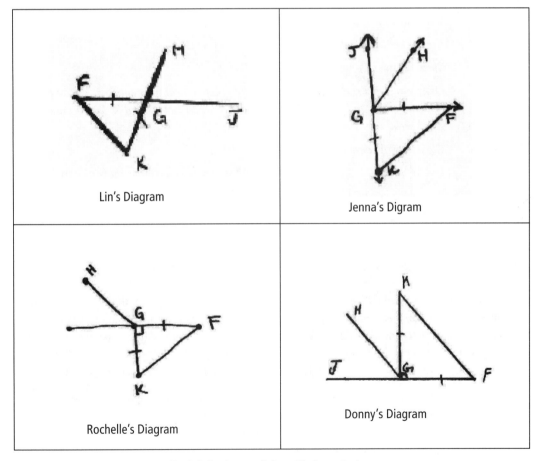

Fig. 3.4. Student work from Mr. Steven's class

Mr. Steven:	*What do you all think?*
Students:	*Yes. . . . No.*
Donny:	*It seems right now, but mine's pretty different, so I'm not sure.*
Mr. Steven:	*Okay, I heard a lot of yesses. Do you think that it's possible that there's more than one correct answer?*
Rochelle:	*Yeah, I think mine is right, and it's different than theirs.*
Mr. Steven:	*Okay, well, if no one sees anything wrong with Lin's ,then let's move on. Jenna, can you come up?* [Jenna goes up to the board.]
Jenna:	*Well, I realized that mine was wrong already, but I know how to fix it.*
Mr. Steven:	*Oh, okay, wait. Can you tell us about this diagram first?*
Jenna:	*Well I don't really know what I was thinking because it's all wrong. FGH is not obtuse. So then the whole thing is wrong.*
Mr. Steven:	*Okay, well, how do you think you can fix it?*
Jenna:	*Okay, if I just switch points F and K, then I think the whole thing works.*
Mr. Steven:	*What do you mean switch them? Move the points?*
Jenna:	*No; F should be K and K should be F. Can I do that?*
Mr. Steven:	*Sure.* [Jenna changes her diagram.]
Jenna:	*Okay now, let's see. FGH is obtuse. Yes. HGJ is a supplement. Yes. FG and GK are congruent and perpendicular. A segment connects F and K. Yup. I think that's good now.*
Mr. Steven:	*Class, any feedback for Jenna? Yes, Charlie?*
Charlie:	*Um, if she says it's perpendicular, don't you need that little square-thingy?*
Mr. Steven:	*Square-thingy? Seanae?*
Seanae:	*I think he means the perpendicular mark. Is that what you mean?*
Charlie:	*Yeah.*
Mr. Steven:	*Okay good, let's try to be precise with our language . . .*

Mr. Steven continues the discussion with the dual goals of making sure that students are able to translate the symbolic text into a diagram and helping students recognize that there is more than one correct way to draw the diagram (e.g., Rochelle's and Donny's diagrams). He also wants the students to construct an informal argument based on the given information about which angles they definitely know are acute angles. Mr. Steven reflected on the discourse of this lesson.

> Well compared to that first lesson that you showed me from a few years ago, I feel much better about this one. I think I am doing about the same amount of talking, which I don't love, but the kids are definitely talking more. Compared to the other one, this task is definitely more interesting. Something I learned is that if I want to have interesting discourse, then I have to give the kids something interesting to discuss. The task not only helps students work with the geometric objects, as the other one did, but also in a more interesting way. It also allows them to begin to work towards proof with some informal reasoning related to the

question about the acute angle. Also, I don't just call on different kids when they're wrong like I did in that other video. Here the whole point of having the kids put their work on the board is so I can see how they are thinking, and by engaging the rest of the class in a discussion, I can learn things about how some of the other students are thinking, using discourse as formative assessment, such as I learned in the PD. I still have some dilemmas, though., For instance, I remember that when Lin asked me if his diagram was correct, I'm never certain when it's appropriate for me to say that. I would like for the students to decide, but I guess what I did could leave some students confused.

As the case of Mr. Steven shows, attending to the tasks, norms, and classroom discourse, can really transform a classroom. His remarks also demonstrate the complexity of doing such work—working to improve your discourse does not happen overnight. As Herbel-Eisenmann and Cirillo (2009) demonstrated through cases of teachers' work to make discourse-related changes, change can be slow, and it is easy to slip back into old habits. Determining when it is productive to provide feedback and when it is not can also produce dilemmas. To this end, professional development goes a long way in supporting shifts in teachers' practices. In the section that follows, we offer examples of teacher education activities, with both preservice and in-service teachers, that can support teachers' capacity to facilitate productive and powerful discourse in their classrooms and to use discourse for formative assessment.

Supporting Purposeful, Productive, and Powerful Discourse in Teacher Development

In our own work with teachers, we have found that supporting teachers' capacity both to facilitate mathematics discussions among students and to make sense of student mathematical thinking is key to realizing the benefits of classroom discussion, including its potential to serve as a powerful formative assessment tool. In the following vignettes, we offer examples of activities we have designed for both preservice and in-service teacher education that can serve to highlight the useful connections between orchestrating classroom discourse and formative assessment. We focus on using discourse for formative assessment related to both students' mathematical learning and equitable engagement in mathematical activity.

Number Talks Rehearsal

The first vignette focuses on mathematical discussion "rehearsals" with preservice teachers where they can pause, rewind, and re-play the discourse moves they use to orchestrate classroom discussion. This ability to pause, rewind, and re-play allows teachers to gain feedback from peers when they feel stuck on how to proceed with orchestrating a discussion. Peers also get the chance to anticipate student strategies by playacting K–grade 12 students during the mathematical discussions.

The vignette described below offers a glimpse of a discussion rehearsal activity where teachers rehearsed number talks with their peers, who playacted the appropriate student age range. Teachers in this activity had the opportunity to rehearse the discourse moves involved in eliciting and probing students' mathematical thinking, inviting new student voices into the discussion, and responding to students' mathematical thinking in ways that support learning. In the activity, teachers are able to "pause" the rehearsal at any point if they are feeling stuck on how to continue facilitation of the discussion. Once paused, teachers can elicit advice from colleagues who are also serving in the role of students. When ready, the teacher can then "un-pause" or "rewind" the rehearsal and try again with a new move. The role of the teachers-as-students is just as important, as it gives teachers the opportunity to anticipate how young learners might approach a particular problem and consider the problem from students' perspectives.

Rehearsing Mathematical Discussions

"Okay, wait, pause," says Sara, punctuating her words with nervous laughter and hand-waving. "I feel like I don't know how to deal with that error." Her colleagues laugh along with her and offer encouragement. "That was a hard one!" Her colleague, Matt, admits, "I've seen students have errors like this before, so I was wondering how you would handle it, since I'm not sure." Ana raises her hand and offers an idea, "I think instead of trying to deal with the error, let the other students respond to his explanation and try to get more voices in." Heads nod. Sara agrees. "Oh, good idea. That way, I can see where the other students are with this. Ok, I want to un-pause and try again. Matt, so you said that one fourth is more than one half because four is greater than two, right? What do you all think about that? Does anyone agree or disagree with Matt?" Another colleague, Tim, performing his best attempt at a third grader's thinking, adds, "Well, I think it's less because I would rather have half of a cookie than a fourth of a cookie because in half a cookie you cut it in two pieces and in a fourth of a cookie you cut it in four pieces. So the half piece is bigger." Sara revoices Tim's explanation and draws two partitioned circles. "So which is the half?" The class points to one of the circles, and Sara labels "$1/2$." "And this one is a fourth?" Heads nod. She labels the other circle "$1/4$." She then turns back to Matt. "Matt, what do you think about that?"

This activity highlights the tight connection between orchestrating a mathematical discussion and using it as a powerful tool to elicit and make sense of students' mathematical thinking. In the vignette, Sara finds herself unsure about both how to respond to a student's error and also whether other students were thinking in a similar way. Rather than evaluate and correct Matt, Sara invites new student voices. In doing so, she gains the opportunity to assess how other students are thinking about denominators while also challenging Matt's thinking without direct evaluation on her part. She returns to Matt, asking what he thinks about Tim's explanation that one-half was more than a one-fourth. In doing so, Sara has the opportunity to assess Matt's thinking even further, once confronted with a potentially more productive way to reason about fractions.

Making student thinking visible through discourse allows teachers to assess and adjust their own instructional choices in-the-moment, increasing the likelihood that students learn. Knowing how to do this work, however, is neither simple nor easy. Rehearsing mathematical discussions with colleagues offers important learning opportunities for teachers. Teachers in Sara's role have the opportunity to practice orchestrating mathematical discussions, trying out discourse moves and responding to student thinking in a low-stakes and supportive environment. When unsure of what to do, Sara had the opportunity to request advice from her colleagues on how to proceed. At the same time, her colleagues, acting in the role of students, also had important learning opportunities. By attempting to engage in the discussion authentically in the role of young learners, Matt, Tim, and others had the opportunities to reflect on how students might actually think about fractional quantities and thereby practice anticipating how their students might actually engage in real mathematical discussions. Practice in both the discourse moves that elicit and probe student thinking and in anticipating student mathematical reasoning prepares teachers to use classroom discourse as a useful tool for formative assessment. They are able to make student thinking visible and to locate their thinking within a range of anticipated possibilities.

Video Club

The second vignette focuses on professional development where K–grade 12 teachers watched videos of their own students' group work discussions to notice collaborative dynamics and reflect on ways to support their students' small group discourse.

This activity can also be done with preservice teachers or in-service teachers, including those with substantial experience in supporting mathematics discourse. With preservice teachers, however, videos used in this activity would not come from their own classrooms, but from a bank of videos provided by the teacher educator. The goals of this activity are two-fold: (a) making sense of student thinking when conferring with small groups of students engaged in collaborative mathematical work and (b) assessing how students position themselves and one another as learners of mathematics during group work, a key concern in equitable teaching practices.

Small groups are an important context for mathematics discourse beyond the whole class discussion. One of the benefits of small group work is enabling far more students to engage in mathematical discussions with peers. At the whole-class level, relatively few students are able to take the floor; in small groups, all students have the opportunity to offer their ideas and respond to the ideas of their peers. The challenge for teachers is to ensure that students engage equitably with one another in their absence as well as productively engage with students' mathematical thinking during their brief time conferring with small groups.

Teachers do not typically have the opportunity to witness small group activity in action and reflect deeply on students' collaborative mathematical work. In this activity, teachers have the opportunity to take a sneak peek at students engaged in collaborative work and to make sense of how students negotiate both mathematical ideas and identities with one another. In this activity, teachers collectively watch videos of students from their own classrooms (or others' classrooms especially in the case of preservice teachers) engaged in small group mathematical discussions. Teachers come together to watch videos and to discuss what they notice about how students engage with one another's ideas, making sense of not only what mathematical ideas are exchanged between students, but also whose ideas are attended to and whose are rejected or ignored by peers. In the vignette that follows, teachers discuss what they notice about students' discussions with one another.

Noticing Ideas and Identities during Collaborative Math Activity

The mathematics teacher educator, facilitating the day's PD, launches the activity. "We'll begin with a clip from Luz's 6th grade classroom. The students at the table have a set of cards with different representations of rational numbers and are tasked with putting the cards in order from least to greatest. In the clip, the students at the focal table are trying to figure out where to place $12/25$. As you watch the clip, I want you to notice how students are getting this work accomplished. What ideas do they offer? Who offers what ideas? What happens to those ideas?"

As the four-minute clip plays, a room of eight teachers, including Luz, watch intently, some jotting down notes rapidly, while others lean forward cupping their chins with their hands as they pay close attention to the students' collaborative dynamics. When the clip ends, Carla, a seventh grade teacher, offers some observations. "I noticed that the boy on the top right of the screen kept trying to get the others to notice how close $12/25$ was to a half, but they wouldn't let him get the words out!" "I noticed that, too" said another teacher, jumping in. "They kept *wanting to turn all of the fractions into decimals and were getting stuck on the computation. I don't think they really noticed what he was saying." She added, "I also noticed that the two who were dominating the conversation were just really stuck on this strategy of converting to decimals. They were huddled over the paper. And the fourth student, the girl with the yellow shirt, she was just shut out totally. Like, spatially, she didn't even look like she was in the group." Luz interjected, "It's interesting. It's interesting because the boy on the top right trying to get them to notice that it's close to a half, Dominic, he doesn't usually see himself as good at math. I'm kinda not surprised they ignored him, but I'm frustrated to see this because he was the only one thinking about it the way I had hoped, I'm actually really impressed, and I'm wondering how I could've, you know, made sure they gave him the chance to offer that idea."*

This activity highlights the power of discourse for formative assessment of both mathematical understandings and issues of equity. Luz and her colleagues had the opportunity to notice which strategies different students were bringing to the task of ordering rational numbers. In noticing how students were talking to one another as they worked together on the task, she saw that one student, Dominic, was anchoring $12/25$ to $1/2$, while two other students were trying to convert the fraction into decimal form. At the same time, she also had the opportunity to notice what was happening to whose ideas—specifically, that a productive idea was being ignored while other students struggled with computation. Luz also had the opportunity to notice that one of the students was largely shut out of the collaboration both spatially and verbally. In bringing these dynamics to the surface through video records of group work and discussing what they notice with colleagues, teachers had the opportunity to reflect on how they might notice and respond to similar mathematical understandings and the collaborative dynamics next time in their own classrooms.

Enhancing Connections between Formative Assessment and Discourse Practices

Classroom discourse offers productive and powerful formative assessment opportunities. However, the connections between classroom discourse and formative assessment are not always illuminated during professional development. We propose three particularly important connections that could be more explicitly leveraged by teachers and teacher educators during professional activities. One, the connection between eliciting and probing student thinking through particular discourse moves can reveal students' mathematical understandings. Classroom discourse can help students develop conceptual understanding, while simultaneously revealing and clarifying students' partial understandings and misconceptions (Chapin et al., 2013). Two, making sense of and responding to student thinking revealed during discussions supports student learning in ways that are immediately responsive to formative assessment. Making good use of classroom discourse and discussion tools enables teachers to inform and adjust instruction in ways that meet students where they are. Three, attending to the dynamics of participation in mathematical discussion offers a way in which to assess equitable learning opportunities. Attending to these three things can support discourse that is purposeful, productive, and powerful.

Topics for Further Study

While much about classroom discourse has been studied and learned over the past few decades, there are many questions that still remain for the field. Just a few examples follow.

- What kinds of discourse moves best propel learners forward and under what conditions?
- What are some guidelines that will support teachers in knowing when to tell students and when to let students struggle?
- How can we assess whether students are engaging in destructive versus productive struggle?
- What is an inclusive set of classroom norms that will prime a classroom where students can engage in productive and powerful discourse?
- What does planning for purposeful discourse look like?
- Under what conditions do particular discourse moves, like revoicing, help or hinder the discourse?
- What is the proper balance of recitation and discussion to maximize student learning?
- How can teachers use discourse to support equitable participation in their classrooms?

Selected Commonly Used Resources

Chapin, S. H., O'Connor, C., & Anderson, N. C. (2013). *Talk Moves: A Teacher's Guide for Using Classroom Discussions in Math*. Sausalito, CA: Math Solutions.

Herbel-Eisenmann, B., & Cirillo, M. (Eds.). (2009). *Promoting Purposeful Discourse*. Reston, VA: National Council of Teachers of Mathematics.

Herbel-Eisenmann, B., Cirillo, M., Steele, M. D., Otten, S., & Johnson, K. R. (in press). *Mathematics Discourse in Secondary Classrooms: A Case-Based Professional Development Curriculum*. Sausalito, CA: Math Solutions.

Kazemi, E., & Hintz, A. (2014). *Intentional Talk: How to Structure and Lead Productive Mathematical Discussions*. Portland, ME: Stenhouse Publishers.

Lee, C. (2006). *Language for Learning Mathematics*. New York: Open University Press.

Smith, M. S., & Stein, M. K. (2011). *5 Practices for Orchestrating Productive Mathematics Discussions*. Reston, VA: National Council of Teachers of Mathematics.

Acknowledgments

We thank the teachers whose classroom videos and professional development sessions formed the basis of the cases in this chapter. We also thank Amanda Seiwell and Zack Murtha, whose math tasks formed the basis of the vignette. The research reported in this chapter was supported with funding from the National Science Foundation (award #0918117, PIs: Herbel-Eisenmann, Cirillo, and Steele; award #1453493, PI: Cirillo), a private donor grant through Stanford's Center to Support Excellence in Teaching (CSET; PIs: Langer-Osuna and Carlson) and an Institute for Research in the Social Sciences (IRiSS) faculty fellowship (PI: Langer-Osuna). Any opinions, findings, conclusions, or recommendations expressed in this material are those of the authors and do not necessarily reflect the views of the NSF, CSET, or IRiSS.

Reflect on Your Practice

1. Initiate-Response-Evaluate (IRE) and "meaningful discourse" are two ways of thinking about talk in mathematics classrooms. To what extent does your practice reflect each of these forms of discourse? How might you move your practice towards more meaningful discourse?

2. In what ways do you already use discourse as a tool for formative assessment? What are some additional things you could do to use discourse as a tool for formative assessment that you are not already doing?

Connect Your Practice with Colleagues

1. In the opening quotation for this chapter, Clare Lee asserts that "Feedback is only formative (i.e., helpful to learning) if the information fed back to the learner is used by the learner in improving their learning."

   - What does it mean for feedback to be used by the learner (rather than just by the teacher)?
   - What are some ways that discourse could be used as a tool to feed information back to the learner?
   - What evidence would tell us that doing so improves students' learning?
   - What important information about students, or "data," exists within classroom discourse that can serve as formative assessment?
   - How might discourse uncover both student understandings and misunderstandings? How might that inform your teaching?

2. In Mr. Steven's two teaching episodes, find evidence in the discourse of where he makes use of the formative assessment strategies described in Table 3.1. Where do you see missed opportunities?

References

Arbaugh, F. (2010). Secondary school mathematics teachers' classroom practices. In J. E. Lobato (Ed.), *Teaching and learning mathematics: Translating research for secondary school teachers* (pp. 45–51). Reston, VA: National Council of Teachers of Mathematics.

Cazden, C. B. (1988). *Classroom Discourse: The Language of Teaching and Learning.* Portsmouth, NH: Heinemann.

Chapin, S. H., O'Connor, C., & Anderson, N. C. (2013). *Talk Moves: A Teacher's Guide for Using Classroom Discussions in Math.* Sausalito, CA: Math Solutions.

Cirillo, M. (2013). "What Does Research Say the Benefits of Discussion in Mathematics Class Are?" A National Council of Teachers of Mathematics (NCTM) Research Brief, edited by S. DeLeeuw, pp. 1–6. Reston, VA: NCTM.

Cirillo, M., Steele, M. D., Otten, S., Herbel-Eisenmann, B., McAneny, K., & Riser, J. (2014). Teacher discourse moves: Supporting productive and powerful discourse. In K. Karp (Ed.), *Using Research to Improve Instruction* (pp. 141–149). Reston, VA: National Council of Teachers of Mathematics.

Dweck, C. (2006). *Mindset: The new psychology of sucess.* Random House.

Herbel-Eisenmann, B., & Cirillo, M. (Eds.). (2009). *Promoting purposeful discourse.* Reston, VA: NCTM.

Herbel-Eisenmann, B., Cirillo, M., Steele, M. D., Otten, S., & Johnson, K. R. (2017). *Mathematics discourse in secondary classrooms: A practice-based resource for professional learning.* Sausalito, CA: Math Solutions.

Jackson, K. J., Shahan, E. C., Gibbons, L. K., & Cobb, P. A. (2012). Launching complex tasks. *Mathematics Teacher, 18*(1), 24–29.

Kazemi, E., & Hintz, A. (2014). *Intentional talk: How to structure and lead productive mathematical discussions.* Portland, ME: Stenhouse Publishers.

Lampert, M. (1990). When the problem is not the question and the solution is not the answer: Mathematical knowing and teaching. *American Educational Research Journal, 27*, 29–63.

Leahy, S., Lyon, C., Thompson, M., & Wiliam, D. (2005). Classroom assessment: Minute by minute, day by day. *Educational Leadership, 63*(3), 19–24.

Lee, C. (2006). *Language for learning mathematics.* New York: Open University Press.

Mehan, H. (1979). *Learning lessons: Social organization in the classroom.* Cambridge, MA: Harvard University Press.

Michaels, S., O'Connor, C., & Resnick, L. B. (2008). Deliberative discourse idealized and realized: accountable talk in the classroom and in civic life. *Studies in Philosophy and Education, 27*(4), 283–297. doi:10.1007/s11217-007-9071-1

National Council of Teachers of Mathematics. (1989). *Curriculum and evaluation standards for school mathematics.* Reston, VA: Author.

National Council of Teachers of Mathematics. (1991). *Professional standards for teaching mathematics.* Reston, VA: Author.

National Council of Teachers of Mathematics. (2000). *Principles and standards for school mathematics.* Reston, VA: Author.

National Council of Teachers of Mathematics. (2014). *Principles to actions: Ensuring mathematical success for all.* Reston, VA: NCTM.

Rose, C. M., & Arline, C. B. (2008). *Uncovering student thinking in mathematics grades 6–12: 30 formative assessment probes for the secondary classroom.* Thousand Oaks, CA: Corwin Press.

Smith, M. S., & Stein, M. K. (2011). *5 practices for orchestrating productive mathematics discussions.* Reston, VA: NCTM.

# Chapter 4

Cognitively Guided Instruction and Formative Assessment

Linda Levi and Rebecca Ambrose

It's impossible to describe Cognitively Guided Instruction without mentioning the crucial elements of formative assessment. Cognitively Guided Instruction (CGI) is a professional learning (PL) program that helps teachers understand their students' mathematical thinking and use information about that thinking in order to guide instruction. Formative assessment is central in CGI classrooms where teachers assess students' thinking within the stream of instruction while they are solving problems, explaining their work, or reflecting on another student's strategy. Information about students' mathematical thinking guides all of the instructional decisions that CGI teachers make. In this chapter, we describe ways in which CGI both uses and provides substantial support for the powerful and effective use of formative assessment in elementary school mathematics classes.

Dylan Wiliam (2007) identified CGI as one of the best-known programs to integrate assessment and instruction. A distinctive feature of CGI is its research-based frameworks that describe how children's understanding of mathematical concepts develops and how problem characteristics influence how children think about these concepts. CGI Professional Learning focuses on supporting teachers' understanding of these frameworks. Over the past 30 years, the CGI frameworks have expanded to incorporate many elementary school mathematics concepts including: addition and subtraction, multiplication and division, operations with multi-digit numbers, base ten number concepts, algebraic reasoning, equations and fractions. Research indicates that understanding these frameworks enables teachers to adjust instruction to guide students towards more sophisticated understandings and plan instruction based on students' thinking (see Fennema, Carpenter, Franke, Levi, Jacobs, & Empson, 1996, for example).

In this chapter, we employ a vignette to help the reader gain insight into CGI and understand how CGI teachers engage in formative assessment. We show how a teacher's knowledge of the CGI framework describing children's base ten understanding supports her formative assessment and how formative assessment is essential to her instruction. We highlight distinctive features of formative assessment in a CGI classroom, as well as connections to the five strategies supporting formative assessment (Leahy et al., 2005).

Thomas Carpenter (1989) wrote "the teaching-learning process is too complex to specify in advance, and as a consequence teaching is essentially problem solving" (p. 199). This complexity makes it impossible to convey every detail of a lesson and all of the decisions that a teacher makes while orchestrating classroom activity. Our vignette illustrates some, but not all, of the formative assessment the teacher engaged in during this lesson. The problem-solving nature of teaching also means that each CGI teacher develops their own approaches to putting the CGI frameworks into play in their instruction. The vignette is only one example of many possible ways in which CGI teachers organize their instruction and engage in formative assessment. The vignette is infused with elements of Leahy's five strategies of formative assessment to allow the reader to see how each of these elements of formative assessment is a part of CGI. Connections to these formative assessment strategies are underlined in the vignette. In addition to the vignette, we discuss CGI Professional Development to show the kinds of activities that are used to support teachers in learning and applying the CGI frameworks. We conclude by highlighting distinctive features of the CGI approach to formative assessment.

Classroom Vignette

Ms. Harris is a second-grade teacher at a Title One school. Ms. Harris participated in three years of CGI professional learning seminars and has been using CGI for six years. The lesson takes place in the fall and focuses on developing students' understanding of base ten number concepts.

Planning for Instruction

When planning for instruction, CGI teachers use assessments of their students' thinking from prior lessons to set a general learning goal for the lesson. They choose a task to engage students in this *general* goal, and set *specific* learning goals for individual children that are aligned with each child's current understanding of the concept in the general learning goal.

Planning for instruction—general learning goal

Ms. Harris's *general learning goal* for this lesson was to develop her students' understanding of how a two- or three-digit number can be decomposed into groups of ten. This learning goal appears in her state standards and the second-grade teachers at her school decided to focus on base ten number concepts at the beginning of the year. As is typical for CGI teachers, Ms. Harris's learning goals differ from standard learning goals in that Ms. Harris does not expect children to master a learning goal in one lesson. She believes that if she were to set learning goals in terms of skills or concepts that could be mastered in one lesson, she would then end up choosing goals that weren't terribly important. She avoids using the term "mastery," holding the view that students can revisit a mathematical idea repeatedly and gain new insights (Franke, 2016). She sets long-term learning goals, which students approach over a period of time. For example, she knows her students began developing an understanding of base ten when they were in kindergarten and that base ten concepts will be revisited many times during students' academic careers as they progress to working with larger numbers and decimals.

After defining a general learning goal, Ms. Harris sets *specific learning goals for individual children* that are based on her formative assessments in previous lessons of each child's current understanding of the concept described in the general learning goal. Since not all of her students were at the same level, setting one learning goal for the entire class would mean that some of her students would either already understand the mathematical content in the learning goal or that the learning goal would not be realistic for other students, or both. Ms. Harris understands that in planning her lesson, she must select a task that can advance the general and specific learning goals for her students.

Planning for instruction—choosing a task

From her experience in CGI professional learning, Ms. Harris knows that multiplicative thinking, treating a group of units as a composite, is at the heart of base-ten understanding. She relies on the CGI research-based framework of problem types and strategies for base ten number concepts to choose a task for this problem. Examples of these problems and the strategies that students use to solve them appear in Table 4.1. (For more information on this framework, and other CGI frameworks, see Carpenter et al., 2015.)

Table 4.1. Word problems with groups of tens and strategies for solving these problems

Strategy Levels	Word Problems	
	Multiplication with 10 in a group Arden had 8 bags of rocks with 10 rocks in each bag. How many rocks does Arden have?	**Measurement Division with 10 in a group** Eve has 67 dollars to spend on books. If each book costs 10 dollars how many books could she buy?
Count by Ones	 Child makes 8 circles and then puts 10 dots in each circle, counts each dot, 1, 2, 3, 4, . . . 80	 Child makes 67 dots, counting 1, 2, 3, . . . 67, circles groups of 10 dots and counts the number of circles to get 6
Count by Tens	"10, 20, 30, 40, 50, 60, 70, 80, she has 80 rocks." (note—child has to keep track of counts in some way)	"10, 20, 30, 40, 50, 60, she can buy 6 books" (note—child has to keep track of counts in some way)
Direct Place Value	80, 8 tens is 80	6, there are 6 tens in 60

The CGI framework of strategy development enables teachers to support children to advance in their thinking when the children are ready to do so. CGI teachers recognize that students' progress will vary and that bypassing any of the stages of development can lead to misconceptions. Based on her learning goals and prior assessments of students' understanding of base ten number concepts, Ms. Harris *engineered the following learning task* for today's lesson.

Keisha has ____ crayons and it takes 10 crayons to fill a box. How many boxes can Keisha fill? (74, 154)

The children in her class understand that when there is a blank (or blanks) in the problem and numbers that follow at the end that they can insert either number (or sets of numbers) into the blank(s) before solving the problem. Sometimes Ms. Harris asks children to choose the numbers for the problem that will challenge but not overwhelm them. She found that the move of asking students to choose appropriate numbers for a problem provides an opportunity to *activate her students as owners of their learning.* Ms. Harris learned that with some initial guidance, most children do an excellent job of choosing numbers appropriate to their current understanding.

Planning for instruction—specific learning goals for individual children

Ms. Harris *engineered this learning task* because she knew that this problem, at least with the smaller numbers, would allow all of her students to engage with the concept of decomposing a number into groups of ten. She set the following specific learning goals for individual children, based on previous formative assessments (see Table 4.2).

Table 4.2. Ms. Harris's learning goals for individual students

Students	Ms. Harris's Learning Goal for these students
Randy, Grant, Cady	**Use a correct strategy to solve this problem:** These children haven't been successful with problems like this in the past. My goal is that they will be able to solve the problem by producing of model that matches the situation described in the story problem text. They won't be ready to engage deeply with base ten number concepts until they can generate a model of what is happening in the story. If they don't produce their own model, my goal is that they understand another student's model when it is presented to the class.
Daniela, River, Eliza, Michael, and Myra	**Use tens rather than ones to solve this problem:** In the past, these children have solved problems like this by Counting by Ones. All of these children can count by tens to 100 by rote but they haven't used Counting by Tens to solve these problems. My goal for them is that they engage with the concept that 1 ten is the same as 10 ones and at least understand a Counting by Tens strategy when another student presents it to the class.
Tylesha, Cameron, Laurel	**Develop proficiency in using tens to solve this problem:** Counting by Tens is a new strategy for these students and its use indicates that they are developing an understanding of ten as a unit. My goal for them is that they use Counting by Tens when the problem involves 74 crayons. Continued use of this strategy indicates that their understanding of ten as a unit is deepening.
Tyrone, Tyler, Kianna, Donovan, Xylia, Maria, Keisha, Michaela	**Use tens to solve the three-digit division problem:** These children routinely use Counting by Tens to solve this type of problem for two-digit numbers. I hope that they will extend the Counting by Tens strategy for three-digit numbers and are able to follow along when another student explains the Direct Place Value Strategy.
Meadow, Anna, Charles	**Use Direct Place Value to solve the 3-digit problem:** I have seen each of these children use Direct Place Value for problems with two-digit numbers. My goal for them is that they are able to use Direct Place Value for the problem with 154 crayons and that they are able to produce a written representation of how they solved this problem.

As is evident in Table 4.2, Ms. Harris had five different specific learning goals, each addressing a different level of development in the students in her class. She set these specific learning goals by matching her observations and interpretations of children's strategies onto the strategy levels in the CGI framework and did not expect that all students will achieve the goal in one lesson. Setting mathematically specific learning goals for individual children without such a framework would be extremely challenging, if not impossible. Ms. Harris usually doesn't write out the learning goals for each of her students. Students will be working toward these goals throughout the school year so writing out these specific learning goals once or twice a month is often enough for Ms. Harris to ensure she is matching instruction to assessments of students' thinking.

Teaching the Lesson

The lesson in this vignette follows the general format of—

- the teacher poses the problem to the class;
- Students solve the problem individually while the teacher monitors progress and has discussions with individual students; and
- the class reconvenes to share strategies for solving the problem.

Although this is a common format for CGI lessons, it is not the only format that CGI teachers use.

Posing the problem

Ms. Harris read the problem to her students assembled on the rug, gave each of her students a sheet of paper with the problem written on it and sent them back to their desks to solve the problem. Ms. Harris posed the problem without providing instruction, either directly or indirectly, on how to solve it. Children had a variety of tools available to them such as linking cubes and base ten materials. Sometimes, Ms. Harris spends more time launching a problem when she feels that her students need support in understanding the context.

Although Ms. Harris didn't share specific learning goals with her students, she described some *performance criteria*. After reading the problems aloud, Ms. Harris said, "You need to solve this problem using a strategy that you can explain. I don't want to see just your answer; I also want to see how you solved the problem. Do your best to make sure that what you write on your paper would show someone how you solved the problem, even if you aren't there to explain it."

Discussions with individual students

After posing the problem, Ms. Harris circulated around the room, took notes about children's solution strategies and worked individually with children during independent problem-solving time. The following interaction with River shows how Ms. Harris *regulated learning interactively*. Ms. Harris saw the following on River's paper shown in figure 4.1. Her strategy for the first problem is at the top of the paper; she had started solving the second problem at the bottom of her paper.

Fig. 4.1. River's strategy when Ms. Harris interacted with her

Ms. Harris's specific learning goal for River was that she engage with the concept that 1 ten is the same as 10 ones. Although River had the right answer for the first problem, she wasn't thinking of 10 as 10 ones.

Ms. Harris:	*River, I see you started the second problem. I am going to interrupt you because I really want to know how you solved the first problem.*
River:	*Keisha had 74 crayons and I just made boxes of ten, I did 1, 2, 3, 4, 5, 6, 7, 8, 9, 10* [points to a line in the first box for each number she says] *that's one box, but that's not all of her crayons, so I did 1, 2, 3, 4, 5, 6, 7, 8, 9, 10* [points to a line in the second box for each number she says] *that's two boxes, so that's 10* [pause] *11, 12, 13, 14, 15, 16, 17, 18, 19, 20 but that's still not all of her crayons.* [River continues describing her strategy of making 10 lines in a box and counting them one by one.]
Ms. Harris:	*I understand what you did and your picture shows me what you did. Good job explaining your thinking. Wow, that is a lot of counting. When we do a lot of counting like that, is it pretty easy to make a mistake?*
River:	*Yes, and now she has 154 crayons for this problem. And I don't even remember how many crayons I used so far.*

Ms. Harris:	[pointing to the second strategy, under the line] *How could you figure that out how many crayons are in these boxes so far?*
River:	*I could count them, 1, 2, 3, 4, 5, 6, 7, 8, 9, 10, 11, 12, 13.*
Ms. Harris:	*I am sorry to interrupt you, but I have a question, is there another way you could count those?*
River:	*I could count them by twos.*
Ms. Harris:	*You could count them by twos, it would be a little faster. Is there any other way?* [Long pause] *Maybe something one of your classmates did?* [Long pause] *Remember how Tylesha shared with us yesterday with the cracker problem?*

River counted by ones instead of by tens, so Ms. Harris's *provided feedback to move her forward* by asking, "Is there another way you could count?" Her feedback then got more specific when she asked, "Do you remember what Tylesha did?" thus allowing for *minimal intervention* when supporting River. We return to the vignette and River now answers Ms. Harris'squestion about what Tylesha did yesterday.

River:	*Tylesha counted by tens. It was really fast.*
Ms. Harris:	*Do you want to try that?*
River:	*Ok, 10, 20, 30, 40, 50, 60*
Ms. Harris:	*So how many crayons have you put in boxes so far?*
River:	*60*
Ms. Harris:	*I wonder if you could use that idea to solve the rest of the problem. I want you to really think about how you could count by tens to solve the rest of the problem.*

Ms. Harris walked away from the discussion so that River could decide for herself how to proceed. This move *provides feedback* to students at a *minimal level of intervention* that doesn't interfere with their learning process.

Just before the group sharing of strategies, Ms. Harris looked at River's paper (fig. 4.2). After her extended interaction with River, a quick glance is all she needed to assess that River began to treat 10 as a composite, achieving the specific goal that Ms. Harris had set for River for the problem.

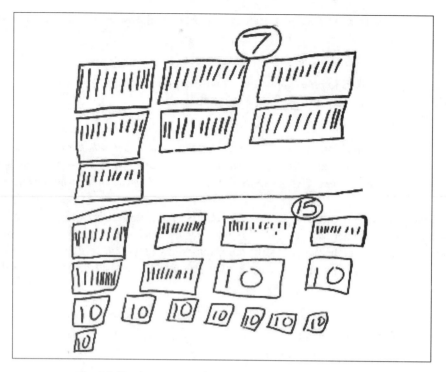

Fig. 4.2. River's strategy at the end of the problem-solving time

Ms. Harris had supportive verbal interactions with three other students as she circulated through the room. She took a quick look at the work of the other twenty-three students to determine what strategy they used. Understanding the CGI framework gave Ms. Harris a structure to quickly interpret the mathematical thinking for the twenty-six children in her classroom. Without understanding this framework, it would be very hard, if not impossible, to consider how twenty-six students solved this problem when engineering an effective classroom discussion of their strategies that would engage all students with the six specific mathematical learning goals that Ms. Harris identified for this problem.

Ms. Harris doesn't usually collect information about every child's strategy for every problem she poses. Even with her understanding of the CGI framework, there were a couple of students whose strategies remained unclear to her; however, she did not have time to follow up during the lesson. She planned to follow up with them on another day. She reviews her notes every couple of weeks and ensures that she isn't systematically missing information on any of her students.

Engineering the whole-group discussion

Before the lesson began, Ms. Harris predicted how her students would solve these problems but because children's thinking is dynamic, these predictions were tentative. She noted who used a strategy that was different from what they used in the past; the names of the children who used different strategies are underlined. Ms. Harris'ssolid understanding of the framework enabled her to see that ten students' strategies changed. Ms. Harris'splanning process enabled her also to gather evidence so she could decide what strategies to have children share, the order in which they would be shared, and the reason for sharing each strategy (see Table 4.3). Ms. Harris considered her specific learning goals to target her interactions during the strategy discussion to further assess her students while also advancing their thinking.

Table 4.3. Ms. Harris's assessment of students' strategies gathered during instruction (underlined names indicate students who used different strategies)

Strategy Used to Solve the Problem	Students who used this strategy
Invalid strategy—child doesn't seem to understand the problem	Randy, Grant, Daniela
Counting by Ones	Myra, Cady
	River starts Counting by Ones but moves to Counting by Tens with help
	Eliza started Counting by Ones but moved to Counting by Tens *without* help from the teacher
Counting by Tens	Michael, Laurel—only solved the problem with 74 crayons
	Tylesha, Cameron, Tyrone, Tyler, Kianna, Xylia, Maria—used Counting by Tens for both problems
Direct Place Value	Michaela—for one problem
	Meadow and Anna—for both problems
Students with unclear strategies	Keisha, Donovan, Charles

Ms. Harris orchestrated the discussion of students' strategies into three different segments.

1. A student shared a Counting by Ones strategy so that Grant, Randy, and Daniela—who didn't use a valid strategy to solve this problem—were able to see a strategy that they were most likely able to understand.

2. A student shared a Counting by Tens strategy so that the group of students who Counted by Ones could see this strategy and further develop their understanding of ten as a unit.

3. The Direct Place Value strategy was discussed with a particular focus on how one can produce a written representation of this strategy.

Readers will notice in the dialogue that follows that *students are activated as resources for each other.* Students make several comments that have the potential to move their classmates forward. Note that when a child shares a strategy with this class, Ms. Harris focused more on the students who needed to understand the strategy rather than the student who was sharing the strategy. Ms. Harris and other students asked questions about the details of the strategy; they weren't only attending to the answer. CGI research shows that engaging with the details of another student's strategy and having classmates engage with your strategy are both positively related to student achievement (Webb et al., 2014).

In the sections that follow, we present a detailed account of the first discussion, and then highlights of the other two. Readers might wish to pay special attention to the following:

• Ms. Harris's questions often serve the dual purpose of assessing what a student understands, as well as potentially moving the student forward.

• Ms. Harris asks different questions and provides different feedback for each student on the basis of the specific learning goal she has for that child.

• *Students are activated as resources* for one another by sharing their strategies with each other and reflecting on each other's strategies.

Segment 1: A student shares a Counting by Ones strategy

Randy, Grant and Daniela didn't use a valid strategy to solve this problem. Ms. Harris started by having Cady share a Counting by Ones strategy (fig. 4.3) and questioned Randy, Grant and Daniela to support them in understanding the problem so that they could have a better chance of understanding the subsequent strategies. Ms. Harris gathered the children to the rug at the front of the room and asked Cady to place her paper on the document camera.

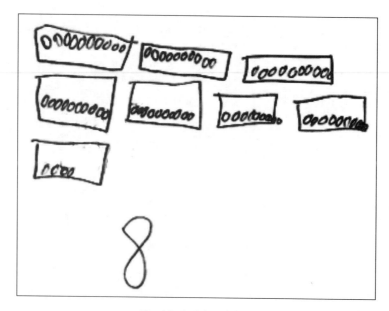

Fig. 4.3. Cady's strategy

Ms. Harris asked Cady to explain how she solved the problem.

Cady:	*Keisha has 74 crayons to put into boxes, so I first made a box, and then I put 10 crayons in that box. That is what you said, 10 crayons go into a box.*
Ms. Harris:	*[Covers up all but the first box on Cady's paper] Randy, Cady said that this is what she did first. Why do you think she did this?*
Randy:	*I bet that is one box full of crayons*
Ms. Harris:	*Cady, is he right?*
Cady:	*Yes, that is what I am doing. Keisha is putting away the crayons, and there are 10 in a box.*
Ms. Harris:	*Grant, what do you think Cady will do next?*
Grant:	*I did 74 plus 10 more.*
Ms. Harris:	*Ok. Let's look at the story. Keisha has 74 crayons and it takes 10 crayons to fill a box. How many boxes can Keisha fill? Does Cady have 74 crayons and gets 10 more?*
Grant:	*No, but I don't know how to do it.*
Ms. Harris:	*Ok, so I want you to watch Cady really closely, because I think watching her will help. Think about the story while you are watching Cady.*

Cady continued to explain her strategy. When she got to the fifth box with 10 in it, Ms. Harris asked Grant another question.

Ms. Harris: *Grant, why do you think Cady made all of those rectangles?*

Grant: *Those are the boxes in the story.*

Ms. Harris: *And what do you think the little circles are?*

Grant: *Those are the crayons. Ten in each box.*

The class discussed Cady's strategy a bit more and then Ms. Harris asked if everyone agreed with Cady's answer. A student said, "No, the boxes have to be full and the last box only had four." Cady didn't understand at first, but then they reread the problem and Cady agreed. She changed her answer to 7.

There are many ways in which Ms. Harris engaged in formative assessment during this discussion. When she questioned Randy, she determined that he didn't need much support to engage with Cady's strategy. Conversely, Grant needed more support to understand Cady's strategy, so Ms. Harris asked him several questions. Rather than pose an open question for anyone in the class to answer or randomly call on students, Ms. Harris targeted specific children during this strategy sharing because she had identified a specific learning goal for them and engineered this part of the discussion to meet their needs.

Segment 2: A student shares a Counting by Tens strategy

Ms. Harris targeted a different group of children when she had Cameron share his strategy of Counting by Tens. While several children used this strategy, Ms. Harris chose Cameron to share because his representation shown in figure 4.4 clearly shows his strategy.

Fig. 4.4. Cameron's strategy

When the class discussed Cameron's strategy, students noted that he not only showed 10 in each box but he also showed how he counted by tens. Several students mentioned that they counted by tens but didn't write how they counted on their papers.

Ms. Harris positioned Cady's strategy next to Cameron's strategy on the document camera and asked Cady how her strategy differed from Cameron's.

Ms. Harris: *Cady, How is Cameron's strategy different than yours?*

Cady: *I don't see the crayons.*

Ms. Harris: *What do you see?*

Cady: *He wrote 10 in a box.*

Ms. Harris: *Why do you think he wrote 10?*

Cady: *[long pause] I am not sure.*

Ms. Harris: *Tyrone, do you know why he wrote the tens?*

Tyrone: *He counted by tens. He didn't write all of the crayons and that was much faster.*

Ms. Harris: *Myra, Tyrone said that there were 10 crayons in each box so that is why Cameron just wrote a 10, what do you think about that?*

Myra: *I did it like Cady but I think I see. 10, 20, 30, 40, 50, 60, 70—70 crayons. That is much faster.*

Ms. Harris: *Is that what you did Cameron?*

Cameron: *Yes, I wrote 10, I didn't write each crayon. That would take a long time and I could have made a mistake.*

Ms. Harris: *Myra, maybe you want to try Cameron's strategy when we have a problem like this again.*

Ms. Harris had Cameron describe his strategy for solving the second problem and the discussion continued.

Again, Ms. Harris engaged in formative assessment in many ways during this segment. Note that Ms. Harris targeted her questions to specific individuals to focus their attention on the advancement that she believed they were ready to make. Again, students who used more sophisticated strategies were not called on during this segment.

Segment 3: The Direct Place Value strategy is discussed

Ms. Harris wondered if some students' written strategies indicated that they Counted by Tens to solve this problem, even though they used Direct Place Value. In order to assess these students' strategy use, she asked the children to stay on the rug and solve a new problem involving 93 crayons put into boxes of 10 and to put up a thumb when they got an answer. She looked for evidence of children's strategies by noticing which children used their fingers, how they used their fingers, and how long it took them to get an answer. She invited Kianna, who put her thumb up right away to share her strategy. Kianna reported knowing that 93 has 90, which is 9 tens, and adds that this is how she solved the problem with 74 crayons; 70 is 7 tens. Ms. Harris then showed Kianna's written work, which is similar to Cameron's, and the group discussed how her representation could be altered to represent Kianna's strategy better.

Ms. Harris's goal for this segment was somewhat different from her goals for the other two. Here she hoped to push students to develop notation so that students using the Direct Place Value strategy can effectively convey that strategy on paper. While this is a specific goal for some of the students in the class, participating in the group discussion allowed all of the students access to this strategy. Ms. Harris did not emphasize that she wants all students to use this strategy, because she knows that not all students are ready to use this strategy with understanding and she did not want them to skip important developmental milestones along the way.

Essential Connections between CGI and Formative Assessment

Throughout this vignette we identified ways in which Ms. Harris used the five formative assessment strategies identified by Leahy et al. (2005). Although CGI teachers use all five strategies, *activating students as owners of their own learning* sets the foundation for all formative assessment strategies. Students solving problems by generating their own strategies is essential to activating students as owners of their learning. When teachers demonstrate and expect students to replicate these strategies, students learn that mathematical ideas start with the teacher. In contrast, when students are presented with problems and expected to generate their own strategies to solve these problems, students learn that they are capable of generating mathematics. Knowing that you are capable of generating mathematical ideas is essential to being in charge of your learning.

Knowing that you are capable of generating mathematical ideas does not mean that you can't learn from others. Students who understand that they are capable of generating mathematical ideas also understand that their classmates are capable of generating mathematical ideas. These students understand the importance of engaging with their classmates' mathematical ideas and are naturally *activated as resources for one another*. When students know that their classmates are only repeating the strategies that the teacher has already demonstrated, we shouldn't be surprised that they don't listen to each other and don't consider other students to be resources for their learning. Activating students as resources for each other starts with activating students as owners of their learning, which starts with students solving problems by generating their own strategies.

Expecting students to use their own strategies to solve problems is also crucial to the formative assessment strategies of *setting learning goals, engineering effective classroom discussions and providing feedback that moves the learning forward,* because the strategy a student generates gives their teacher a window into their level of understanding. When teachers demonstrate a strategy to students, teachers can assess whether or not students can replicate the demonstrated strategy but they can't assess if this strategy is appropriate to how a student understands the concepts in the problem. Often students can replicate strategies that they don't understand. (These students might be able to replicate the strategy right after they have been shown the strategy, and then forget it later.) Alternatively, some students are able to use strategies that are more sophisticated than those presented in curriculum materials.

Understanding the importance of students' generating their own strategies for solving problems influences how teachers *communicate learning goals* to their students. Ms. Harris could have posted the learning goal, "students will develop an understanding of how a number can be decomposed into tens," on her board but it is unlikely that seeing this learning goal would have been useful to her students. There are different levels of understanding how a number can be decomposed into tens that were reflected in Ms. Harris's specific learning goals for individual students. Teachers wouldn't write specific learning goals for individual students on the board for a variety of reasons, one of which is that sharing such goals could detract from the process of students generating their own strategies because students might try to use the strategy that their teacher wanted them to use.

start here CGI teachers do *clarify and share intentions and criteria.* These criteria remain the same for every lesson, specifically that children solve problems in a way that makes sense to them, that they represent their strategies, and they are ready to explain their thinking to their teacher and classmates.

We acknowledge the high cognitive demands on the teacher when using the formative assessment strategies of *setting learning goals, engineering effective classroom discussions,* and *providing feedback that moves the learning forward.* The CGI frameworks significantly support this challenging work by helping teachers first locate students' current understandings, suggesting next learning goals and providing problem types to engage students with the concepts in these learning goals. For example, knowledge of the CGI frameworks enables teachers to effectively *activate students as instructional resources for one another* as they *engineer effective classroom discussions,* because teachers can identify which strategies will be useful for particular groups of students to engage with, and structure discussions to ensure that these students interact with those strategies by responding to questions or making comments about them, or both. As illustrated in the vignette, Ms. Harris questioned one group of students about the first strategy and a different group of students about the second strategy because she wanted students to have access to the next strategy along the developmental trajectory. Ms. Harris makes her discussion equitable by being attentive to the individual needs of her students and strategically drawing them into the discussion when it will be most advantageous to them. Teachers need great facility with the CGI frameworks to achieve this level of expertise. Not all CGI teachers are as skilled in working with the CGI frameworks as Ms. Harris.

CGI Teacher Professional Development

Formative assessment requires that teachers see themselves as engineering the learning environment in the classrooms rather than implementing the provided curriculum. As one teacher noted, "I'm a decision maker. I need to decide where the kids are and then I have to use my knowledge about . . . where they are at in my class . . . and then I have to come up with the story problem to get these kids to . . . build on what they already know" (Fennema et al., 1996, p. 419).

We teach CGI professional learning (PL) using the same principles that CGI teachers use when teaching children. Activating teachers as owners of their own learning sets the foundation for all of our PL work. Just as CGI teachers do not demonstrate strategies for children, we do not prescribe teaching procedures in CGI professional learning. Rather, we engineer the professional learning environment so that teachers develop a knowledge base that supports them to make decisions that enhance their students' understanding. We understand that teachers develop ideas at their own pace and advance in their thinking at various times depending on their experiences, dispositions, and knowledge. CGI frameworks that describe the progression of teachers' learning help us formatively assess the teachers we work with and make decisions about supporting teachers' progress.

CGI professional learning is focused on supporting teachers as they develop an understanding of CGI research-based frameworks describing students' mathematical thinking. Although CGI professional learning follows a variety of formats with different activities included in these different formats, there are some activities that typically occur in CGI professional learning. Here we discuss three of these activities: (1) analyzing video of individual children's problem solving, (2) conducting problem solving interviews with individual children, and (3) classroom embedded work. These activities start with a simple environment, where teachers can concentrate on using the CGI framework to assess the development of a single child on a video and gradually build in complexity so that, ultimately, teachers encounter the complicated domain of a live classroom full of children. In each of these descriptions, the reader is encouraged to read for examples of the formative assessment process in action, the use of the CGI frameworks in the process, and in particular, the use of the five Leahy strategies.

Analyzing Video of Individual Children Solving Problems

Early in CGI professional learning, teachers watch videotapes of individual students solving problems and discuss the details of the students' strategies. Investigating video of students doing mathematics deepens teachers' understanding of CGI frameworks and contributes to knowledge associated with the formative assessment process, namely, identifying where a student is within a CGI framework in order to plan next instructional steps. Using video episodes allows us to select the examples we watch carefully and permits viewing the episodes several times. Before watching a clip, teachers discuss problem characteristics that affect children's thinking and anticipate the different strategies that children might use to solve the problem. This work begins to add depth to the individual elements of the CGI framework, a depth of understanding needed to assess accurately where students are currently in order to advance their learning as part of the formative assessment process.

After watching a clip, facilitators support teachers as they distinguish critical aspects of students' activity in order to link the student's strategy to a CGI framework. For example, after watching a child on a video, a teacher might make the observation that the child made a drawing to solve a problem. The facilitator would press for elaboration to focus the teacher's attention on how the child represented a group of ten in her drawing. After generating a detailed account of the child's work, the teachers use the CGI framework to determine how far along the child is in strategy development on the learning trajectory. Associating specific strategies with each level of development helps teachers develop their own understanding of the CGI framework so that it becomes an interpretative tool for the formative assessment process that they can use on the fly in their classroom as Ms. Harris did in the vignette.

In our videos[1] of individual children solving problems, the child typically solves the problem independently, and the interviewer requests an explanation and may ask some clarifying questions. The child does most of the talking. As is always true in formative assessment, the attention is focused on the child's thinking rather than the teacher's activity. So, one of the important lessons of the videos is for teachers to begin formative assessment by doing more observing and less talking.

Interviewing Children

Once teachers have experience with video examples, we move to interviews with individual children. Interviews are considerably more complex than the video examples and provide teachers

---

[1] Carpenter et al. (2014) provides readers with access to web-based videos.

with an opportunity to deepen their understanding of the CGI frameworks by applying them in the midst of formatively assessing a student.

CGI professional learning facilitators formatively assess teachers to determine how much support to provide to the teachers during the interview. When teachers are in the early stages of learning these frameworks, the interviews are done in pairs so that one teacher can interact with the child and the other teacher can take notes. Teachers might be given a list of problems to pose in a particular order. When teachers are further along in their understanding, they are given a list of problems and asked to choose problems that are appropriate to the strategies the child uses and may even design some problems in the stream of the interview. When teachers are new to posing problems without first teaching strategies, CGI professional learning leaders may direct the teachers only to pose the problem and ask clarifying questions. As teachers gain experience, CGI professional learning leaders ask teachers to enact moves that offer support to the students and ask questions to extend students' thinking. When the CGI frameworks are new to the teachers, they need time to interpret a child's strategy use. This is typically done after the interview when teachers can confer with other teachers about their observations of the child's work. This way, they can apply the CGI framework and determine where the child is in terms of his or her strategy development.

In the interviews teachers experience the predictive power of the CGI framework both in terms of predicting which problems will be more difficult for children and predicting children's strategy use. Interviewing individual students both deepens teachers' understanding of CGI frameworks and contributes to the knowledge and skills associated with the formative assessment process, in that teachers have to formulate questions on the spot to accurately assess what a student understands about a particular concept. As is the case with formative assessment in classrooms, these questions can't be designed beforehand because they are dependent on what the teacher observes when interacting with the child. After interpreting students' thinking in terms of the frameworks, teachers further develop their formative assessment skills when they discuss the next step in the child's development and consider which problems to pose or questions to ask that have the potential to advance the child's thinking.

In addition to providing teachers the opportunity to internalize the CGI framework, interviews also support teachers in developing a belief that children can figure things out for themselves and that they enjoy doing so. Many teachers are surprised that children need much less help than they anticipated.

Classroom Embedded Work

As teachers develop a deeper understanding of the CGI frameworks, experiencing authentic classroom situations further enhances their understanding of the frameworks and their ability to use these frameworks for formative assessment. In our classroom embedded work, a group of teachers collectively engages in planning a lesson. Since the teachers in the PL session don't know the students in the classroom, we start with an interview to assess students' thinking. When there isn't time for an interview, the assessment may be limited to analysis of students' written work collected the day before or collected as teachers observe students in the classroom during independent problem solving. We explain that the information gained during this assessment is the type of information that they could gather from their own students from formative assessment during math instruction.

Teachers interpret the results of the assessment and each student is categorized along a developmental trajectory, similar to what we saw Ms. Harris produce in Table 4.2. Specific learning goals are set for each group of students or for a focus group of students. The CGI professional learning facilitator supports the teachers in writing a problem that will engage students in the learning goals. Sometimes different number choices are needed for different groups and sometimes the same numbers work for all groups. Using the CGI framework, teachers anticipate the strategies students will use to solve this problem. The strategies that will be shared are selected and the reason for sharing each strategy described. The group decides which students will be drawn in to different portions of the lesson, according to the specific learning goals established for various individuals. We return to the classroom where the lesson is taught, either by the students' usual teacher or the CGI professional learning facilitator. The person teaching the lesson engages in formative assessment during the lesson and alters the plan accordingly.

The classroom embedded work deepens teachers' understanding of CGI frameworks at the same time that it contributes to the knowledge and skills associated with the formative assessment process. With the support of their colleagues and the CGI professional learning leader, teachers consider how to use information obtained from the initial assessment of a whole classroom of students to set a general learning goal. They engineer effective instruction by designing a problem to pose, and then set more specific learning goals for individuals by using their previous work to anticipate the strategies they will use to solve the problem, and choosing which strategies will be shared with the entire class to advance the thinking of various individuals. The teachers see formative assessment in action when the lesson is taught and they are able to reflect further on how the strategies associated with it are used in a classroom.

When the teachers reconvene after observing the lesson, they discuss the lesson and then consider their own classrooms. They have brought student work on a similar concept with them and begin by categorizing it along the same developmental trajectory used earlier in the day and then set a general learning goal for their classroom and specific learning goals for individual students. Teachers work with other teachers whose students fell into similar spots on the learning trajectory to design a problem to engage their students with their learning goal and anticipate strategies that these students will use to solve this problem. They plan the sharing of these strategies and decide which students will be drawn into different portions of the lesson. Teachers are encouraged to teach their planned lesson soon after their experience in the CGI professional learning session.

In our classroom embedded work, we spend 90–120 minutes analyzing students' strategies and planning a lesson. We ensure that teachers in our PL session know that we understand that teachers can't spend this long when planning one lesson. We explain that the process we are engaged in is similar to being coached on how to improve one's golf swing in that we slow down the process in order to improve performance. Our classroom embedded work differs a great deal from solely visiting and observing another teacher's class in that the teachers who observe understand the reasons for the teacher's actions during the lesson.

In discussions of student work, facilitators press teachers to share details about students' thinking. At first, this can be difficult because they have not honed their skills at noticing these details. As they internalize the CGI frameworks, which can take several years, teachers become more adept at remembering and capturing these details. They begin to see the range of levels of mathematical development in their classrooms as an asset because most students have models to emulate as they advance in their thinking.

Concluding Comments

We started this chapter by stating that is impossible to describe CGI without mentioning elements of formative assessment. Cognitively guided istruction is instruction guided by students' mathematical thinking; formative assessment is also instruction that is guided by students' thinking.

Students' generating their own strategies, rather than replicating a procedure they have been shown by the teacher, is at the heart of CGI. These solution strategies give the teacher a window into their students' thinking, and the teacher can formatively assess where the children are in the developmental trajectory articulated in the CGI framework. Alternatively, when a teacher models a strategy that students replicate, it becomes unclear whether the child could generate the strategy on his or her own, and whether the child understands the strategy. Expecting students to generate their own strategies activates them as owners of their learning because they choose which tools or representations they want to employ, and they decide when they are ready to try a new approach.

CGI teachers' approach to learning goals warrants special mention. They don't have the same specific learning goal for the entire class; rather, as was evident in the vignette, they specify learning goals for groups of students. Moreover, teachers do not expect students to master the learning goal in one lesson, and teachers don't share their learning goals with students. Although CGI teachers share some criteria for success with students, there are other learning goals that are only appropriate for the teacher to know. Teachers constantly adjust their goals for their students and rather than limit their aspirations to grade level standards, they strive to have their students constantly growing including surpassing standards when possible.

We know that the CGI approach to formative assessment can't yet work for all math contents or all grade levels. We focus on number, operation, and algebraic thinking in the elementary school where there are well-established research frameworks describing children's mathematical development. There are many content areas where such frameworks don't yet exist. In these areas teachers will be hard-pressed to devise learning goals for specific children or anticipate where children are likely to move next without such frameworks. While other researchers have been mapping out teaching and learning progressions in school mathematics, their programs tend to provide teachers with problems to use with their students. A hallmark of CGI is that teachers author their own problems based not only on their students' mathematical developmental but also on their interests and activities. Readers interested in learning more about CGI are encouraged to consult the recommended reading listed below and contact the authors to find professional development opportunities in their region.

In CGI classrooms, teachers and students appear to be enjoying themselves. Students might be using manipulatives or drawing while solving problems. Discussions tend to be lively. This cheerful environment leads some educators to interpret CGI as "anything goes," with teachers providing problems to students, and then conducting a show and tell of strategies. As we hope is evident from this chapter, this is far from the case. There is a great deal of intention shaped by formative assessment in a CGI classroom. While CGI teachers assess students by closely observing and listening during individual interactions with children, they also convey high expectations for children by prompting them to attempt more sophisticated strategies when the time is right. While the children do most of the talking during whole group discussion, due to their formative assessment efforts before and during the lesson, the teacher is able to stimulate individuals to notice particular aspects of strategies that are one level above the strategies they are presently using. Expert CGI teachers make this look easy, leading some observers to underestimate the time it takes to develop the knowledge of the CGI frameworks that is necessary to be able to formatively assess students on-the-fly, as well as skills in establishing classroom norms for productive group discussions.

Reflect on Your Practice

1. Look ahead in your math curriculum materials and find a unit that introduces a new math concept. Choose a problem from this unit. How do you think your students would solve this problem if you asked them to solve it without first teaching the new concept? Would all of your students solve the problem using the same strategy?

2. What information might you gain through formative assessment if you posed this problem without first teaching the new concept or strategy? How is the information that you would gain different from the formative assessment information that you would gain if you first taught the concept and then posed the problem?

3. Consider posing this problem to your students without first teaching the new concept, and then examine your students' strategies. (It might be helpful to find some quiet time to examine these strategies rather than trying to do this in the flow of instruction if this process is new to you.) Would you modify the learning goal for any of your students based on how they solved the problem before you taught the concept? Did you learn anything that could help you engineer effective classroom discussions surrounding this problem?

4. Why do CGI professional learning activities emphasize *attending to the details* of children's thinking? What opportunities might you have to emphasize attending to the details of children's thinking in teacher preparation courses, professional learning conversations, or in my lesson planning?

Connect Your Practice with Colleagues

1. In what ways does Ms. Harris **activate students as owners of their own learning** while also **activating other students as resources** during the lesson in the vignette? How might we similarly activate students as **owners of their own learning** and **as resources for others** in our classrooms?

2. How does Ms. Harris ensure that students understand the strategies that they are using as opposed to simply replicating the actions of another student? What strategies do we use now, or could we learn to use, to ensure that students in our classrooms understand the strategies they are using?

References

Carpenter, T. P. (1989). Teaching as problem solving. In R. I. Charles & E. A. Silver (Eds.), *The teaching and assessing of mathematical problem solving* (pp. 187–202). Reston, VA: National Council of Teachers of Mathematics & Lawrence Erlbaum Associates.

Fennema, E., Carpenter, T. P., Franke, M. L., Levi, L., Jacobs, V. R., & Empson, S. B. (1996). A longitudinal study of learning to use children's thinking in mathematics instruction. *Journal for Research in Mathematics Education*, 403–434.

Franke, M. (2016). *Keynote address*. Cognitively Guided Instruction Conference of Los Angeles. May, 2016.

Wiliam, D. (2007). Keeping learning on track: Classroom assessment and the regulation of learning. In F. Lester (Ed.), *Second handbook of research on mathematics teaching and learning* (pp. 1051–1098). Charlotte, NC: National Council of Teachers of Mathematics & Information Age Publishing.

Webb, N. M., Franke, M. L., Ing, M., Wong, J., Fernandez, C. H., Shin, N., & Turrou, A. C. (2014). Engaging with others' mathematical ideas: Interrelationships among student participation, teachers' instructional practices, and learning. *International Journal of Educational Research*, *63*, 79–93.

Recommended Reading

Carpenter, T. P., Fennema, E., Franke, M. L., Levi, L., & Empson, S. B. (2014). *Children's Mathematics: Cognitively Guided Instruction.* Second Edition. Portsmouth, NH: Heinemann.

Carpenter, T. P., Franke, M. L., Johnson, N. C., Turrou, A. C., & Wager, A. A. (2016). *Young Children's Mathematics: Cognitively Guided Instruction in Early Childhood Education.* Portsmouth, NH: Heinemann.

Carpenter, T. P., Franke, M. L., Johnson, & Levi, L. (2003) *Thinking Mathematically: Integrating Arithmetic and Algebra in Elementary School.* Portsmouth, NH: Heinemann.

Empson, S. B., & Levi, L. (2011). *Extending Children's Mathematics.* Portsmouth, NH: Heinemann.

Chapter 5

Distinguishing Features of Culturally Responsive Pedagogy Related to Formative Assessment in Mathematics Instruction

Thomasenia Lott Adams and Emily P. Bonner

Culturally responsive teaching, in idea and action, emphasizes localism and contextual specificity. That is, it exemplifies the notion that instructional practices should be shaped by the sociocultural characteristics of the settings in which they occur, and the populations for whom they are designed.

G. Gay, 2013, p. 63

Students, teachers, and all others present in a learning community have characteristics of culture. As such, it is necessary and valuable for teachers to give attention to the ways in which culture interacts with schooling and the teaching-and-learning processes. Culturally responsive pedagogy (CRP) is a framework that supports this idea, insisting that all instructional decisions are made with explicit focus on culture and ways of knowing that are reflective of the participants in the learning community. In this chapter, we will describe the ways in which CRP supports and is supported by formative assessment, and how these practices can be used together effectively to support learning for each student.

Our foundation for CRP is Ladson-Billings' (1994) definition of CRP as " . . . a pedagogy that empowers students intellectually, socially, emotionally, and politically by using cultural referents to impact knowledge, skills, and attitudes" (pp. 17–18). We will work from this definition to describe CRP's primary elements (authentic tasks, teacher knowledge, focus on communication, and fluidity of power) and subsequently provide further discussion to support the application of CRP in the mathematics learning environment. It is important to note that while we will present distinguishing features of CRP, characteristics of CRP are iterative and evolving, and they are deeply connected to each other. Furthermore, CRP can be represented in various ways, depending on the diversity of cultural perspectives, norms, and lived experiences of the participants in the learning community. As such, we take a general approach to framing this theoretical perspective for the mathematics classroom. Throughout the chapter, vignettes and activities are included to highlight the ways in which these concepts can be operationalized through effective formative assessment practices that support student learning. Next, we provide discussion questions centered on CRP and formative assessment to contribute to understanding their connection.

Primary Elements of CRP

Authentic Tasks

CRP is not intended to be an "add on" or modification to traditional mathematics instruction; rather, CRP is a paradigm shift towards validating and building on students' funds of knowledge (Moll, Amanti, Neff, & Gonzalez, 1992) in order that each student's learning is empowered by his or her own connection to the curriculum and instruction. As such, CRP is rooted in relevant, authentic tasks, ideally generated from knowledge of the communities in which students live. There are examples of this type of lesson in the literature. Civil and Kahn (2001), for example, described developing mathematical ideas around a garden theme, which introduced rigorous mathematics through building on students' funds of knowledge related to their experiences of interacting with nature in their communities. In this context, students were engaged in problem solving around issues such as finding the area of an irregular shape using non-standard units—one such task was to build a protective fence around a garden to protect it from animals and other natural intruders. This idea was presented to and supported by parents and drew on a familiar context for students and the community. Simic-Muller, Turner, and Varley (2009) described an after-school mathematics program that engaged Latino students in the exploration of local businesses through field trips and problem-solving activities that were purposeful and related to the students' home community. Not only did students in this club brainstorm and generate the ideas for these experiences, they also generated their own mathematics problems based on the context. For example, one group visited an auto shop and investigated the methods used for enlarging a design to cover the hood of a lowrider, engaging in proportional reasoning in an authentic context. The mathematics in these examples remained rigorous, but was generated from the students themselves, making learning more meaningful. Further, the tasks presented were group-worthy with multiple entry points, allowing for a variety of solution strategies, points of view, and representations.

These examples reflect the possibilities of tapping into ways of developing or selecting tasks that are embedded in students' experiences. The goal of these tasks is to provide students access to mathematics through building on shared, culturally based experiences. It is important to note that the focus of these activities is the connected and rich mathematics embedded in the tasks. Indeed, these are not simply "fun" or "engaging" activities without depth. Teachers who use task-based CRP must know their students and consider ways in which students can have meaningful interaction with mathematics through tasks and other learning experiences that have authentic connections to students. This can be achieved through communication with students about mathematics and lived experiences, and is enhanced when there is a constant and structured method for gathering and analyzing student information on a continual basis.

Teacher Knowledge

Teachers who strive to facilitate CRP benefit from having a deep understanding of mathematics content and an intimate knowledge about students' mathematical funds of knowledge. From this vantage point, teachers can acknowledge student culture as the basis from which other knowledge is constructed. For example, when the teacher has a deep understanding of mathematics content, he or she is better able to make connections and recognize qualities of student's mathematical knowledge. With this awareness, the teacher can constantly communicate with students and refine the teacher's knowledge about students' cultural practices, family lives, and experiences. Teachers can then validate mathematical ideas resulting from diverse cultural perspectives and help develop examples that provide students an opportunity for further understanding of mathematics. The constant aim is to value students as they are and what they bring to the learning community in order to enhance curriculum and make mathematics more accessible. This process is necessary to build tasks and experiences that connect community (mathematical ideas that students already know and bring to school with them), critical (sociopolitical realities), and classical (formal, traditional) mathematics knowledge (Gutstein, 2006).

As an example of this approach to teacher knowledge, consider the phrase "couple of." In a mathematics task, the phrase "couple of" might be assumed to mean two, as we often consider a statement like "A couple of people sat on the park bench" to communicate that a couple (i.e., two people) sat on the park bench. However, in some instances in students' home culture, "couple of" is not necessarily a phrase that lends itself to the quantity of two. For example, a parent might say to his son, "You can have a couple of cookies." The son might take four cookies, and the parent is satisfied that the son was in line with the parent's expectations, because "couple of" to the parent allowed for a quantity reasonably greater than two. Interpretation of quantity-related phrases can then become a source of instruction for all students. So, use of language in the mathematics is a prime opportunity for teachers to validate and expand students' understanding within contexts that are meaningful for the students. Instruction related to language in the mathematics might include students participating in an interactive word wall. For each major mathematics topic, the teacher can solicit words and phrases from students to post on the word wall. When students contribute words or phrases that are unique or not commonly used, this provides an opportunity to the teacher to take advantage of the students' funds of knowledge to expand the knowledge for all in the learning community. Consider the list of words and phrases that students might contribute for a money word wall (see fig. 5.1). Rather than dismissing students' home and community language as a barrier, the teacher can use students' language about money as a platform for starting lessons to help students to develop formal language about money.

Common Terms for U.S. Currency	Colloquial Terms for U.S. Currency
money, pennies, dimes, nickels, dollars, fives, tens, twenties, make change for (a dollar)	cheese, bread, Benjamin, paper, case quarter, bo dollar, break (a dollar), bacon, dough, moolah, fin, sawbuck, C-note, two bits

Fig. 5.1. Terms for U.S. currency

Focus on Communication

Communication is a key aspect of instruction at all levels and contributes to teachers' cultural knowledge that is used in the learning community and students' ability to apply mathematics to problem solve and justify solutions. CRP that is grounded in task-based instruction will help teachers facilitate productive discussions around deep mathematical ideas on multiple levels. This focus on communication between students, students and teachers, students and the whole class, and the teacher and the whole class, lead to more understandings and increased cultural knowledge and capital. Further, students are empowered through communicating ideas in ways that are relevant and make sense to them on a personal level. This promotes constructive discussions around mathematics that readily allow teachers to listen for what and how students understand during a lesson (Leahy et al., 2005). Further, by asking questions and communicating in culturally responsive ways, teachers are more likely to get a true idea of students' thoughts about mathematical concepts that are not misinterpreted because of cultural or linguistic disconnects. This leads to more authentic formative assessment practices through which teachers gain important information for use in teaching. Moreover, this type of interaction allows for teachers to build relationships with students that are essential to CRP.

One way to strengthen communication in the learning community is for teachers to promote norms that provide a safe space for discourse. Dixon and colleagues (2016) suggest these three norms to promote healthy discourse:

1. Explain and justify solutions.
2. Make sense of each other's solutions.
3. Say when you don't understand or when you don't agree. (p. 10)

When students know that these are the expected norms for discourse, the learning community is established as a place where different ideas, perspectives, ways of knowing and ways of doing mathematics are welcomed and valued. This type of instruction, which provides real-time feedback to the teacher, empowers students to take control of their own learning. Students are given permission not only to express their ideas, but to ask questions to understand the ideas of others. When students productively struggle to make sense of others' ideas, they become analysts of their own work and, inherently, critical thinkers. Ultimately, when given this power, students can self-assess more beneficially (Leahy et al., 2005) while providing productive feedback to other students.

Fluidity of Power

In a learning environment where teachers are culturally responsive, power is explicitly shifted to students as meaning-makers and owners of mathematical knowledge. Traditionally underserved students often feel disenfranchised in school and disempowered in mathematics, so CRP focuses on student empowerment to address the needs of each and every student in the learning community. Mathematical and communication-based power, including ownership of ideas, generation of knowledge, and taking responsibility for learning pass from student to student and between student and teacher. Further, this fluidity of power allows for trust and relationships among teachers and students in ways that support deep mathematical thinking.

When teachers use formative assessment in a culturally responsive classroom, this power shift is activated. For example, teachers who are culturally responsive hold deep-seated beliefs that their students can understand and use high-level mathematics, and these teachers hold students to this standard. As such, culturally relevant open-ended problems with multiple solutions and entry points drive instruction. Embedded in these problems are opportunities for students to discuss mathematical ideas in ways that make sense to them, which not only generates productive discussion, but also provides the teacher with insight into how students are making sense of mathematical ideas (Leahy et al., 2005). Moreover, students become the engineers of the discussion—the solutions that they present become the content of the class. This empowers students to take ownership over their own and others' learning, and to persist in problem solving.

Other Considerations

CRP is a framework from which all instruction is built; as such, it is important that mathematics teachers understand their own mathematical stories and how these might inform key aspects of instruction. Communication, knowledge about students and their lives and relationships are foundational to CRP, and can be facilitated through effective formative assessment practices. The focus of CRP is on integrating student funds of knowledge into the learning community in ways that allow students to explore and understand complex mathematical ideas, and communicating with students about mathematics in culturally congruent ways can enhance these understandings through empowerment and self-regulation. Ultimately, CRP asks teachers to question the status quo mathematics teaching practices that favor particular cultures and calls for each and every student to have access to high-level, connected, rigorous mathematics.

Connect CRP to Formative Assessment

Because formative assessment is developed through an ongoing stream of interactive occurrences that thread through teaching and learning, it is important to acknowledge formative assessment more explicitly within the context of CRP. In a learning community where CRP is vibrant, teachers and students can engage in formative assessment with recognition of the diversity and variation of ways (e.g., style, pace, connections) that students think about and learn mathematics. Hence, the evidence of student learning will mirror this diversity and variation. In this section, we will discuss the connections between CRP and formative assessment from three perspectives: process, gathering of evidence, and informing teaching and learning (fig. 5.2).

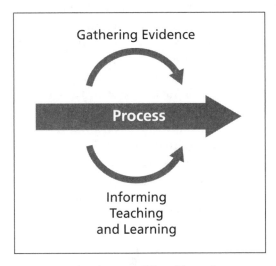

Fig. 5.2. Connections between CRP and formative assessment

Process

CRP supports teachers as they operate from the foundation that (a) all cultural perspectives are valued and used in learning, (b) mathematics tasks are relevant and informed by the teachers' knowledge of students' lived experiences, and (c) students' learning of mathematics is the primary objective. The relevancy of the tasks helps students develop and understand context for how mathematics might be useful in the everyday lives of students and others. To help teachers develop the skill of determining relevant tasks, teachers might find self-reflection about their own mathematics learning experiences beneficial. Teachers might recall asking themselves this question about mathematics: "What does this have to do with me?" Sometimes, the response can point to something explicit (e.g., "I can use mathematics to understand how the final score in a football game could have been acquired"). Other times, finding the relevancy or application of mathematics takes some willingness to think creatively or through extension to the lives of others. When teachers take care to select tasks that provide meaningful mathematics experiences for students, then students are better positioned to use either their background knowledge from lived experiences or imagination of possibilities, or both, to explore the mathematics. When this process occurs, students are able to provide evidence of their mathematics learning that is a reflection of who they are and to reveal the lens through which they interact with and come to understand mathematics.

The teacher who regards formative assessment as a key component of teaching and learning mathematics applies effort to anticipate how students might respond to tasks. In constructing culturally responsive problem-solving sessions, the teacher uses his or her knowledge to provide access to high-level mathematics in culturally congruent ways. Using formative assessment explicitly during these sessions allows students to provide the teacher with "feedback that moves learners forward" (Leahy et al., 2005). Students are constantly providing the teacher with feedback about mathematical thinking *and* cultural norms by presenting and discussing their work.

Gathering Evidence

As students engage in mathematics learning, the teacher constantly gathers evidence of student learning as students interact in the learning community where all students' perspectives about mathematics are valued and where students know their different ways of thinking about mathematics can be heard (recall the previously stated norms suggested by Dixon et al., 2016), In gathering evidence of student learning, teachers are looking for information that will provide inference about students' development of mathematics knowledge or their underlying struggles, misconceptions, or misunderstandings about mathematics. There is a multitude of ways to collect evidence of student learning and, particularly, to collect evidence that honors the cultural diversity in the learning environment. Some alternative approaches to formative assessment include (a) listening to students' discussions, (b) arranging students' solutions strategically based on knowledge about progressions in mathematics, (c) encouraging students to present their solutions to the class which provides the teacher with evidence for connections and extensions to students' lived experiences, and (d) allowing students to discuss with the class their expectations and appreciation of diverse perspectives. In addition, students may present first in their home language to support additional clarity and then another student can translate. When students can do so with clarity and comfort, both presenter and class benefit.

Informing Teaching and Learning

Formative assessment has many important roles in the learning community. One such role is to inform teaching to support teachers improving and enhancing how and what they teach as well as how and what students learn. The activity of teaching provides an opportunity for teachers to change the course of instruction to meet the needs of students. For instance, teachers might apply formative assessment by using students' responses, discussions, and conceptions to identify and present an extension task or to design another task targeting areas that need more attention. Using real-time evidence in this way helps teachers tailor lessons to students (Leahy et al., 2005). Altering the progression of instruction happens holistically and moment by moment. For example, student feedback can lead a teacher to pose new questions to the class as new connections are identified to inform the task (e.g., filling the gaps, explicitly addressing misconceptions, or following up based on students' interests). In the context of CRP, teachers can use formative assessment to provide all students an opportunity to engage and share their perspectives and lived experience using mathematics. This empowers learners as the drivers of instruction (Leahy et al., 2005) and builds trust between teacher and students. Culturally responsive classrooms naturally lend themselves to tasks in which formative assessment is embedded in instruction. Consider the vignette in figure 5.3 to illustrate this perspective.

It is a typical day in Ms. Pace's class. Her sixth-grade students are sitting in groups of three or four working on a warm-up activity in preparation for a mathematics lesson. When the students have completed the warm-up, Ms. Pace says, "Recently, I have asked you to think about problems that we see in your community, and how we might be able to use mathematics to solve them. In your groups, I want you to write down two such problems and share them with the class."

After two minutes, student groups take turns discussing what they are seeing in their community. There is a lot of discussion around City Park, located just one block from the school. The students really enjoy playing there, but would like to build a short fence around the playground area because of the high number of unleashed dogs in the area. After some initial discussion about this, the teacher launches the following task:

You are a city planner, and you want to know how much it will cost to build a short fence around the playground area at City Park. What information do you need to solve this problem? What is a good estimate of the cost of building a fence?

Students are given time to walk to the park and gather measurements. Students investigate the costs of materials based on a given cost per linear foot of the fence.

Along the way, they present their findings and discuss plans with the class. After two days of working on the project, groups of students present their solutions and plans to the class. As each group presents, Ms. Pace orchestrates a discussion around the big mathematical ideas (related to geometry, area, perimeter, cost, etc.) that are mentioned. Finally, the class has one final task, which is to write a letter to the city planner requesting funding for this project.

Discussion questions:

What are several benefits or drawbacks to leaving the task open-ended?

In what ways does this lesson mathematics illustrate the tenets of CRP and formative assessment?

Adapted from (Bonner, 2014)

Fig. 5.3. CRP and formative assessment in action

Here's a snapshot of the discourse that emerges from this task:

Group 1: (Jaida, Sasha, Jaxon, Michael)

Jaida poses this question to her group: "How much fence do you think we will need?"

The teacher listens to the group discussion and asks the group a probing question: "What area would you fence off to play in?"

Jaida:	*This area over here.* [She points to the map they drew of the park on grid paper.] *It is where the swings are.*
Teacher:	*Do you have the measurements that you took from the field? Would it be helpful to place those on the map?* [The teacher points to their drawing of the map.]
Jaida:	*Yes.*
Jaxon:	*I think we will need about 100 feet of fence based on our measurements.*

Teacher:	*Jaxon, that's a good thought; let's test it out and see if we have enough fence. What should we do?* [The teacher provides these probing questions to help students engage the task.]
Michael:	*We took lots of measurements of different areas of the park. I think we should first find the area of the park we want to fence in and draw it. We need to include the basketball hoops, too. That's where I like to hang out, and I am sick of dogs running there.*
Teacher:	*Good point Michael. So, does that increase the area we want or only change its location? What shapes are on our drawing of the park? Remember some of the shapes we already know. The distance around that the fence will enclose is called the what?*
Michael:	*Perimeter.*
Sasha:	*Ok, and we should include the swings and tables. Let's draw the shape we are enclosing.* [Sasha takes the initiative and draws a rectangle around the area on the map to show where the fencing will go.]
Teacher:	*What is the unit we are using for measuring? Do we remember what we discussed?*
Michael:	*We measured the distance in feet.*
Teacher:	*Michael told us the distance we want to fence is called the perimeter, what is the enclosed area called? This might be kind of a trick question.*
Sasha:	*Area. Perimeter is like the rim or outside. Area is the inside.*
Teacher:	*Yes, that's right. So, have you decided on the kind of fence you are going to use?*
Jaida:	*Wait, I have an idea. Let's do the opposite. Why don't we just fence in a small area for the dogs to play in and we get the rest of the park! We will use a chain fence, right?*
Sasha:	*So instead of making a fence to keep the dogs out, we make a fence to keep the dogs in!*
Jaxon:	*Right!*
Michael:	*Yea, we agreed on a chain fence.*
Jaxon:	*We can get the chain fence for about $3 a linear foot.*
Teacher:	*How can we figure out how much the fence will cost?*
Sasha:	*If we know the perimeter, we can just multiply it by the cost of the fence at $3.*

The group draws the area they plan to enclose to present to the class. They include their calculations for the cost of the fence. On a poster paper the group draws a place where the dogs can play. The teacher circulates and engages each group in similar discussions.

After students have completed the posters, the teacher asks each student to stand at their poster and engage in a chalk talk. Students walk around providing quiet feedback. As students return to their original posters they read the comments that were provided. The teacher makes inferences about students' understanding based on these responses. The groups summarize the comments that their peers made and share their strategies for solving the problem, including the steps they took.

Other Considerations: Formative Assessment within the Context of Cultural Practices

Throughout the teaching and learning experience, as teachers focus on determining what students are learning (or not learning), formative assessment occurs within the context of the cultural practices students experience in their lives. For example, during a debate about the validity of mathematics ideas between the teacher and students, the teacher takes into consideration that some students might have norms in their families that do not support children debating with adults. Hence, it is important to understand how to empower students (e.g., students debating with students) without penalizing them for their different perspective. Of fundamental importance is that students are supported when they engage in discourse with and about mathematics. Hence, while formative assessment promotes the use of questioning and probing, CRP promotes the engagement of all students in the processes of questioning and probing and the acceptance that students will present diverse responses based on their background knowledge and experiences to questioning and probing.

Connection Between Culturally Responsive Pedagogy and Leahy et al. (2005) Formative Assessment Strategies

Culturally responsive pedagogy is a very flexible construct that does not disrupt teaching and learning with a list of dos and don'ts. Rather, it can interact well with other purposeful activities in the learning community such as the formative assessment process (as previously discussed). In this section, we dig a little deeper to describe how CRP connects with Leahy et al. (2005) strategies for formative assessment.

Learning Intentions and Criteria

When culturally responsive pedagogy is employed, mathematical tasks are relevant and explicitly connected to students' lives and cultures, and the tasks value students' funds of knowledge. The role of the teacher is to (a) connect to authentic expectations for student learning, (b) refine as students engage in learning, and (c) be considerate of students' ability to communicate and justify mathematical ideas. Teachers have clarity about learning goals and objectives, and these are explicitly connected to student perspectives and cultures.

Effective Learning Community

In effective learning communities, relevant problem-solving activities provide a connected way to incorporate three criteria: (a) tasks have multiple entry points and are relevant, and students must discuss their thinking (i.e., contribute to mathematical discourse); (b) the solution strategy becomes the source of discussion with the class, questions are posed, and mathematical ideas are elicited through discourse; and (c) structured tasks provide a platform for students to grapple with and justify complex mathematical ideas (and pose new questions based in their own cultural context). For example, tasks might be based on experiences (e.g., playing games, shopping, taking a trip, cooking, building a shed, fixing a car, etc.) students have in their daily lives that connect to mathematics. Tasks can explicitly focus on issues, such as race, if it is relevant or of concern to students (i.e., rethinking mathematics curriculum), or can be more focused on community needs and events. As such, mathematics teachers must have knowledge of students and of content that allow them to design these types of problem tasks. Further, the role of the teacher is to set students up for success, in terms of engaging in mathematical discourse, rather than to impart knowledge that is grounded only in the teacher's cultures and understandings.

Feedback That Moves Learners Forward

When feedback is designed to move learners forward, solutions are connected as representations of similar ideas (i.e., the teacher makes these connections with the students). For example, solutions can be arranged to provide constant feedback on the mathematical ideas that are presented; solution strategies can be recorded publicly so that students can revisit these in future sessions; and "incorrect" solutions are seen as learning opportunities and are utilized to frame further discourse. Teacher action is based on this feedback, and can be immediate (during student justification and discussion), or action can be applied over time to new tasks. For example, if a misunderstanding or good connection is presented during the solution sharing portion of a lesson, the teacher may decide to go more in depth with that idea, or to pose an extension problem based on that content that emphasizes the new idea. If an idea comes out of the discussion across solutions, then the teacher may address and emphasize this idea by choosing tasks that center on the idea.

Students as Owners of Their Learning

Students engaged in relevant problem solving are continuously self-assessing their own work and the work of their peers. In this sense, there is personal ownership of learning and collective ownership of learning. Since the mathematics in CRP is rooted in cultural experiences, the personal connections are explicit and constant. Disposition, confidence, efficacy, student belief in self as a doer of mathematics, and focus on the individual as a valuable contributor are all foci. Empowerment through cultural relevance leads students to believe they can do mathematics and that mathematics is a tool that can impact their lives and communities, and is not just a disconnected tool that someone is making them use and learn. As such, teachers should engage in self-reflection and gain a deeper understanding of students' cultures. This will allow the lines of communication to open, and knowledge and power become more fluid.

Students as Resources for One Another

In a learning community where students are resources for one another, most tasks should be worked on within small groups and require justification within and between groups when discussed. Teachers can also ask students to do "gallery walks" where groups can review and discuss their strategies and solutions. As students learn to critically review their work, they strengthen the culture of the learning community as a place where all students' conceptions of mathematics are valuable. Teachers can facilitate this type of interaction by posing relevant questions and honoring the student's right to say only what makes sense to him or her (Kalinec-Craig, 2016) in a culturally congruent manner. Further, teachers can reinforce this type of productive struggle by structuring problems in ways that encourage discourse. Student contributions to discourse should be rewarded as well so that more emphasis is placed on the process rather than the product, or "correct" answer.

Other Considerations: The Empowerment of Students

It can be argued that culturally responsive pedagogy's primary contribution to formative assessment strategies is the empowerment of students to engage actively in doing and learning mathematics and subsequently showcase their learning in response to the formative assessment strategies. When CRP is present, students are each given the opportunity to succeed in the mathematics classroom, and teachers' formative assessment strategies enhance students' learning.

Connections among Culturally Responsive Pedagogy, Formative Assessment, and NCTM's Principles to Actions

The National Council of Teachers of Mathematics'(NCTM) *Principles to Actions* (2014) outlined five essential elements of effective mathematics programs and eight essential research-based teaching practices that promote deep understandings of mathematical ideas. These elements and practices align with the tenets of CRP, especially as CRP connects to task-based instruction that focuses on formative assessment.

NCTM (2014) described the five essential elements of effective mathematics programs as (1) access and equity, (2) curriculum, (3) tools and technology, (4) assessment, and (5) professionalism. Access and equity, a central focus of CRP, underlies all the essential elements. Furthermore, the central goal of CRP is to provide access to a high-quality, deeply connected mathematics curriculum that empowers students personally and academically. From this standpoint, relevant and effective curricula are developed using tools and technology, and assessment is ongoing and informative. In these ways, the framework of CRP uses formative assessment as an essential component while encouraging and supporting students. Teachers who are culturally responsive hold the student at the center of everything they do and design curricula in ways that inherently support professionalism and collegiality for the good of the learning community. Indeed, culturally responsive pedagogy and formative assessment both support the guiding principles set forth by NCTM.

The eight research-based mathematics teaching practices described in *Principles to Actions* (NCTM, 2014) promote deep understandings of mathematical ideas. Consider how these teaching practices interact with culturally responsive pedagogy and formative assessment:

1. **Establishing mathematics goals to focus learning.** Culturally responsive pedagogy makes explicit the focus on using mathematics as a means for empowerment and social justice. Further, the formative assessment element of this approach allows students to grow as problem solvers, adjusting solutions to big problems and connecting major ideas through socio-constructivist principles. Teachers who are culturally responsive have clear, high expectations for students related to these foci.

2. **Posing purposeful questions.** One of the main goals of culturally responsive pedagogy is to provide access to deep, connected mathematical ideas for traditionally underserved students. As such, teachers who are culturally responsive draw on students' funds of knowledge and students' mathematical experiences to design high-level mathematics tasks. Though this may not look the same in every classroom, the teacher uses his or her knowledge about the students (gained through communication and relationships) to create experiences that allow for students to problem solve in meaningful ways while exploring mathematics in relevant ways.

3. **Implementing tasks that promote reasoning.** Culturally responsive pedagogy is task-based, drawing on relevant tasks with multiple entry points. As such, students access the mathematics through open sharing strategy sessions (Kazemi & Hintz, 2014) and class discussion. Learning occurs through problem solving, and student justifications are elicited and used as generalizable mathematical ideas.

4. **Elicit and use evidence of student thinking.** Teachers who are culturally responsive pose relevant tasks and use these to elicit student solutions that are then justified by students. Students are often encouraged to design innovative strategies and then publicly defend these strategies to the class. Student representations, then, become the basis of the mathematical concept and serve as a scaffolding mechanism towards efficiency.

5. **Facilitate meaningful mathematical discourse.** Through task-based explorations, students must present, justify, and connect their solutions. Students are the holders of the knowledge, and the teacher's role is to elicit this knowledge and develop inferences about student learning. Further, in sequencing and connecting student solutions in careful ways, the teacher can guide the discussion in highly productive ways.

6. **Use and connect mathematical representations.** In culturally responsive classrooms, students are asked to design solutions to tasks in ways that make sense to them. Thus, culturally responsive pedagogy inherently differentiates and accounts for various learning styles and allows for a variety of valid and justifiable solutions. Student solutions are publicly discussed and serve as the basis of understanding for the concept. The teacher and students collaborate to connect different representations that are elicited from the students and work to find more efficient or practical ways, if applicable.

7. **Support productive struggle.** Productive struggle is inherent in culturally responsive pedagogy. As discussed previously, students are required to justify their solutions and are encouraged to ask questions, using "mistakes" as opportunities for refinement and learning. In choosing developmentally and socially appropriate tasks, teachers can encourage this type of discourse.

8. **Build procedural fluency from conceptual understanding.** Just as student solutions and representations serve as the basis of discussion in culturally responsive pedagogy, the ultimate goal is to move students to efficient, procedural understandings. Instruction begins where the students have understandings. For example, students may be using manipulative models to solve two-digit addition problems. Teachers who are culturally responsive will then connect that model to an invented or transitional algorithm that may rely on place value representations, such as expanded notation, and then eventually to the traditional algorithm which is then just a shorthand version of the concept. In these ways, teachers build on student understandings to develop essential mathematical skills.

Hence, NCTM's effort as considered through the lenses of CRP and formative assessment created a platform by which teachers are equipped to make decisions about selecting tasks. Consider the two tasks in figure 5.4.

Task 1

What is the area of a rectangle with a width of 30" and a length of 40"?

Task 2

Delvin and his friend Monica are helping Delvin's mom cover her 40" $\times$ 30" porch table with new self-sticking square tiles. She can buy individual tiles in various sizes, but wants all the tiles to be uniform. What size tiles could Delvin's mom use to cover her table evenly? Please suggest at least three options.

Fig. 5.4. Selecting tasks through the lenses of NCTM, CRP, and formative assessment

Both tasks address the mathematical concepts of area, measurement, geometry, and perhaps multiplication; yet the first task does not readily offer the kind of opportunity provided in the statement of Task 2 for students to consider how the task might relate to their lived experiences. Task 2 suggests a context in which to use mathematics to solve a problem that might arise in real life. Furthermore, because Task 2 has multiple plausible responses, the importance of the explanation is magnified. Moreover, students have an opportunity to relate Task 2 to similar situations they might encounter in their lives. It can be argued also that Task 2 sets the stage for deeper connections in mathematics in ways that promote critical thinking, justification of solutions, new ways of thinking, and transformative learning.

Importance of this Connection for Preservice and In-Service Education

In a mathematics content course for preservice teachers, modeling by the instructor to identify what is understood or misunderstood through listening to students and filling the content gaps is a valuable exercise in helping preservice teachers to develop their own craft of teaching that aligns with diverse learners. Techniques such as connecting to standards, eliciting mathematical ideas, and making connections in terms of content and representations to help students find relevancy in mathematics are important for supporting preservice teachers to develop skills of communicating with students and facilitating formative assessment strategies. For example, in a mathematics methods course, instructors should model this practice through their teaching and elicit the following connections from preservice teachers: (a) explicit focus on the idea that the whole experience is one big cycle of formative assessment and feedback (i.e., after teachers engage in a task, they should reflect on where and why the formative assessment happened, and discuss benefits and challenges of teaching in this way); (b) explicit association between student funds of knowledge and mathematics; and (c) examination of one's own cultural awareness and how this plays into mathematical perspectives.

In light of the mathematics education community's focus on the preparation of preservice teachers and the ongoing development of in-service teachers, the next section describes activities (e.g., task analysis, vignette, mathematical autobiography, and action research project) that support both preservice and in-service teachers.

Activities for Preservice and In-Service Teachers That Connect Culturally Responsive Pedagogy and Formative Assessment

Activity 1: Task Analysis

In order to engage in culturally responsive formative assessment, teachers must be skilled in developing and selecting appropriate tasks that capitalize on students' funds of knowledge. To support the development of this skill, we suggest a task analysis activity that pushes teachers to think not only about the mathematics of a task but also about the cultural context or social justice, or both, that frames the work. After presenting the task and asking teachers to work through it, the facilitator leads a discussion based on the following prompts:

- For whom is this task most appropriate? Why?

- What modifications might you make? Why?

- What conceptions/misconceptions based in cultural knowledge might exist?

- What types of student responses would you anticipate from different groups of students?

- What would these tell you about student understanding?

- How would you use these to drive the student discussion that would follow?

Try your hand at this task analysis activity using the tasks in figure 5.5.

> When April went to the county fair, she discovered that she had to pay $7 to enter the fair and then buy tickets for rides and games. Each ticket was 25 cents. Each ride or game required from 4 to 6 tickets. April suggested that she'd rather pay more, perhaps $15, to enter the fair than to pay to enter and buy tickets for rides and games. Do you agree or disagree with April? Explain.

Fig. 5.5. Task

Activity 2: Mathematical Autobiography

Teachers and students bring rich histories and varied, intersecting identities to the classroom. These identities influence the ways that we learn and teach mathematics (Aguirre, Mayfield-Ingram, & Martin, 2013). It is important that teachers engage in reflective practices that provide opportunities to understand their own cultural, mathematical, and social backgrounds and how those backgrounds impact their instructional practice, mathematical understandings, and interactions with students. From a culturally responsive standpoint, this understanding is especially vital, as awareness of one's own identity and how it is supported by status quo educational practices will provide a new lens through which to view the educational system at large.

One way to engage preservice and in-service teachers in this type of reflective practice is to ask them to complete a written or oral mathematics autobiography. During this exercise, teachers are asked to think back about their own mathematics history, starting from when they were young, and reflect on how those experiences impacted their attitudes towards and understandings of mathematics. Simultaneously, teachers are asked to reflect on their cultural identities related to home and school, and how those identities shaped their mathematical practices. Ultimately, teachers are asked to discuss how their history might have impacted their work as mathematics teachers. Some examples of questions that might guide this assignment are listed below.

- How do you feel about mathematics?
- How do you think your school mathematics experiences affected your perceptions and attitudes about mathematics?
- How do you think your school mathematics experiences affected your understandings of mathematical concepts?
- Did you receive mathematics instruction that connected to your home life or language? If so, how? If not, then how did this affect your experiences?
- Describe one positive and one negative experience you had in learning mathematics.
- How do you think your experiences and beliefs about yourself as a mathematics learner might impact the kind of mathematics teacher that you will be, or the kind of teacher that you want to be?

When asked to describe her autobiography of mathematics learning, a teacher shared the following:

I grew up in a small town and never dreamed I would one day be a teacher in a big city. I remember how we used to play with mud pies and pick blackberries right off the bush on the side of the road. We would pick a whole bunch and hold them in our shirts, so our shirts would be stained blue on most summer days. School was not that fun for me, because it didn't really seem to matter that much, and I really hated math anyway. None of it made much sense, and all our teachers really wanted us to do was to just memorize stuff. I guess if someone had tried to show me how mathematics really worked, I might have paid better attention in school. Anyway, when I got to high school, I learned about a program for students who thought they might want to be teachers. You would enroll in the program and then have an opportunity to visit schools and learn about teaching, and if you did well, you might get accepted to the local college to study how to be a teacher. I decided to try out for the program, and I was accepted. I remember when I visited my first class. It was a sixth-grade class, and the teacher was teaching about dividing fractions. She was telling the students that its just like division with whole numbers, except you are working with fractions. I was like, "Wow!" I wish I'd had that understanding when I was in sixth-grade. I just remember that I needed to follow a rule: invert and multiply. I had no idea really what I was doing. So anyway, the teacher gave an example of $3/4$ divided by 3. First she said to consider 15 divided by 3. She asked a student what the student would do if she had three groups and wanted to share 15 equally in the groups, how much would be in each group. That was easy; there would be 5 in each group. Then she said that $3/4$ divided by 3 works the same way. If you have three groups and $3/4$ is shared equally among the three groups, how much would be in each group? That was easy too; it would be $1/4$ in each group. Except then I realized that I didn't get that answer from inverting and multiplying, but I got the answer from making sense of the problem! I was hooked on mathematics from that day—the day I realized that I could make sense of mathematics without depending on memorization of rules. Now that I am a mathematics teacher, I try to remind myself that my students might be just like me when I was growing up, and so I need to be understanding and patient and give them opportunities to think about the mathematics rather than just showing them the rule on how to do the mathematics and expecting the students to just catch on!

As a follow-up to sharing their stories, teachers can consider how they have common backgrounds, experiences and perspectives. When students build on commonalities with their peers as well as with students, there is support for strengthening the learning community.

Activity 3: Action Research Project

Teachers who are culturally responsive constantly examine their own practice, formally and informally, to answer specific questions about their own practice. In order for each student to have access to high-quality, rigorous mathematics education, it is critical that teachers, administrators, districts, and beyond engage in reflective work, with a focus on equity. This "grass roots" research is grounded in student data, often gathered through a variety of formative assessment strategies that have been designed to answer particular questions. In aggregate, this type of data can provide important insights into the mathematical understandings of students and the inner workings of classrooms and schools.

Action research is a powerful tool that can combine CRP and formative assessment to promote equitable practice addressing gaps in opportunity and achievement that are prevalent in mathematics. Teams of teachers, administrators, district personnel, and other stakeholders can collect context-specific data, and utilize this data to respond to specific issues or happenings at a particular place (Caro-Bruce, Flessner, Klehr, & Zeichner, 2007). Collecting and using data allow the teacher, school, or district to create an action research program to address specific problems or goals in fluid ways that explicitly support their students. Engaging preservice and in-service teachers in action research work takes time and promotes opportunities for collaboration. We recommend that teachers first be introduced to the idea of action research, and then have discussions about what "equity" means, if this is the focus. Teachers can also focus on formative assessment questions, which often inherently encompass issues of equity like communication, high expectations, and rigor.

Through this discussion process, teachers and administrators will work together to develop working action research questions that will inform the specific goals they hope to achieve. Ways of collecting data can be discussed and implemented, and progress can be documented. Efron and Ravid (2013) presented an iterative six-step process:

1. State the problem.
2. Collect necessary information.
3. Develop a plan for the research.
4. Engage in data collection.
5. Analyze the data.
6. Put the findings into action and share with others.

Action research allows for (and thrives on) subjectivity; researchers are intimately tied to the data, and are not trying to control the environment in any way. Further, action research is iterative and fluid, so there is room for adjustment and change in focus along the way. Once the research plan is in place, teachers begin collecting and analyzing data. Given the nature of action research, these often occur simultaneously and inform one another. Lastly, teachers implement what they have learned and share their findings before identifying a new or slightly different problem to assess. Below are several action research questions combining CRP and formative assessment that teachers might consider; however, we would like to emphasize that action research questions should be elicited from practitioners based on their unique needs, and the needs of their students.

1. How can I use formative assessment to increase my English Language Learners' engagement in solving contextual mathematics tasks?

2. How do sharing and discussing solutions affect students' abilities to understand and communicate mathematical ideas? Does it help all groups equally?

3. How can I facilitate more productive mathematical discussions among students that will empower them as learners while providing formative feedback about their learning?

Conclusion

Culturally Responsive Pedagogy (CRP) has at its heart the goal of positioning each and every student to be successful in school. By stating "each" student, we honor the importance of the individual student with all of his or her characteristics and cultural distinctions to be able to achieve successfully in mathematics. By stating "every" student, we honor the importance of the collective of students who have common and differing characteristics and cultural distinctions to be supported to attain success in mathematics. This necessitates that we examine mathematics curriculum and instruction and aim to align our practices with attentiveness to who the learners are, the cultural funds of knowledge (e.g., language, lived experiences, diverse perspectives, etc.) that learners bring with them to the classroom. Formative assessment—a process through which we employ strategies to determine what students are or are not learning and develop ways for pushing students forward in their learning is at the center of classroom activity. Hence, the relationship between CRP and formative assessment is refined as students engage in learning and showcase diversity of thought and activity. NCTM provides insight on effective programs and teaching practices that both support and receive support from CRP and formative assessment in the preparation of future teachers of mathematics and in the enhancement of current teachers of mathematics. Teaching mathematics to reach each and every student is the most endeared outcome of culturally responsive pedagogy, and formative assessment uniquely joins culturally responsive pedagogy to accomplish this goal.

Reflect on Your Practice

1. According to Ladson-Billings (1994), CRP "empowers students . . . by using cultural referents to impact knowledge, skills, and attitudes." What are some specific practices that you employ to empower students in this way? What do you use as evidence of the effectiveness of these practices?

2. How do you encourage productive mathematical discussions in your classroom? How do you know they are productive? What measures do you take to ensure that *all students* have the opportunity to engage in such discussions?

3. How can you enhance your questioning techniques to (1) formatively assess students to gather evidence about their mathematical understandings while also (2) gathering information about students' lived experiences to build a cultural knowledge base that will support CRP?

Connect Your Practice with Colleagues

1. Communication is essential to both CRP and formative assessment. Why is communication so essential to both practices? How do the communication patterns involved in each practice intersect and interact to create a productive mathematics classroom environment?

2. What interactions between and tenets of CRP and formative assessment does figure 5.2 represent?

3. The authors suggest that open-ended tasks may promote a classroom environment rooted in CRP and ripe for innovative formative assessment practices. Do you agree or disagree with this claim? What evidence would be convincing in this regard?

Additional Readings

Cartledge, G., & Kourea, L. (2008). Culturally responsive classrooms for culturally diverse students with and at risk for disabilities. *Exceptional Children, 74,* 352–371.

Gay, G. (2000). *Culturally responsive teaching: Theory, practice, & research.* New York, NY: Teachers College Press.

Irvin, J. J. (2003). *Educating teachers for diversity: Seeing with a cultural eye.* New York, NY: Teachers College Press.

Ladson-Billings, G. (1995). Toward a theory of culturally relevant pedagogy. *American Educational Research Journal, 32*(3), 465–491.

Ladson-Billings, G. (2006). Yes, but how do we do it? In J. Landsman & C. W. Lewis (Eds.), *White teachers, diverse classrooms* (pp. 29–42). Sterling, VA: Stylus.

References

Aguirre, J., Mayfield-Ingram, K., & Martin, D. (2013). *The impact of identity in K–8 mathematics: Rethinking equity-based practices.* Reston, VA: National Council of Teachers of Mathematics.

Bonner, E. P. (2014). Investigating practices of highly successful teachers of traditionally underserved students. *Educational Studies in Mathematics, 86*(3), 377–399.

Caro-Bruce, C., Flessner, R., Klehr, M., & Zeichner, K. (Eds.). (2007). *Creating equitable classrooms through action research.* Thousand Oaks, CA: Corwin.

Civil, M., & Kahn, L. (2001). Mathematics instruction developed from a garden theme. *Teaching Children Mathematics, 7,* 400–405.

Dixon, J. K., Nolan, E. C., Adams, T. L., Brooks, L. A., & Howse, T. D. (2016). *Making sense of mathematics for teaching (Grades K–2).* Bloomington, IN: Solution Tree Press.

Efron, S. E., & Ravid, R. (2013). *Action research in education: A practical guide.* New York, NY: Guilford Press.

Gay, G. (3013). Teaching to and through cultural diversity. *Cultural Diversity and Multicultural* Education, *43,* 48–70.

Gutstein, E. (2006). *Reading and writing the world with mathematics: Toward a pedagogy for social justice.* New York, NY: Routledge.

Kalinec-Craig, C. A. (2016). *The rights of the learner: A Sociocultural framework for promoting equity through formative assessment in mathematics classrooms.* North American Chapter of the International Group for the Psychology of Mathematics Education, Tucson, AZ.

Kazemi, E., & Hintz, A. (2014). *Intentional talk: How to structure and lead productive mathematical discussions.* Portland, ME: Stenhouse Publishers.

Ladson-Billings, G. (1994). *The dreamkeepers: Successful teachers of African American Children.* San Francisco, CA: Jossey-Bass.

Leahy, S., Lyon, C., Thompson, M., & Wiliam, D. (2005). Classroom assessment: Minute by minute, day by day. *Educational Leadership, 63*(3), 19–24.

Moll, L. C., Amanti, C., Neff, D., & Gonzalez, N. (1992). Funds of knowledge for teaching: A qualitative approach to connect homes and classrooms. *Theory into Practice, 31*(1), 132–141.

National Council of Teachers of Mathematics. (2014). *Principles to actions: Ensuring mathematical success for all.* Reston, VA: Author.

Simic-Muller, K., Turner, E. E., & Varley, M. C. (2009). Math club problem posing. *Teaching Children Mathematics, 16*(4), 206–212.

Chapter 6

Using Learning Trajectories to Elicit, Interpret, and Respond to Student Thinking

Caroline B. Ebby and Marjorie Petit

A team of sixth-grade math teachers gathers for their monthly planning meeting. At their last meeting, they decided to administer a formative assessment task to their students and bring the work back to discuss as a group. As they begin the meeting, excitement abounds about sharing student solutions. Some of the teachers had sorted the work by correct and incorrect responses and were eager to share some interesting correct solutions. Other teachers had done no organization of the work before the meeting. As a result of the lack of clarity around the purpose of looking at student work, the conversation was dominated by the sharing of interesting and exciting solutions and discussion of which students had not reached proficiency. Before they realized it, the time was over; everyone left thinking it was an interesting meeting that they would repeat in the future.

From a formative assessment perspective, this meeting was a failure. Some teachers left having never looked at their own students' solutions and most important, they all left having made no instructional decisions based on the evidence in the student solutions—the cornerstone of formative assessment. As Wiliam (2011) states:

> An assessment functions formatively to the extent that evidence about student achievement is elicited, interpreted, and used by teachers, learners, or their peers to make decisions about the next steps in instruction that are likely to be better, or better informed, than the decisions would have been in the absence of evidence. (p. 43)

This chapter demonstrates how learning trajectories can enhance the formative assessment process in ways that help teachers interpret the evidence that they collect to make informed instructional decisions that can impact student learning. We illustrate this through an example of a set of learning trajectory-based tools and routines that have been developed for classroom use by the Ongoing Assessment Project (OGAP). We show how using these formative assessment tools and routines can help teachers go beyond merely identifying which students need extra help to adapting instruction to meet students' diverse needs, thereby ensuring both access and equity (NCTM, 2014). Additionally, we describe examples of professional learning activities that develop instructional practices around linking learning trajectories with the use of formative assessment in classroom settings.

The impact of systematic and intentional use of formative assessment has been well established and is widely known (as discussed in Chapter 1). Less well known at the K–grade 12 levels is the impact of knowledge and use of learning trajectories on teacher practice. Multiple researchers are finding that knowledge and use of learning trajectories positively improves teacher's knowledge and instruction, as well as student achievement and motivation (Clarke et al., 2001; Clements, Sarama, Spitler, Lange, & Wolfe, 2011; Fennema, Carpenter, Levi, Jacobs, & Empson, 1996; Wilson, Sztajn, Edgington, & Myers, 2015).

A learning trajectory describes a progression of student thinking and strategies from least sophisticated to more efficient and generalizable strategies, while also developing procedural fluency through understanding. Founded on the mathematics education research of how students develop understanding and fluency, common errors that students make, and pre-conceptions or misconceptions that interfere with students learning new concepts or solving related problems, learning trajectories describe the pathway from the student's prior knowledge to the mathematical goals or standards (Daro, Mosher, & Corcoran, 2011). Learning trajectories are found in the research literature for several mathematical domains including counting, addition and subtraction, fractions, multiplicative reasoning, measurement, geometry, proportionality, and algebraic thinking and were used, in part, in the development of the CCSSM (CCSSO, 2010; Daro et al., 2011).

Before unpacking formative assessment that is based on learning trajectories more fully, let us return to a 1990s classroom after the release of the *Curriculum and Evaluation Standards for School Mathematics* (NCTM, 1989). Stein et al. (2008) referred to this time period as the "first generation of practice and research," where the emphasis in reform classrooms was on valuing student thinking by eliciting multiple solution methods and allowing students to share and explain their solutions. More recent "second generation" practice "reasserts the critical role of the teacher in guiding mathematical discussions" (p. 319). Another way to view this shift from first- to second-generation practice is as a shift from *eliciting* evidence of student thinking to *eliciting and responding* to student thinking, with the goal of moving students to a more sophisticated understanding of mathematics. This is where learning trajectories can provide much needed guidance for teachers who are adopting a formative assessment lens. In formative assessment, everything students do (e.g., classroom discussion, independent or group work, projects, exit slips) has the potential to provide evidence of student thinking (Leahy, Lyon, Thompson, & Wiliam, 2005). Understanding and using a learning trajectory to analyze evidence of student thinking provides research-based evidence to inform instruction and student learning that has the potential to move practice towards a second-generation use of knowledge of student thinking. For example, review the student solutions to the multiplication problem in figure 6.1. You will notice that while the answers to the problem are all correct, the strategies that students use are quite different.

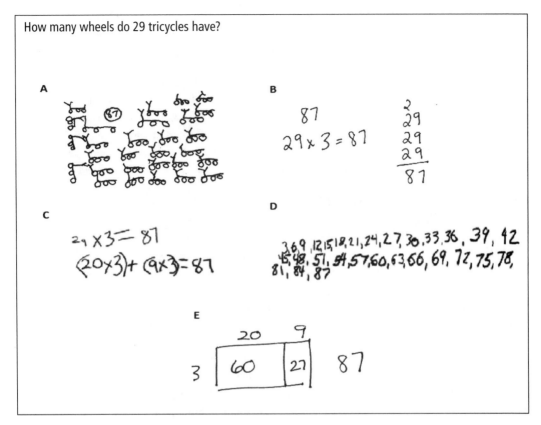

How many wheels do 29 tricycles have?

A

B

$$87$$
$$29 \times 3 = 87$$

$$\begin{array}{r} 2 \\ 29 \\ 29 \\ 29 \\ \hline 87 \end{array}$$

C

$$29 \times 3 = 87$$
$$(20 \times 3) + (9 \times 3) = 87$$

D

3,6,9, 12,15,18,21,24,27, 30,33,36, 39, 42
45,48, 51, 54,57,60,63,66, 69, 72,75,78,
81, 84, 87

E

Fig. 6.1. Multiple solutions for solving the problem, all with the correct answer of 87 tricycles

From a "first generation" reform lens, we might celebrate the fact that students can arrive at the correct answer to this problem in multiple ways, can clearly show their thinking, and do not necessarily need to be taught a specific method to solve this problem successfully. In addition, asking students to share their solutions to this kind of task creates opportunities to increase the range of students who participate in classroom discussion and for students to have their thinking validated and to learn from each other. Unfortunately, merely sharing or celebrating multiple solutions is no guarantee that students will learn important mathematics or develop procedural fluency with understanding.

Looking at these solutions through a learning trajectory lens offers a somewhat different perspective. When students first solve multiplication problems, they may sketch out the problem situation and then count each object. Example A exemplifies a solution at this level. The solution shows evidence of understanding the problem situation by drawing each tricycle and then count-ing each wheel. This answer was correct, but the strategy was inefficient. As students move away from counting by ones they recognize and begin to count by the groups, first by using repeated addition, and then later by skip counting; this is illustrated by solutions B and D respectively. Solution E represents a strategy—the open area model—that is based on and supports a firm understanding of grouping by larger quantities and place value. The open-area model provides the final link to the development of procedural fluency based on conceptual understanding. These concept-building strategies are replaced with more abstract and efficient strategies, as exemplified by Solution C, which shows evidence of using place value understanding and the use of the distributive property.

Importantly, the value added to formative assessment of using a learning trajectory is the way in which the progression embedded in the trajectory both helps teachers and students understand the ultimate learning goals and informs the next instructional step. When thinking about the solutions in figure 6.1 from a lens of accuracy, the solutions are all equal. Yet, it is clear from the learning trajectory perspective they are not equal, and based on the evidence, the instructional action should be substantially different. The levels of the learning trajectory can provide guidance on what kind of support is needed to move student understanding and strategy sophistication forward. For example, the evidence in Solution A suggests the student is counting by ones. Instruction, therefore, should focus on moving the student away from seeing the wheels as a collection of ones to conceptualizing the composite units and using repeated addition or skip counting to find the total. In contrast, the evidence in Solution B and D suggests instruction focused on helping students see the factors as dimensions of arrays and area models to move beyond these additive strategies.

This example might give the impression that performance on learning trajectories over time is linear, that first students learn to use one strategy and then the next, and so on. However, researchers have found that as students interact with new contexts and problem structures, their performance moves back and forth within the trajectory until understanding stabilizes regardless of the context or structure (Kouba & Franklin, 1995; Petit, Laird, Marsden, & Ebby, 2016). In multiplicative reasoning, for example, the goal by the end of fifth grade is for students to have efficient and flexible strategies for solving a range of whole number multiplication and division problems that will position students to engage successfully in middle school mathematics topics such as ratio and proportions. Figure 6.2 represents this movement on a trajectory over time.

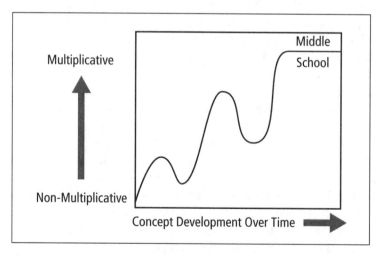

Fig. 6.2. Hypothesized movement on the progression as whole number multiplication and division concepts are introduced and developed across grades (Hulbert, Petit, Ebby, Cunningham, & Laird, 2017)

The use of learning trajectories within the context of formative assessment supports the implementation of the strategies for effective use of formative assessment (Leahy et al., 2005) in significant ways. Table 6.1 summarizes some of ways in which learning trajectories can be used to enhance each of the five formative assessment strategies discussed in Chapter 1.

Table 6.1. Learning trajectory enhanced strategies for effective formative assessment (Leahy et al., 2005)

Formative Assessment Strategy	How LT's Enhance the Formative Assessment Strategy
Clarifying and sharing learning intentions and criteria for success	Learning trajectories provide the long-range target (fluency and flexibility with a range of contexts and structures) and the short-range goal based upon current levels on the trajectory for both teachers and students.
Engineering effective classroom discussions, questions, and learning tasks	Learning trajectories provide an analytical framework to anticipate, elicit, interpret and respond to evidence of student thinking through discussions and written work.
Providing feedback that moves learners forward	Learning trajectories provide descriptive evidence that teachers can use to provide actionable feedback to students that can help them progress to the next level of a trajectory or understand an error evidenced in their solution.
Activating students as the owners of their learning	Student can use a learning trajectory to self-assess their solution strategies, leading toward increasingly sophisticated strategies or thinking.
Activating students as resources for each other	Students can peer assess student work using a trajectory and help each other understand and use more sophisticated strategies or thinking.

In the remainder of this chapter, we describe tools and strategies from the Ongoing Assessment Project (OGAP) that were developed at a grain size to make learning trajectories usable at the classroom level, and were specifically designed to be used in the context of formative assessment to inform instruction and student learning.

Using Learning Trajectories to Provide Actionable Evidence: The Ongoing Assessment Project (OGAP)

OGAP is an intentional and systematic approach to formative assessment based on mathematics education research, including (1) how student understanding and strategies develop, (2) how errors and misconceptions may interfere with learning new concepts or solving problems, (3) how to make instructional decisions based on development on the progressions, and (4) how to vary problem structures and contexts given the evidence in student solutions.

This research has been translated for use by teachers in the OGAP Frameworks for fractions, additive reasoning, multiplicative reasoning, and proportionality. The OGAP formative assessment system involves using learning trajectories to analyze a pre-assessment to inform initial planning, and then systematically and intentionally analyzing evidence of student thinking on an ongoing basis. Evidence of student thinking is elicited during classroom discussions and through strategies such as administering daily exit problems. The problems are designed specifically for formative assessment and are based on findings from research on student learning to elicit students' developing understanding, common errors and misconceptions or preconceptions.

The OGAP Frameworks include information on problem contexts and structures that teachers should consider when designing and using formative assessment tasks, as well as learning trajectories that have been translated into a grain size that is usable at the classroom level. (See figure 6.3 for a depiction of these components for the OGAP Multiplicative Reasoning Framework.) The OGAP Progressions are visual representations of the learning trajectories that can be used to make sense of evidence of student thinking and can act in concert with problem structures and contexts. That is, as teachers design or select tasks to use for formative assessment based on evidence in student work along the progression, they consider the different multiplication contexts and problem structures found in the framework. For example, when selecting a follow-up task based on the evidence in Response E of figure 6.1, a teacher might select an equal groups task with larger numbers (e.g., 2-digit × 2-digit) or a problem in a different context (e.g., measure conversion) to gather additional information about the students' flexibility in different contexts or different magnitude factors. When the context is changed, for example, to a measure conversion problem, is student performance at the same level on the progression?

Interpreting Evidence and Informing Instruction

OGAP Progressions

- Multiplication Progression (see Figure 6.4)
- Division Progression
- Issues and Errors

Task Considerations

Problem Contexts	**Problem Structures**
• Equal groups	• Types of items
• Equal measures	• Understanding and use of relationships
• Measure conversions	• Factors
• Multiplicative comparisons	• Language
• Patterns	• Types of division
• Rates	• Divisors
• Rectangular area	• Representations
• Volume	• Properties of operations

Fig. 6.3. Components of the OGAP Multiplication Reasoning Framework

Consider the OGAP Multiplication Progression shown in figure 6.4 which represents a learning trajectory for multiplication. (There is a corresponding progression for division.) In particular, focus on the levels in the progression, and the arrows suggesting growth and movement along the progression. Each has meaning when making instructional decisions.

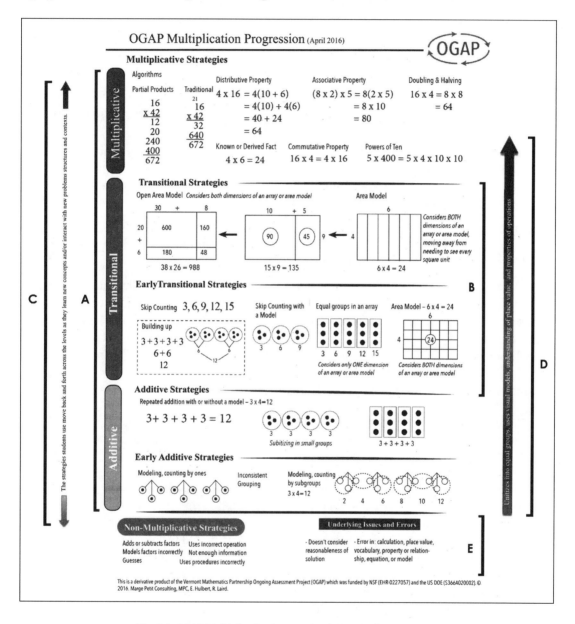

Fig. 6.4. OGAP Multiplication Progression (OGAPMath LLC, 2016)
(For an electronic copy go to www.ogapmathllc.com.)

Notice the following about the OGAP Multiplication Progression:

a) The levels reflect strategies that go from least sophisticated and most inefficient (early additive) to flexible and efficient strategies (multiplicative). Returning to figure 6.1, for example, Solution A (counting by ones) is at the early additive level while solution D (skip counting) is at the early transitional level.

b) The use of visual models at the Transitional level plays a critical role in the development of fluency at the multiplicative levels (e.g., equal groups, to equal groups in an array, to the area model, to the open area model) .

c) The double arrow at the left of the progression levels is a reminder that performance may move back and forth across the progression until it stabilizes at the multiplicative level regardless of the problem context or problem structure.

d) The arrow on the right provides some guidance on instructional foci to move performance from one level to the next (e.g., when moving a student from an early additive strategy such as counting by ones, the instructional emphasis might be on unitizing into composite units and counting by groups, rather than by ones.)

e) In addition to gathering evidence of strategies along the progression, note the list of underlying issues and errors at the bottom. This includes recognizing solutions that are non-multiplicative (e.g., adding factors).

"Eliciting evidence of student thinking to inform instruction" is one of the eight mathematical teaching practices promoted by NCTM's *Principles to Actions* (2014). Specific strategies for how to gather evidence to inform instruction using the OGAP Progression are explored later in this chapter, but first we look at how learning trajectories can support another important mathematical teaching practice: "build fluency from conceptual understanding."

Building Procedural Fluency from Conceptual Understanding

> Effective teaching of mathematics builds fluency with procedures on a foundation of conceptual understanding so that students, over time, become skillful in using procedures flexibly as they solve contextual and mathematical problems. (NCTM, 2014, p. 42)

A learning trajectory shows the path or steps to procedural fluency based on conceptual understanding. In the case of the OGAP Multiplication Progression, fluency is built on understanding developed through research-based instructional strategies, such as using visual models, placing an emphasis on unitizing, deepening place value understanding, and focusing on the properties of operations (shown on the arrow at the right side of the progression). In contrast, if procedural fluency is built through rote memorization or repeated practice of algorithms without an underlying understanding of place value or properties of operations, it is fluency with a limited shelf-life.

The evidence in the student work in figure 6.5 shows the pre- to post-assessment response to the same question by Karen, a fourth-grade student. When asked about the evidence in this student's work the teacher said that her instruction had focused on introducing the traditional algorithm. She noted that Karen, like many of her students, solved all the problems in the pre-assessment using repeated addition or skip counting. She was surprised to see that every post assessment response by Karen demonstrated a lack of foundational understanding of the standard algorithm she had worked so hard to establish.

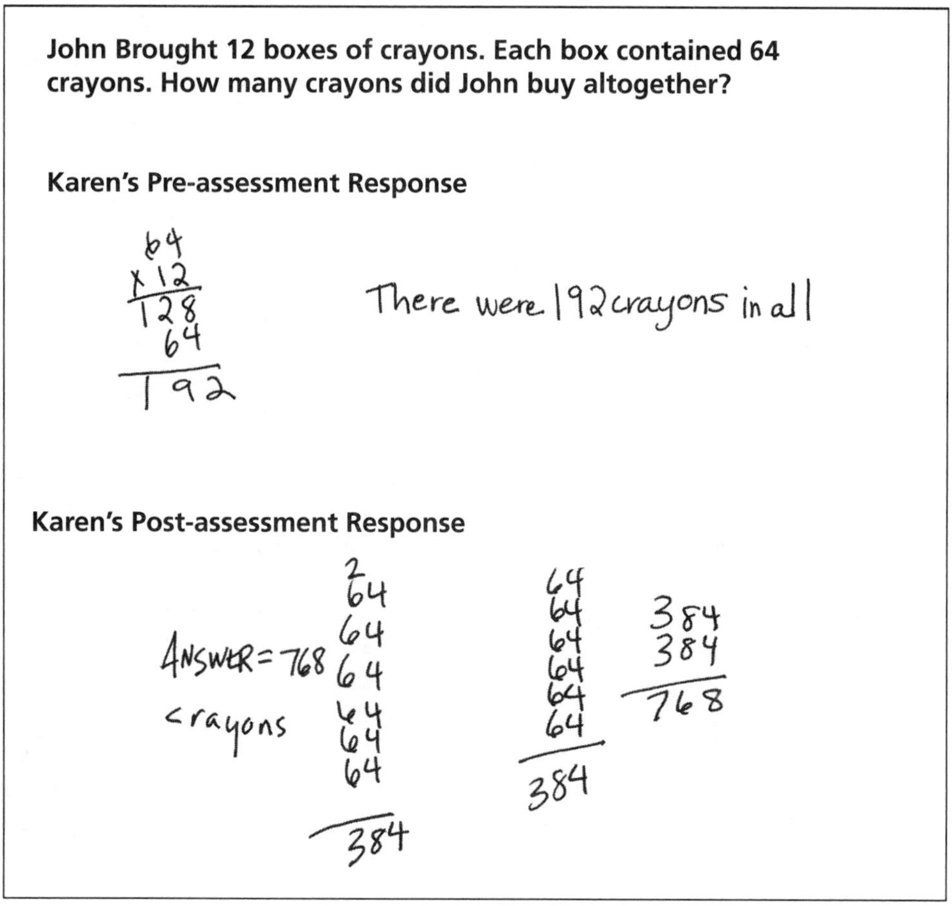

John Brought 12 boxes of crayons. Each box contained 64 crayons. How many crayons did John buy altogether?

Karen's Pre-assessment Response

$$
\begin{array}{r}
64 \\
\times 12 \\
\hline
128 \\
64 \\
\hline
192
\end{array}
$$

There were 192 crayons in all

Karen's Post-assessment Response

ANSWER = 768
< rayons

$$
\begin{array}{r}
2 \\
64 \\
64 \\
64 \\
64 \\
64 \\
64 \\
\hline
384
\end{array}
$$

$$
\begin{array}{r}
64 \\
64 \\
64 \\
64 \\
64 \\
64 \\
\hline
384
\end{array}
\qquad
\begin{array}{r}
384 \\
384 \\
\hline
768
\end{array}
$$

Fig. 6.5. Karen's pre- to post-assessment response shows evidence of attempting to use the U.S. traditional algorithm in the post-assessment without understanding

What this teacher failed to consider is how to help her students build from repeated addition or skip counting towards more efficient and generalizable strategies while also building place value understanding. Learning trajectories can provide a roadmap for teachers to help guide their instructional decisions based on the evidence of students' developing understanding while keeping the focus on the ultimate goal of developing procedural fluency with understanding. In multiplicative reasoning, once students have developed an understanding of equal grouping, it is important to build unitizing and place value understanding through visual models, such as the area model. From there, they can make connections to more abstract strategies and procedures that are efficient and generalizable. Skipping too soon to the multiplicative stage without building understanding is like constructing a building without a foundation, which may have been the situation in Karen's instruction.

What is most striking in Karen's example is that the teacher had not realized that Karen was struggling with understanding the algorithm until she gave the post-assessment. She admitted to not having given formative assessment questions throughout the unit or analyzed her work in a way that would provide her a clue as to Karen's misunderstanding. In many ways, this example is exactly why formative assessment, as a regular part of instruction, is so critical.

Karen's example reminds us that the "gathering of evidence should neither be left to chance nor occur sporadically" (NCTM, 2014, p. 53). We now turn to ways that we can we help both prospective and experienced teachers become versed in the use of learning trajectories to gather, interpret, and respond to evidence of student thinking as part of their daily mathematics instruction. As mentioned earlier, this evidence can be found in many places during a lesson: classroom discussion, independent or group work, and formative assessment strategies, such as exit cards.

Using Learning Trajectories in the Design of Professional Learning Activities

OGAP professional development for each content area is extensive, focusing on related concept understanding, mathematics education research that underpins the trajectory for each of the content strands, mathematics education research that underpins understanding of the selection or design of formative assessment tasks, strategies to analyze student work and make instructional decisions, strategies to analyze instructional materials for alignment with mathematics education research, and classroom-based case studies that model the formative assessment cycle using a learning trajectory (Hulbert, Petit, Ebby, Cunningham, & Laird, 2017; Petit et al., 2016; Petit & Zawojewski, 2010; Wiliam, 2011). While these professional learning foci and the activities exemplified in this section are specific to OGAP, they are appropriate for any professional development involving the application of learning trajectories to formative assessment. This section includes a detailed explanation of three professional learning activities that can be used with in-service or preservice educators: (1) analyzing student work and making instructional decisions using a *learning trajectory* (2) developing understanding of the influence of problem structures, and (3) conducting and analyzing a clinical interview of a student from a learning trajectory perspective.

Analyzing Evidence of Student Thinking with a Learning Trajectory: The OGAP Sort

The first professional learning activity involves introducing preservice or in-service teachers to a systematic way to analyze evidence of student thinking and strategies on mathematics problems in order to inform their instruction on an ongoing basis. Typically, when teachers look at student work, they begin with the accuracy of a solution, looking for whether students have provided the correct answer, and then looking more closely at incorrect solutions to find errors (Crespo, 2000; Ebby, 2015). However, the student work samples in figure 6.1 illustrate that correct answers alone can provide a false positive. All of the solutions have the correct answer; however, a fifth-grade student who is using repeated addition or skip counting to solve a multiplication problem is not in a position to engage successfully in middle school concepts, such as solving ratio and proportion problems.

In the *Principles to Actions*, the following three elements are described in relation to what "counts" as evidence of student thinking:

1) Teachers attend to more than just the correctness of the solution (Crespo, 2000).

2) Teachers collect evidence using learning trajectories (Clements & Sarama, 2004; Sztajn et al., 2012).

3) Teachers collect evidence of patterns of difficulties, errors, and misconceptions (Swan, 2001 as cited in NCTM, 2014, p. 53).

The OGAP process described here for collecting and analyzing evidence of student thinking is consistent with these ideas. To focus analysis of evidence using a learning trajectory during instruction means to listen and look interpretively for evidence of students' strategies and thinking. Analyzing student work from a formative assessment perspective using a learning trajectory requires a shift, therefore, from the normative ways that teachers analyze student work. Teachers can practice this analysis in the context of professional development, preservice methods courses, or school-based professional learning communities.

The OGAP Sort is a process of analyzing evidence in student work using a learning trajectory to attend to student strategies as well as identify errors and misconceptions that may interfere with learning new concepts or solving problems. This process, which counteracts the tendency to sort student work into correct and incorrect solutions, was refined through extensive piloting and feedback from hundreds of teachers. Teachers are introduced to the OGAP Sort by working collaboratively to sort preselected sets of actual student work into piles that represent each of the levels on the OGAP Progression (fig. 6.6). After practicing this process, they can use the progressions to sort student work in their own classroom or school settings.

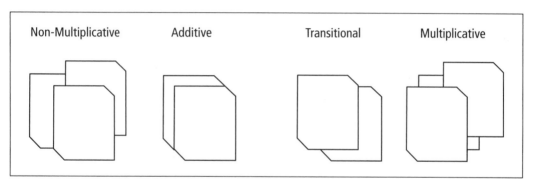

Fig. 6.6. An illustration of how student work would be sorted using the
OGAP Multiplicative Progression. (Hulbert et al., in press 2017)

After sorting into the four main categories, the transitional and additive piles can then be further sorted into early transitional and transitional and early additive and additive. Next, the work in each pile is analyzed for the specific strategy used and for errors and other issues that should be addressed. Once the work is sorted, teachers have a picture of the evidence across their class in relation to the learning trajectory.

The information from OGAP Sorts can also be recorded on an evidence recording sheet such as the one shown in figure 6.7. The sample in figure 6.7 also shows that the teacher has underlined or highlighted incorrect solutions. Written or electronic records provide the opportunity to look for trends across students, questions, and time.

Items #	Content (e.g., context, type of number)	Multiplicative	Transitional		Additive		Non-multiplicative Reasoning
			Transitional	Early	Additive	Early	
i	Equal group 8×12	Open area model	Ethan Natalie Grace Lucas Abdi Nathan	Emma ⎤ skip Claire ⎦ Counting Kelyn – Area Model	Tyler ⎤ Jacob ⎦ Sophie Alexis	Repeated addition Logan ⎤ Eli ⎦ Counting by ones	Charlotte – Added factor 208? used procedure incorrectly

Underlying Issues or concerns									
Unreasonable	Misinterpret meaning of remainders	Place value error	Units inconsistent or absent	Property or relationship error	Calculation error	Equation error	Model error	Vocabulary error
		Abdi			Ethan Grace			

Fig. 6.7. Sample of completed OGAP Student Work Evidence Collection Sheet.
Student names are listed under strategy evidenced, sub-strategies are noted, student names are listed under Underlying Issues or Errors if evidenced, and incorrect solutions are highlighted. (Hulbert et al., 2017)

Whether or not the evidence is recorded, it is critical that the sort is used to inform instruction and provide feedback to students. The following questions can be used in professional development or to structure PLCs to help teachers think about the evidence across the class once they have completed a sort: (1) What are developing understandings that can be built upon? (2) What issues or concerns are evidenced in the student work? (3) What are the potential next instructional steps based on the evidence?

Teachers who have followed this process have been able to locate the evidence in the student work on the progression, identify any errors or misconceptions, or both, and generate specific and targeted instructional goals based on the evidence. For example, when analyzing evidence in Karen's post-assessment response (fig. 6.5) teachers first acknowledge that the student recognized the situation as multiplicative and that the student may be able to apply the first step of the algorithm when there is no regrouping (e.g., 2×64). This evidence can be built upon as they consider what to do next based on the evidence in the second step that the standard algorithm was incorrectly applied and the reasonableness of the solution was not considered. Using the OGAP multiplicative progression for guidance, teachers recognize that they need to rebuild understanding of the algorithm by using the open area model and distributive property to develop place value understanding. While the strategy the student attempted to use was at the multiplicative level, the actions to consider are found on the right arrow and at the transitional level on the progression. Additionally, the teacher may consider the problem structures to check for understanding of the first step of the algorithm by asking a question that involves regrouping in the first step of the procedure (e.g., 6×64 crayons). This is an example of generating instructional strategies that are based directly on evidence in the student's work. The aim is to move students towards more sophisticated strategies and understanding based on a learning trajectory.

While this process is an integral part of OGAP professional development, its real purpose is to provide a structure and process for analyzing evidence in student thinking in relation to learning trajectories as a part of the ongoing formative assessment process in the classroom. Imagine, for example, how differently the sixth-grade monthly planning meeting described in the beginning of this chapter would have been if the teachers had arrived having sorted the work using a trajectory with explicit questions for help on the next instructional steps. As one OGAP participant noted:

> My participation in OGAP has helped me in giving immediate feedback and has given me the chance to identify children who need more help and to really look, in detail, as to what their needs are and how I can push them to that next level. Identifying the different levels that students may come in at and where I need to get them has made a significant difference in my instruction.

Additionally, while this professional learning activity centers around sorting actual written work, in classrooms where OGAP Progressions are an integral part of practice, teachers are using the levels of progressions to respond to student questions, to listen to classroom discussion, to use visual models and representations, and to make "on the spot" instructional decisions without the need for explicitly sorting the evidence. In classrooms where OGAP is effectively used students are also familiar with the progression, know where their performance is along the progression and recognize their goals based on the progression. It is not uncommon for conversations between students to include advice on how to move from one level to the next. In this way, the use of the learning trajectories embedded in classroom instruction helps "activate students as owners of their own learning" and "as resources for each other" (Leahy et al., 2005).

Understanding the Influence of Problem Structures

Another key element of formative assessment and the use of learning trajectories is selecting and using tasks that are designed to elicit student thinking and strategies (Leahy et al., 2005; NCTM, 2014). Earlier in the chapter, we explored how problem context and structures strongly influence student performance. That is, as students interact with new contexts and problem structures their performance moves back and forth within the trajectory until understanding stabilizes regardless of the context or structure (Kouba & Franklin, 1995; Petit et al., 2016). Teachers are intuitively aware that different problem structures influence their students' performance. A teacher's first response to students having difficulty is often to simplify the numbers or contexts. The example of Karen's post assessment evidence shows a more nuanced teacher response: rather than making the problem easier, by increasing the complexity of the first step of the algorithm so that regrouping is necessary, the teacher can elicit additional information about the students' use and understanding of the procedure when multiplying single and multi-digit quantities. On the other hand, a student who has successfully used an open area model to solve a multi-digit equal groups problem might benefit by being asked to solve a multiplicative comparison problem with numbers of the same magnitude. An important research finding that often surprises teachers is that students will continue to use immature strategies if problem contexts and structures are not varied (Cobb, Yackel, & Wood, 1988; Peterson, Carpenter, & Fennema, 1989). Figure 6.3 shows examples of problem structures and contexts that should be considered when selecting a task for students to solve.

A professional learning activity that introduces the underlying research on the influence of specific structures involves having participants interact with a selection of problems with varied contexts, structures, and numbers (shown in Table 6.2) in the following ways: (1) solving each of the problems individually; (2) sorting the problems into three categories: easiest, moderate, and most challenging; (3) collaboratively identifying the features in the problem that led to sorting into each of the categories, and; (4) debriefing as a whole group.

The point of this activity is not to agree on the categorization of the difficulty of each of the problems; Rather, the point is for participants to identify the features of the problems that influenced their decisions. The facilitator then elicits features from participants and records them so that the group can then analyze the list in relation to the problem structures and contexts in the OGAP Framework and add features to that list as needed. Engaging participants in this way prepares them to understand and use the research about the importance of problem structures to be more purposeful in selecting mathematical tasks based on evidence in student work.

Table 6.2. A variety of tasks for sorting activity

Problem Structure, Context, and Features	Example Problem
Multi-step step area problem involving multiples of ten and measurements	Carmen is painting her bedroom walls. Her room is 15 feet long and 10 feet wide. Her ceiling is 8 feet high. If a can of paint covers 300 square feet, how many cans of paint does she need to buy?
Equal measures and measure conversion with extraneous information	Abby has 8 quarts of ginger ale. She plans to use all the ginger ale to make the punch recipe below. How many gallons of juice does Abby need to buy? **Fruit Punch recipe:** 3 quarts juice, 1 quart ginger ale, 4 scoops sherbet (4 quarts = 1 gallon)
Equal groups problem with three factors and multiples of powers of ten	Mr. Jones ordered office supplies. He ordered 7 cases of paper. There are 10 packages of paper in each case. Each package contains 500 sheets of paper. How many sheets of paper did he order?
Two-part equal groups problem involving different size factors and relationship between factors	A) Mark bought 12 boxes of crayons. Each box contained 8 crayons. How many crayons did Mark buy all together? Show your work. B) Mark bought 12 boxes of crayons. Each box contained 64 crayons. How many crayons did Mark buy all together?
Rate problem	During migration, humpback whales swim about 6 miles per hour. After 25 hours, about how far have they traveled? Show your work.
Measure conversion involving fractions	How many millimeters are in 5½ centimeters? (10 millimeters = 1 centimeter)
Multiplicative comparison involving rate, decimal numbers, and extraneous numbers (dates).	The price of gas in 1960 was $ 0.19 per gallon. The price of gas in 2014 was about 15 times as much as the price of gas in 1960. What was the price of gas in 2014?

These problems were selected specifically to elicit a range of features as shown in the left-hand column. Typically, teachers identify the magnitude or nature of the numbers, the language in the problems, the number of steps in the problem, the context of the problem, and the implicit or explicit models in the problem as features that affect the problem difficulty. Once those features are elicited from the group and recorded on chart paper, participants are directed to study the problem contexts and structures section of the OGAP Framework (see page 1 on the framework), identifying structures and contexts they identified and ones they did not.

Notably this is the first introduction to problem structures and contexts in OGAP professional development. Participants also engage in additional activities, including selecting formative assessment items from an item bank and analyzing questions in mathematics instructional materials for the different features. For example, teachers review their instructional materials to ascertain the extent to which students have the opportunity to engage in a range of contexts and other problem structures (e.g., magnitude of factors). Teachers have consistently told us that understanding the research about problem structures, contexts, and the OGAP Progression changed the way they interact with their instructional materials. It is not uncommon for teachers to find that one context (e.g., equal groups) is overemphasized, or some contexts are not included at all (e.g., multiplicative change), or that there are no problems involving powers of ten that are so important for reinforcing place value understanding. Consequently, teachers can fill the identified gaps as the unit of study progresses.

Conducting and Analyzing a Clinical Interview

The third professional learning activity involves using a learning trajectory to analyze student responses to a one-on-one or clinical interview (Ginsburg, Jacobs & Lopez, 1998). Conducting a clinical interview of a child is a common assignment in mathematics methods courses that can help preservice teachers understand and use research on student learning to make sense of student thinking (Jenkins, 2010; Schorr & Ginsburg, 2000). The student interview has also been widely used as a way to help prospective teachers develop the kinds of skills and practices in relation to questioning, listening, and responding that are important components of effective classroom mathematics instruction (Buschman, 2001; Crepso & Nicol, 2003; Moyer & Milewicz, 2002). While it may not be practical for teachers to conduct interviews with every child in a classroom, there is much to be learned from even one or two in-depth interviews. This is also an assignment that can be embedded into ongoing professional development for in-service teachers.

To illustrate how learning trajectories can enhance this activity, we describe a version of the interview assignment in a mathematics methods course for elementary preservice teachers who were student teaching in a fieldwork classroom while taking the course. The assignment asked them to use a given interview protocol that focused on number and operations appropriate for the grade level they were teaching and to provide students with manipulatives and paper and pencil to solve the problems. Many of the interview prompts were contextual word problems. In the methods class, the preservice teachers read and learned about research on students' learning of number and operations. They also watched and analyzed interview clips of one-on-one interviews and learned about effective questioning and probing strategies. In the report of the interview, they were expected to use research to interpret and make sense of the student's thinking, problem solving strategies, and understanding of foundational concepts and then make instructional recommendations based on this analysis.

This assignment had been used in the methods course for many years and was found to be a useful way to help preservice teachers focus deeply on children's thinking. However, developing appropriate instructional implications based on this evidence tended to be more of a challenge and was often a weaker part of the preservice teacher reports. We found that introducing and exploring the OGAP Progressions in the methods class further supported the depth and quality of the analysis that preservice teachers conducted on the interviews.

Preservice teachers drew on these learning trajectories both to make sense of the student's reasoning and to think about appropriate instruction based on that evidence. For example, in analyzing an interview of a first-grade child, one preservice teacher explained an interesting strategy for determining the number of cookies if there are three plates and two cookies on each plate. The student said "I just put my 2 fingers up like that [*holds up two fingers*] and then I was like "1, 2 . . . 3, 4 . . . 5, 6 [*indicates the three separate groups by pausing in between each*]." The preservice teacher located this strategy in relation to the OGAP Progression:

> Although [she] still seemed to need to count by ones, she modeled the problem by breaking up the phrasing of her count sequence rather than by using a physical representation, aside from modeling the initial group of two. Thus, it seems as if she is just on the cusp of developing the ability to use repeated addition or skip counting to understand multiplicative situations involving small quantities.

After analyzing what the student had done with her fingers in relation to what she was saying out loud, and looking across other interview problems that involved grouping, the preservice teacher again located her reasoning strategies on the OGAP Progression to help think about the next instructional steps: "the next step will be to transition from counting by ones with a model to using repeated addition and eventually skip counting with a model."

The sample strategies and visual models on the OGAP Progressions also helped to support preservice teachers in developing more specific recommendations for instruction. For example, after noting that a student was using an additive strategy to solve problems involving equal groups, another preservice teacher wrote that she would "help her arrange her drawings in rectangular arrays, as an entry point to area models and an introduction to the commutative nature of multiplication."

One common error that preservice and in-service teachers tend to make is to use the progressions as if they indicate the level of a child rather than the level of a child's strategy for a problem (i.e., stating that child is at the early additive level). It is important to reinforce continually the idea that children's strategies will move up and down the progression, depending on the context, problem structure, problem situation, and complexity of the numbers. This also reinforces the need to collect multiple forms of evidence across varied contexts to obtain an accurate picture of a child's learning and development. This is one of the important shifts in learning to use a learning trajectory to inform formative assessment.

Additional Professional Learning Activities

Below we briefly describe some additional activities that can be used to support in-service and preservice teachers in using learning trajectory enhanced formative assessment to inform instruction.

Analyzing and making connections between visual models and algorithms. This activity is designed to help teachers understand the conceptual links between the strategies at different levels in the progressions. For multiplication, participants are asked to solve a multidigit multiplication problem using the traditional U.S. algorithm, an open area model and the partial products algorithm and then make connections between the three different strategies. Focusing on the links between these strategies helps teachers see how to use place value understanding and the open area model to move students from transitional to multiplicative strategies while also illustrating the importance of transitional strategies in building conceptual foundations (Hulbert, et al., 2017). The same activity—comparing standard algorithms to model-based strategies—can also be used to explore the development of procedural fluency with conceptual understanding for addition and subtraction, division, fraction operations, and proportional reasoning.

Case studies that embed the formative assessment cycle into examples of classroom instruction. OGAP case studies have been developed to model the formative assessment cycle for teachers using the OGAP Progressions. Each case is introduced with a brief description of a lesson and the teacher's goals. Participants then engage in (1) analysis of a formative assessment task used to gather evidence of student thinking during the lesson or as an exit card at the end of the lesson in relationship to the lesson and the lesson goals; (2) analysis of student work from the formative assessment task using an OGAP Progression; and, (3) discussion of instructional actions in relationship to the evidence in the student work. The set of cases are constructed to model and engage participants in decision-making around a range of instructional actions (e.g., selecting and sequencing student solutions to strengthen understanding of a concept or to make connections between levels on a trajectory, adapting the goals of the next lesson, or choosing a formative assessment item to use at the beginning or end of the next lesson). These case studies allow participants to experience the whole formative assessment cycle—from instruction to analysis of evidence of student thinking to instructional adjustment.

Planning, teaching, and reflecting on lessons. For this activity, participants engage in using learning trajectories to inform all three phases of instruction and carry out the complete formative assessment cycle. Before teaching a lesson, they use the learning trajectory to anticipate student strategies for the mathematical task (Smith & Stein, 2011) and consider how they will collect evidence of student learning during the lesson. During the lesson, they use the learning trajectory to listen, interpret, and make sense of student contributions and observe students while they are working on the tasks. At the end of the lesson, they collect evidence of student thinking, ideally in the form of an exit question designed for formative assessment. After the lesson, they then analyze student work to reflect on the lesson and develop goals for future lessons. This activity can be an assignment in a preservice methods course or embedded within lesson study for in-service teachers.

Action research projects. As part of a course for in-service teachers, participants conduct action research projects that focus on student progress over time. These projects allow teachers to do an in-depth analysis on a small set of students, studying their performance in relation to a learning trajectory across time. The analysis allows teachers to see clear links between evidence of student growth in relation to the progression and instructional actions (i.e., which instructional strategies worked and which may not have been as effective). Teachers indicate that conducting action research on a subset of students in this manner helped them understand more broadly the value of using learning trajectories in the context of formative assessment.

Topics for Further Study

An ongoing large-scale two-year randomized control trial (RCT) and implementation study of OGAP shows significant impacts on both teacher and student learning, despite wide variation in implementation across classroom and schools (Supovitz, 2017). Understanding how to strengthen and deepen both implementation and impacts of formative assessment enhanced by learning trajectories is an important next step and can enhance the design of approaches to support teacher learning and growth.

There is also a need for more tools, resources, and approaches to professional learning that make learning trajectories accessible and usable by teachers in classroom settings. Elementary teachers are faced with the challenge of knowing how to draw on and use learning trajectories across a wide variety of topics and grain sizes (e.g., number, operations, geometry, rational numbers, data, measurement, and algebraic thinking). There is much progress to be made in terms of consolidation and integration—for example, how can teachers monitor student progress across multiple learning trajectories (Daro et al., 2011)? In addition, the fact that most of the existing learning trajectories focus on elementary grade levels poses a challenge for teachers at the secondary level.

Finally, while there is accumulating evidence around the importance of the use of learning trajectories, there is still much to be learned. We know relatively little about how teachers make sense of learning trajectories and understand their students' thinking in classroom settings, or about the relationship between their interpretations of student thinking and the planning and execution of instructional responses. Decomposing formative assessment practices or specifying the *core practices* that expert teachers engage in during this process (Grossman et al., 2009) could help us design professional learning experiences where teachers can investigate, rehearse, enact those practices in classroom or professional development settings.

Selected Commonly Used Resources Related to Learning Trajectories and Formative Assessment

- OGAP Frameworks and sample professional development materials for additive reasoning, multiplicative reasoning, fractions, and proportional reasoning. (See www.ogapmathllc.com.)

- Hulbert. E., Petit, M., Ebby, C. B., Cunningham, E., & Laird, R. (2017). *A Focus on Multiplication and Division: Bringing Research to the Classroom.* Routledge.

- Petit, M., Laird, R., Marsden, E., & Ebby, C. E. (2016). *A Focus on Fractions: Bringing Research to the Classroom 2nd edition.* New York: Routledge.

- Battista, M. T. (2012). *Cognition-Based Assessment and Teaching: Building on Student Reasoning.* Series for grades K–6. (Addition and Subtraction, Multiplication and Division, Place Value, Fractions, Geometry, Measurement). Portsmouth, NH: Heinemann.

- Clements, D., & Sarama, J. (2014). *Learning and Teaching Early Math: The Learning Trajectories Approach, 2nd Edition.* New York: Routledge.

- *Developing essential understanding for teaching mathematics.* Series that includes books on a variety of content domains for Pre-K–2, 3–5, 6–8 and 9–12. Reston, VA: NCTM.

- *Marilyn Burns Math Reasoning Inventory* (MRI). Free, Web-based, formative assessment tool that focuses on conducting interviews to assess students' numerical reasoning strategies and understandings. https://mathreasoninginventory.com/

Reflect on Your Practice

1. Administer one of the questions from this chapter or a multiplication word problem from your math program materials to a group of students for formative assessment purposes.

    a.   Use the OGAP Multiplication Progression to sort the work by strategy, and then note evidence of errors or underlying issues.

    b.   How does this process help you think about implications for your instruction? What are some next instructional steps based on the evidence?

2. Some researchers have observed that students will continue to use immature strategies if problem contexts and structures are not varied (Cobb, Yackel, & Wood, 1988; Peterson, Carpenter, & Fennema, 1989).

    a.   To what extent and in what ways do you intentionally vary the context of the problems you ask your students to solve?

    b.   How can you increase or decrease problem difficulty by varying problem structures? Provide some examples.

3. Learning trajectories can be used to help plan for and interpret the evidence collected from clinical interviews with students. Construct a clinical interview by selecting a range of problems with varying contexts. (See fig.4.3 or the CCSSM, or both, for more on this). Carefully observe and document the student's solution processes. For each problem, where do the students' solution strategies fall on the learning trajectory? What patterns do you see across responses? What are some appropriate instructional response based on the evidence and the learning trajectory?

Connect Your Practice with Colleagues

1. In what ways can learning trajectories help teachers be more purposeful in their analysis and use of evidence in student work?

2. The chapter makes the point that, "Movement on a learning trajectory is not linear." Explain what this means and what the implications are for analysis of evidence in student work and for making instructional decisions.

3. In what ways can learning trajectories be used to support teachers to build students' procedural fluency linked to conceptual understanding?

References

Buschman, L. (2001). Using student interviews to guide classroom instruction. *Teaching Children Mathematics, 8*(4), 222–227.

Clarke, D. M., Clarke, B., Cheesman, J., Gervasoni, A., Gronn, D., & Horne, M. (2001). Understanding, assessing, and developing young children's mathematical thinking: Research as a powerful tool for professional growth. In J. Boris, B. Perry, & M. Mitchelmore (Eds.), *Numeracy and Beyond: Proceedings of the 24th Annual Conference of the Mathematics Education Research Group of Australasia, Vol. 1* (pp. 9–26). Sydney: MERGA.

Clements, D. H., & Sarama, J. (2004). Learning trajectories in mathematics education. *Mathematical Thinking and Learning, 6*(2), 81–89.

Clements, D., Sarama, J., Spitler, M., Lange, A., & Wolfe, C. (2011). Mathematics learned by young children in an intervention based on learning trajectories: A large-scale cluster randomized trial. *Journal for Research in Mathematics Education, 42*, 127–166.

Cobb, P., Yackel, E., & Wood, T. (1991). Curriculum and teacher development: Psychological and anthropological perspectives. *Integrating Research on Teaching and Learning Mathematics* (pp. 83–120). Madison: Wisconsin Center for Education Research.

National Governors Association Center for Best Practices, Council of Chief State School Officers. (2010). *Common Core State Standards: Mathematics.* Washington, DC: National Governors Association Center for Best Practices, Council of Chief State School. Retrieved from http://corestandards.org/

Crespo, S., & Nicol, C. (2003). Learning to investigate students' mathematical thinking: The role of student interviews. In N. A. Pateman, B. Dougherty, & J. T. Zilliox (Eds.), *Proceeding of the International Group for the Psychology of Mathematics Education, 27*, Vol. 2 (pp. 261–268).

Crespo, S. (2000). Seeing more than right and wrong answers: Prospective teachers' interpretations of students' mathematical work. *Journal of Mathematics Teacher Education, 3*(2), 155–181.

Daro, P., Mosher, F. A., & Corcoran, T. B. (2011). Learning trajectories in mathematics: A foundation for standards, curriculum, assessment, and instruction. Philadelphia, PA: Consortium for Policy Research in Education.

Ebby, C. B. (2015, April). *How do teachers make sense of student work for instruction?* Paper presented at the NCTM Research Conference, Boston.

Fennema, E. H., Carpenter, T., Levi, L., Jacobs, V., & Empson, S. (1996). A longitudinal study of learning to use children's thinking in mathematics instruction. *Journal for Reserach in Mathematics Education, 27*, 403–434.

Ginsburg, H. P., Jacobs, S. F., & Lopez, L. S. (1998). *The Teacher's Guide to Flexible Interviewing in the Classroom: Learning What Children Know about Math.* Boston: Allyn and Bacon.

Grossman, P., Compton, C., Igra, D., Ronfeldt, M., Shahan, E., & Williamson, P. (2009). Teaching practice: A cross-professional perspective. *Teachers College Record, 111*(9), 2055–2100.

Hulbert, E., Petit, M., Ebby, C. B., Cunningham, E. P., & Laird, R. (in press). *A Focus on Multiplication and Division: Bringing Research to the Classroom.* New York: Routledge.

Jenkins, O. F. (2010). Developing teachers' knowledge of students as learners of mathematics through structured interviews. *Journal of Mathematics Teacher Education, 13*(2), 141–154.

Kouba, V. L., & Franklin, K. (1995). Multiplication and division: Sense making and meaning. *Teaching Children Mathematics, 1*(9), 574–578.

Leahy, S., Lyon, C., Thompson, M., & Wiliam, D. (2005). Classroom assessment: Minute by minute, day by day. *Educational Leadership, 63*(3), 19–24.

Moyer, P. S., & Milewicz, E. (2002). Learning to question: Categories of questioning used by preservice teachers during diagnostic mathematics interviews. *Journal of Mathematics Teacher Education, 5*, 293–315.

National Council of Teachers of Mathematics. (1989). *Curriculum and Evaluation Standards for School Mathematics.* Reston, VA: NCTM.

National Council of Teachers of Mathematics. (2014). *Access and equity in mathematics education*: Position paper. Reston, VA: NCTM.

National Council of Teachers of Mathematics. (2014). *Principles to Actions: Ensuring Mathematics Success for All.* Reston, VA: National Council of Teachers of Mathematics.

OGAPMath LLC. (2016). *Multiplicative Reasoning Framework.* Available at www.ogapmathllc.com

Petit, M., Laird, R., Marsden, E., & Ebby, C. B. (2016). *A Focus on Fractions: Bringing Research to the Classroom 2nd edition.* Routledge, New York City and London.

Petit, M., & Zawojewski, J. (2010). Formative assessment in elementary classrooms. In F. Lester (Ed.), *Teaching and Learning Mathematics: Translating Research for Elementary School Teachers.* NCTM: Reston, VA.

Schorr, R. Y., & Ginsburg, H. P. (2000). Using clinical interviews to promote preservice teachers' understanding of children's mathematical thinking. In M. L. Fernández (Ed.), *Proceedings of the Twenty-Second Annual Meeting of the North American Chapter of the International Group for the Psychology of Mathematics Education* (pp. 599–605). Columbus, OH: ERIC Clearinghouse for science mathematics and environmental education.

Smith, M. S., & Stein, M. K. (2011). *Five Practices for Orchestrating Productive Mathematics Discussions*. Reston, VA: National Council of Teachers of Mathematics.

Stein, M. K., Engle, R. A., Smith, M. S., & Hughes, E. K. (2008). Orchestrating productive mathematical discussions: Five practices for helping teachers move beyond show and tell. *Mathematical Thinking and Learning*, *10*(4), 313–340.

Supovitz, J. (2017). Impacts of the Ongoing Assessment Project (OGAP) on teacher and student learning. Paper presented at the Annual Meeting of the American Educational Research Association, San Antonio, TX.

Swan, M. (2001). Dealing with misconceptions in mathematics. In P. Gates (Ed.), *Issues in Mathematics Teaching* (pp. 147–165). London: Routledge.

Sztajn, P., Confrey, J., Wilson, P. H., & Edgington, C. (2012). Learning trajectory based instruction: Toward a theory of teaching. *Educational Researcher*, *41*(5), 147–156.

Wiliam, D. (2011). *Embedded Formative Assessment*. Solution Tree Press.

Wilson, P. H., Sztajn, P., Edgington, C., & Myers, M. (2015). Teachers' uses of a learning trajectory in student-centered instructional practices. *Journal of Teacher Education, 66*(3), 227–244.

Chapter 7

The Mathematical Tasks Framework and Formative Assessment

Michael Steele and Margaret S. Smith

The tasks in which a teacher chooses to engage students frames the mathematics that students have the opportunities to learn and their beliefs about what mathematics is (Lappan & Briars, 1995). The Mathematical Tasks Framework (Stein, Grover, & Henningsen, 1996; Stein & Smith, 1998) is a research-based tool that allows for the analysis of those opportunities to learn during an instructional episode. The Mathematical Tasks Framework (MTF) acknowledges that different types of tasks provide different learning opportunities, and introduces the construct of *cognitive demand of mathematical tasks* as a means to identify the learning potential that a task provides for students (Stein & Lane, 1996). The MTF also identifies discernable phases through which a task passes, from how the task appears in print form, to how the task is set up or launched by the teacher, to how it is implemented by students and the teacher, and to what students learn from their experiences with the task. Figure 7.1 shows a graphical representation of these phases. In this chapter, we describe the aspects of teaching and learning that the MTF makes visible. We connect these aspects to opportunities for formative assessment and research-based effective mathematics teaching practices (National Council of Teachers of Mathematics, 2014) and present a set of activities that can be used to connect the MTF with formative assessment.

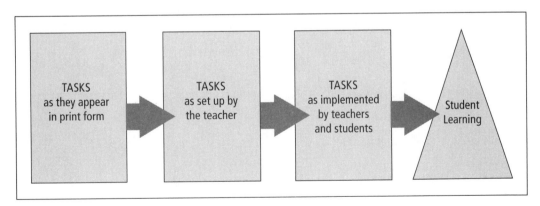

Fig. 7.1. The Mathematical Tasks Framework (Stein & Smith, 1998, p. 270)

Cognitive Demands of Tasks: The Task Analysis Guide

The mathematical tasks that students are asked to complete as a part of instruction can range from routine exercises that demonstrate previously learned procedures to complex non-algorithmic problems that build or make use of important mathematical ideas and practices. Stein and colleagues (Stein et al., 1996; Stein & Smith, 1998) identified four categories of tasks that describe the thinking and reasoning opportunities that tasks afford. The Task Analysis Guide (see fig. 7.2) provides the characteristics of tasks in each of these four categories. High-cognitive demand tasks (i.e., doing mathematics, procedures with connections) ask students to engage in complex thinking and to make decisions about what mathematical tools to use and how to use them. These tasks require significant cognitive effort and self-monitoring, and have the potential to develop understanding. Low-cognitive demand tasks (i.e., procedures without connections, memorization) ask students to recall facts and procedures and make use of them in answering routine questions that require that knowledge. There is little ambiguity about what to do or how to do it, and successful performance rests more on recall and proper sequencing of steps than it does any deep mathematical thinking and reasoning.

Task Analysis Guide

Lower-level demands: Memorization

- Involve either reproducing previously learned facts, rules, formulas, or definitions or committing facts, rules, formulas or definitions to memory.
- Cannot be solved using procedures because either a procedure does not exist or the time frame in which the task is being completed is too short to use a procedure.
- Are not ambiguous. Such tasks involve the exact reproduction of previously seen material, and what is to be reproduced is clearly and directly stated.
- Have no connection to the concepts or meaning that underlie the facts, rules, formulas, or definitions being learned or reproduced.

Lower-level demands: Procedures without Connections

- Are algorithmic. Use of the procedure is either specifically called for or is evident from prior instruction, experience, or placement of the task.
- Require limited cognitive demand for successful completion. Little ambiguity exists about what needs to be done and how to do it.
- Have no connection to the concepts or meaning that underlie the procedure being used.
- Are focused on producing correct answers instead of on developing mathematical understanding.
- Require no explanations or explanations that focus solely on describing the procedure that was used.

Higher-level demands: Procedures with Connections

- Focus students' attention on the use of procedures for the purpose of developing deeper levels of understanding of mathematical concepts and ideas.
- Explicitly or implicitly suggest pathways to follow that are broad general procedures that have close connections to underlying conceptual ideas, as opposed to narrow algorithms that are opaque with respect to underlying concepts.
- Usually are represented in multiple ways, such as visual diagrams, manipulatives, symbols, and problem situations. Making connections among multiple representations helps develop meaning.
- Require some degree of cognitive effort. Although general procedures may be followed, they cannot be followed mindlessly. Students need to engage with conceptual ideas that underlie the procedures to complete the task successfully and that develop understanding.

Higher-level demands: Doing Mathematics

- Require complex and non-algorithmic thinking—a predictable, well-rehearsed approach or pathway is not explicitly suggested by the task, task instructions, or a worked-out example.
- Require students to explore and understand the nature of mathematical concepts, processes, or relationships.
- Demand self-monitoring or self-regulation of one's own cognitive processes.
- Require students to access relevant knowledge and experiences and make appropriate use of them in working through the task.
- Require students to analyze the task and actively examine task constraints that may limit possible solution strategies and solutions.
- Require considerable cognitive effort and may involve some level of anxiety for the student because of the unpredictable nature of the solution process required.

These characteristics are derived from the work of Doyle on academic tasks (1988) and Resnick on high-level-thinking skills (1987), the Professional Standards for Teaching Mathematics (NCTM, 1991), and the examination and categorization of hundreds of tasks used in QUASAR classrooms (Stein, Grover, & Henningsen, 1996; Stein, Lane, & Silver, 1996).

Fig. 7.2. Task Analysis Guide (Smith & Stein, 1998, p. 348)

Figure 7.3 provides an example of four tasks related to solving systems of equations that exemplify the four levels of cognitive demand. Task A asks students to examine the two solution methods to a given system of equations and to identify the names of the methods used (i.e., Kenyon-substitution; Marissa-elimination). To successfully complete this task, a student must know the names of the two methods and what each one looks like. It is not necessary to reproduce these methods or even to make meaning of each step. Task A would be classified as memorization since a student simply needs to recall a name and a procedure. Task B exemplifies procedures without connections to meaning. The task begins with a context and provides the two equations that represent the seat and wheel counts for the bicycles and tricycles. Students are then asked to determine the number of bicycles and tricycles by solving the system of equations using elimination. To be successful with this task, students simply need to be able to complete the elimination procedure on the two equations listed and identify their answer. They do not need to consider why they might execute the procedure, what other possible solution paths might be, or how the answer connects to the problem's context.

Tasks C and D represent high-level cognitive demand versions of the task. Task C represents procedures with connections to meaning. This task starts out identically to Task B, in providing the system of equations. The task then includes a graph of both equations, and asks students to determine which line is represented by which equation, what the points on the line represent, whether the graphs accurately depict the solution to the equations and if not to suggest a modification, and what the point of intersection means. To complete this task successfully, students must understand that the combination of bicycles and tricycles that make each equation true is the same as the points on each of the two lines that represent whole number values for bikes, trikes, and wheels. They must be able to relate those pairs of values/coordinate pairs (from the equation or the graph) to the context of the problem, understanding that the values describe combinations of bicycles and tricycles that meet the conditions related to seats and wheels. Further, they must be able to describe the point of intersection as the value for which both conditions are true and relate the ordered pair to the context of the problem. This requires students to make sense of and connect multiple representations, and in contrast to Task B, the solution cannot be obtained by executing a set of steps without considering their meaning.

Task D gives students the same scenario as presented in Tasks B and C and asks them to identify how many bicycles and tricycles are in the shop. No representations are given or specified, nor is a particular procedure suggested or implied. This task requires significant cognitive effort, as students must make sense of what the problem is asking, be able to identify and mobilize a solution strategy of their choice appropriate to the task, and connect the outcome of that strategy to the problem situation. Students have to monitor their progress throughout their work on the task, asking and answering the question, "Is this strategy moving me towards an answer?" Both Tasks C and D represent meaningful opportunities to engage with the conceptual ideas behind systems of equations, including when they are appropriate to use and the ways in which the solution to a system can be determined and represented.

Task A (memorization)

Identify the methods Kenyon and Marissa used for solving the following system of equations:

$$2b + 3t = 61$$
$$b + t = 24$$

Kenyon's Method

$$b = 24 - t$$
$$2(24 - t) + 3t = 61$$
$$48 - 2t + 3t = 61$$
$$48 + t = 61$$
$$48 + t - 48 = 61 - 48$$
$$\boxed{t = 13}$$
$$b + 13 = 24$$
$$\boxed{b = 11}$$

Marissa's Method

$$2b + 3t = 61$$
$$-2(b + t = 24)$$

$$2b + 3t = 61$$
$$-2b - 2t = -48$$
$$\overline{}$$
$$\boxed{t = 13}$$
$$b + 13 = 24$$
$$\boxed{b = 11}$$

Task B (procedures without connections)

You work for a small business that sells bicycles and tricycles. Bicycles have one seat, two pedals and two wheels. Tricycles have one seat, two pedals and three wheels.

On Monday, there are a total of 24 seats and 61 wheels in the shop. Using the two equations shown below, determine the number of bicycles (b) and tricycles (t) in the shop on Monday using elimination.

$$2b + 3t = 61$$
$$b + t = 24$$

Task C (procedures with connections)

You work for a small business that sells bicycles and tricycles. Bicycles have one seat, two pedals and two wheels. Tricycles have one seat, two pedals and three wheels. On Monday, there are a total of 24 seats and 61 wheels in the shop. How many cycles and how many tricycles are in the shop?

Karla set up the following equations to solve the task:

$$2b + 3t = 61$$
$$b + t = 24$$

She then used her computer to make the graph below:

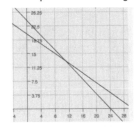

1. Determine which line represents which equation and what the points on each line represent.

2. Do all the points on each line make sense in the context of the problem? How would you change the graph of each line so that it accurately describes the set of solutions to the equation in this context?

3. Explain what the point of intersection (11, 13) means in the context of this problem.

Task D (doing mathematics)

You work for a small business that sells bicycles and tricycles. Bicycles have one seat, two pedals and two wheels. Tricycles have one seat, two pedals and three wheels.

On Monday, there are a total of 24 seats and 61 wheels in the shop. How many bicycles and how many tricycles are in the shop? Show all your work using any method you choose and explain your thinking.

Fig. 7.3. Four tasks involving solving systems of equations at differing levels of cognitive demand
Tasks adapted from New York City Department of Education—The Cycle Shop
http://schools.nyc.gov/NR/rdonlyres/0D9AA86E-F601-4F26-9598
-CF57C4FA7CAB/0/NYCDOEHSAlgebraTheCycleShop_Final.pdf

Tasks of high-cognitive demand, when implemented by teachers in thoughtful ways, have the potential to engage students in reasoning and problem-solving and in mathematics practices that support the development of conceptual understanding (National Council of Teachers of Mathematics, 2000; National Governors Association Center for Best Practices, & Council of Chief State School Officers (CSSO), 2010). Tasks of low-cognitive demand can play important roles in developing fluency and efficiency with procedures, but should be preceded by opportunities to make meaning of those procedures through the use of high-cognitive-demand tasks. In the sections that follow, we focus our discussion on the implementation of high-cognitive-demand tasks as a vehicle for formative assessment.

Implementing High-Cognitive-Demand Tasks: A Focus on Classroom Practice

High-cognitive-demand tasks are a necessary, but not sufficient, condition in order to ensure student learning. As Boston and Wilhelm (2015) note, a high cognitive demand task is almost always a critical starting point to meaningful student learning, as compared to a low-cognitive-demand task:

> Low-level tasks are rarely implemented in ways that result in high-level thinking and reasoning. In general, the potential of the task sets the ceiling for implementation—that is a task almost never increases in cognitive demand during implementation. This finding, robust in its consistency across several studies, suggests that high-level instructional tasks are a necessary condition for ambitious mathematics instruction. (Boston & Wilhelm, 2015, p. 24)

Tasks do not always live up to their potential as written for a number of reasons. Figure 7.4 shows an elaborated version of the MTF that notes the key phases in the enactment of a mathematics lesson within which cognitive demand can either be maintained or declined.

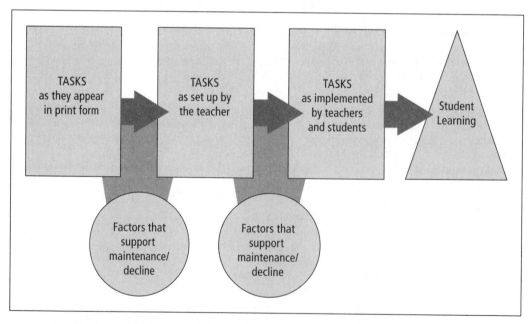

Fig. 7.4. Elaborated Mathematical Tasks Framework (adapted from Stein & Smith, 1998, p. 270)

When teachers move from selecting a task from an instructional resource to thinking about the implementation in a lesson, one of the first considerations is how to set up or launch the task. The set up or launch of a high-cognitive-demand task should support students in activating background knowledge, resources, and practices that will be useful in supporting their work on the task. At times, a teacher might launch a task with implicit or explicit hints towards particular solution paths to pursue or tools to use, which can constrain students' thinking and lower the demand of the task. For example, a teacher launching task D (see fig. 7.3) might suggest that students start by writing two equations. While this move is well meaning and intended to support students in getting started, it may unduly focus students on symbolic solution methods as compared to approaches using tabular, pictorial, or graphical representations.

As teachers and students engage in the task, a number of factors come into play that support either the maintenance or decline of the cognitive demand. A high cognitive demand task requires that students decide on an approach to take, determine a course of action, continually monitor their progress towards the goal, and justify their solution. This requires that students persevere when a pathway is not immediately evident and make meaningful connections between the mathematics that they know and the question that the problem intends for them to answer.

The teacher's role is to find ways to support students in persevering when faced with a high-level task without taking away the thinking and reasoning opportunities from them. Students, however, may experience frustration when faced with a task they cannot immediately solve. In such situations, they may press the teacher to provide assistance that inadvertently takes away from the meaning-making processes. For example, students might ask teachers to do one or more of the following: provide them with a starting point for their work, evaluate the correctness of their answer, or specify particular steps to take to move towards a solution. Other pedagogical decisions made by teachers can support or inhibit the cognitive demand as students work, such as asking questions and providing support that may or may not build on students' prior knowledge and holding students accountable (or not) for high-level processes. Figure 7.5 summarizes the factors most commonly associated with maintenance and decline of cognitive demand during the set-up and implementation of a lesson.

Factors Associated with Maintenance	Factors Associated with Decline
1. Scaffolding (task is simplified so student can solve it; complexity is maintained, but greater resources are made available). Could occur during whole class discussion, presentations, or during group or pair work.	1. Problematic aspects of the task become routinized (e.g., students press teacher to reduce task complexity by specifying explicit procedures or steps to perform; teacher "takes over" difficult pieces of the task and performs them for the students or tells them how to do it).
2. Students are provided with the means of monitoring their own progress (e.g., rubrics are discussed and used to judge performance; means for testing conjectures are made explicit and used).	2. Teacher shifts emphasis from meaning, concepts, or understanding to correctness or completeness of the answer.
3. The teacher or capable students model high-level performance.	3. Not enough time is provided for students to wrestle with the demanding aspects of the task or too much time is provided and students flounder or drift off task.
4. Sustained press for justifications, explanations, meaning through teacher questioning, comments, feedback.	4. Classroom management problems prevent sustained engagement.
5. Tasks are selected that build on students' prior knowledge.	5. Task is inappropriate for the group of students (e.g., lack of interest, lack of motivation, lack of prior knowledge needed to perform, task expectations not clear enough to put students in the right cognitive space, etc.).
6. Teacher draws frequent conceptual connections.	6. Students not held accountable for high-level products or processes (e.g., although asked to explain their thinking, unclear or incorrect student explanations are accepted; students were given the impression that their work would not "count" (i.e., be used towards a grade).
7. Sufficient time to explore (not too little, not too much).	

Fig. 7.5. Factors associated with the maintenance and decline of high-level demands
(Stein & Smith, 1998, p. 274)

Interacting with students while they are working on a cognitively demanding task provides teachers with opportunities to gather evidence of student thinking in the moment and to provide students with feedback that helps them make continued progress. Teacher moves, consistent with the maintenance factors shown in figure 7.5, are also more likely to provide high-quality formative assessment information to the teacher. However, if the teacher takes over the thinking for students by providing them with specific instructions for what to do, little can be learned about what the student knows and can do without being told. The factors associated with decline in figure 7.5 tend to limit students' opportunities to think and reason, and thus provide limited formative assessment information to a teacher.

In sum, two elements play a critical role in students' opportunities to learn meaningful mathematics: the nature of the task selected by the teacher, and the actions and interactions between students and teachers as the task unfolds during a lesson. Planning for and teaching lessons with formative assessment processes in mind can help ensure that a task that has the potential to elicit student thinking and reasoning is selected (the first phase of the framework); that a task with potential to engage students in high-level process is set up in ways that maintain those processes and communicate expectations to students (the second phase of the framework); and that the support provided while students work on the task (the third phase framework) serves to elicit and shape student thinking such that opportunities to learn afforded by high-level tasks are realized and the key mathematical ideas at the heart of a lesson are made public. It is during the setup and implementation phases of the lesson that a teacher has the opportunity to collect data regarding what students know and understand and use the data in ways that support and advance the thinking of students, both individually and collectively.

What Do Tasks Have to Do with Formative Assessment?

Formative assessment is the practice of gathering information during instruction that can inform teaching and learning. The effective mathematics teaching practice *eliciting and using evidence of student thinking*—arguably at the heart of formative assessment processes—makes salient the need for teachers to "assess progress toward mathematical understanding and adjust instruction continually in ways that support and extend learning" (NCTM, 2014, p. 53). Towards this end, the analytical lens of the Mathematical Tasks Framework illuminates several aspects of strategies supporting the formative assessment process (i.e., information gathering and use) noted in Leahy et al. (2005): clarifying and sharing learning intentions and criteria for success; engineering effective classroom discussions, questions, and learning tasks; providing feedback that moves learners forward; activating students as the owners of their learning; and activating students as resources for one another. In the sections that follow, we connect the five formative assessment strategies with the phases described by the MTF.

Considering Task Selection and Set-Up: The Role of Learning Intentions and Success Criteria

Tasks are a critical factor in formative assessment, because it is the nature of the task that determines the level of thinking in which students can potentially engage (first phase of the framework) and the way in which the task is set-up (second phase of the framework) that support task potential. A teacher selecting a mathematical task must carefully consider several aspects of the task: (a) the level of thinking required to engage with the task, (b) how the task builds meaningfully on prior knowledge, (c) the extent to which the task provides broad, and (d) multifaceted access to each and every student, and what students will learn about mathematics as a result of engaging in the task. The setup of the task connects with the formative assessment strategy of *clarifying and sharing learning intentions and criteria for success* with students as they begin a lesson. The set-up must make clear to students what the learning targets are without taking away the challenge of the task by providing a solution path. This can be a delicate balance. For example, consider again the Task D version of the Cycle Shop task in figure 7.3. A teacher might hold as a goal for this task for students to make connections between symbolic, tabular, and graphical representations of the solution to a system of equations. Stating this goal as a part of the learning intentions might guide students towards the use of those specific three representations, possibly to the exclusion of other pathways. Students may be more likely to focus on generation of those specific representations rather than the mathematical thinking and reasoning that would lead them to discover the utility of those representations, and the connections between them. One possible learning intention for Task D that strikes this balance would be, "Students will explore strategies for finding a solution to a problem that has two sets of constraints. In this case, the solution has to yield the correct number of wheels and the correct number of seats." In identifying what the learning intention is for students and sharing it with them, the teacher focuses students' attention on the important mathematical ideas to take away from the lesson and can make decisions during lesson implementation that will keep students moving productively towards those goals.

Similarly, it is important that teachers consider aspects of the factors that support maintenance of cognitive demand when they describe the criteria for success for students. In particular, factor 2 in figure 7.5 states that students should be provided with a means to monitor their own progress, which may consist of a rubric for assessing performance, or specific types of mathematical thinking that a teacher will be looking and listening for (e.g., precise mathematical language in general, specific language that identifies the number of seats and wheels as constraints, and clarity with respect to what the solution means in context), or a clear description of what needs to be included in the final product (e.g., a clear written explanation that is supported by mathematical representations including tables, graphs, equations, drawings, calculations). These criteria for success should be shared with students before they begin their work, and should focus both on the meaning-making and conceptual understanding that is a part of the work on high cognitive demand tasks as well as the accurate applications of mathematical procedures and processes. These criteria for success should connect to the *mathematical residue* (Hiebert et al., 1996) that the teacher hopes for students to take away from the lesson, which include insights into the structure of mathematics, problem solving strategies, and dispositions towards mathematics connected to the mathematical learning goals. For Task D, the criteria for success might include the following: written explanation of the solution and how it was determined; an explanation of the meaning of the point of intersection as it relates to the quantities in the problem, and the use of two or more mathematical representations that are connected through the student's explanation. A teacher could use these three criteria during small-group monitoring, a whole-class discussion, and the evaluation of students' written work to determine whether they had met the goals of the lesson. In so doing, the teacher is using the success criteria that they have established and communicated as foci for collecting data on the extent to which a student has met these criteria.

Sharing learning intentions and success criteria with students makes clear what their targets are for their mathematical work and provides them with tools to monitor their progress towards these targets, both of which help maintain the cognitive demand of the task. Moreover, the learning intentions and criteria for success can play important roles in the implementation of a lesson as bellwethers for teacher decision-making. Specifically, the data that is collected can make salient the ideas students are and are not struggling with and help the teacher make decisions regarding the current lesson (e.g., specific questions to ask and mathematical points to illuminate) and subsequent lessons (e.g., what ideas seem to be clearly understood, where more work is needed, etc.) As Wiliam (2007, p. 1054) noted, "formative assessment is an essentially interactive process, in which the teacher can find out whether what has been taught has been learned, and if not, to do something about it."

Considering Task Setup and Implementation: Making Student Thinking Public

The thinking of students, communicated verbally and in written form, provides evidence of what students know and understand about the mathematical ideas at play in a task. During task setup (also referred to as the launch), the teacher can formatively collect evidence regarding what knowledge and experience students bring to a task. This phase of the lesson offers teachers an opportunity to make use of another of the Leahy et al. formative assessment strategies: *activating students as owners of their own learning*. The set-up or launch should maintain the cognitive demand and provide a forum to discuss the key ideas and contextual features of the task and to agree on a common language for discussing those key ideas (Jackson, Shahan, Gibbons, & Cobb, 2012). For example, a teacher launching the Task D version of the Cycle Shop task (see fig. 7.3) might begin by asking students what they know about bicycles and tricycles, showing pictures of bicycles and tricycles, and by having students describe how they are the same and how they are different. This would provide students with the opportunity to access their practical knowledge about bicycles, discuss why a shop owner might be interested in the answer to such a question, gain knowledge that they may not have (e.g., they may think tricycles are only for small children), and clarify key distinctions between them (i.e., the number of wheels). The teacher could then show the prompt and invite students to discuss what they see as the important contextual quantities in the task, why the pedals in this particular case may not be helpful, and the ways in which the number of each type of cycle and the component parts might be related. Students can then be asked what it is they are trying to accomplish in the task. By launching the task in this way, students are active participants in exploring the context and determining the important aspects of the task, and are prepared to begin work on the task with a clear sense of what needs to be done. Through the process, the teacher gains valuable information about what students bring to the task and has the opportunity to provide clarity as needed that will ensure that they know what they are expected to do and allow them to focus on the key mathematical ideas at play. Hence, students have been positioned as owners of their own learning.

During both the set-up and implementation phase of the lesson, the teacher has several opportunities to engage in the strategy of *activating students as resources for one another*. At the setup or launch phase, a teacher makes decisions about the modes in which students will work (individual, small group, whole class), the focus and products of that work, and the interactions that students can expect with the teacher as they move forward. For example, the teacher may want to make it clear that students cannot ask them a question until they have first exhausted the group resources in determining an answer or that all students in the group should be able to explain any solution that the group has found. The factors that support the maintenance of cognitive demand suggest specific ways in which teachers can activate students as resources, such as modeling of high-level performance. This modeling can occur during small or whole group discussion when the teacher asks one student to explain what they have figured out and how, and holds the other students accountable for restating or explaining the idea that has been shared.

The formative assessment strategy of *engineering effective classroom discussions, questions, and learning tasks* is at the heart of the implementation phase of the lesson as defined by the MTF. In work that builds on the phases of a lesson, Smith and Stein (2011) identify five practices for orchestrating productive discussions around high cognitive demand tasks. Two of these practices, anticipating student thinking and monitoring students as they work, connect directly to the formative assessment strategy of engineering effective classroom discussions, questions, and learning tasks. By considering the solution paths or strategies that students might enact for a task and preparing questions that will assess and advance student thinking as they work on the task in small groups, teachers can gather formative assessment data that guides instructional decision making during small- and whole-group discussion.

In addition, the use of a monitoring tool as described by Smith and Stein (2011) can support the formative assessment strategy of *providing feedback that moves learners forward*. While planning for a lesson, teachers can use the monitoring tool to anticipate specific strategies, misconceptions, and other roadblocks that students might experience during a lesson and create questions tailored to specific solution paths that can be used to assess and advance student thinking. During the lesson, the tool can then be used by teachers to keep track of what students actually do—the strategies they use, the ideas they discuss, the difficulties they run into—and as a source of questions to ask in helping students move forward. These questions are critical in providing a sustained press for justifications, explanations, and meaning—a factor associated with the maintenance of high level tasks noted in figure 7.5. The questions are also critical in implementing the formative assessment process of gathering, and then using, data related to students' current thinking to advance the learning during a lesson. An example of a monitoring tool for Task D is shown in figure 7.6.

Anticipated Solutions	Instructional Support		Who What	Order
	Assessing Questions used to gather evidence of student learning	Advancing Questions used to move the learning forward toward the lesson goals		
Guess and Check Start with a guess of bikes and trikes that totals 24 then figure out the number of wheels. If the guess is too many wheels then lower the number of trikes and increase the number of wheels.	• Can you explain what you are doing? • How are you determining the number of wheels for each of your combinations? • Why did you lower the number of trikes when you had too many wheels?	Can you find a way to keep track of your guesses or to organize them so that you could see a pattern?		
Draw a Picture 24 seats 0 each seat has at least 2 wheels – that uses up 48 wheels so 61-48 or 13 wheels are left These go with the triangles. There are 13 tricycles and 11 bicycles.	• Can you explain your drawing? • Why did you give each cycle two wheels to start with? • How did you know the number of cycles that have three wheels?	• Can you describe the relationship between the number of bikes, the number of trikes and the total number of seats? • Can you describe the relationship between the total number of wheels and the number of wheels on the bikes and the number of wheels on the trikes?		
Make a Table Start with 1 bike and 23 trikes and find the total number of wheels; continue with 2 bikes and 22 trikes and continue the table until you get 61 wheels when you have 24 total bikes and trikes.	• Can you explain your table? • How did you determine the number of wheels for each of your combinations? • Why didn't you continue your table beyond 11 bikes and 13 trikes?	• Can you describe the relationship between the number of bikes, the number of trikes and the total number of seats? • Can you describe the relationship between the total number of wheels and the number of wheels on the bikes and the number of wheels on the trikes?		

Fig. 7.6. continues on the next page

Anticipated Solutions	Instructional Support		Who What	Order
	Assessing Questions used to gather evidence of student learning	Advancing Questions used to move the learning forward toward the lesson goals		
Create Equations and Graph $2b + 3t = 6 \quad b + t = 24$ 	• How did you get your two equations? • How did you get your graph? • How does your graph relate to the equations? • What is (11, 13)?	• What does (11, 13) mean in the context of the problem? • What does it mean to have a point of intersection? • Do all the points on the line $b + t = 24$ represent solutions to the equation in this context? • Do all the points on the line $2b + 3t = 24$ represent solutions to the equation in this context?		
Create Equations—Solve Algebraically —substitution —elimination	• How did you get your two equations? • How do you know that the process you used gave you the correct solution? • Can you try it? (This will help the student see whether or not they have made an error in performing the procedure.)	• Why does your procedure work? • What are you doing when you substitute $24 - t$ for the variable b in the equation $2b + 3t = 6$? • What are you doing when you multiply one equation by -2 so that when you add the two equations together one of the variables in eliminated? • What would the graph of your system of equations look like?		
Cannot Get Started	• What was in the shop on Monday? (24 seats; 61 wheels) • What does it mean to have 24 seats? (24 cycles since each has 1 seat) • So how many bikes and how many trikes could there be? (some combination of 24)	Can you figure out how many wheels you would have for some combination of bikes and trikes?		

Fig. 7.6. continues on the next page

Anticipated Solutions	Instructional Support		Who What	Order
	Assessing Questions used to gather evidence of student learning	Advancing Questions used to move the learning forward toward the lesson goals		
Ignores a constraint—finds a number of bikes and trikes that equals 24 but does not consider the number of wheels	• Can you explain what you did here? • Why did you decide on x bikes and y trikes? (equals 24) • What else do you know about what was in the shop on Monday? (61 wheels)	• How can you find the number of wheels there would be if you had x bikes and y trikes? • Does this combination satisfy the condition of the problem? • What else could you try?		

Fig. 7.6. A monitoring tool for the Cycle Shop task (version D)

The monitoring tool can function as a planning document, as an instructional support, and as an assessment record. As a planning artifact, the monitoring tool supports teachers in anticipating specific solution pathways students are likely to take and identifying in advance questions that they intend to ask students related to those solution strategies that will help assess what they currently understand and advance toward the lesson target. As an instructional support, the monitoring tool provides the teacher with questions to ask as she interacts with individuals and groups.It also serves as a systematic approach to eliciting and keeping track of the formative assessment information collected (recorded in the who/what column) during the monitoring process that can then help inform the discussion by making clear what mathematical thinking is available within the class. As a formative assessment record, a completed monitoring tool provides a snapshot of student thinking individually and collectively on the task at a particular moment in time, which could be used to rearrange groups, identify individuals or groups that required additional support, and track student progress over time.

As a teacher transitions from individual and small-group work towards a whole-class discussion of the task, the formative assessment data available on the monitoring tool can guide the key decisions the teacher must make in supporting the debriefing of the task, in order to ensure that the mathematical ideas targeted during the lesson are made public. The monitoring tool provides important information for three of the five practices identified by Smith and Stein (2011) as supporting productive discussions including: selecting student responses to share, sequencing the responses in a particular order, and connecting those responses in ways that make visible the key mathematical ideas. In particular, a teacher at this moment should return to the learning intention and success criteria, and alongside the formative assessment data collected, consider questions such as the following:

- What are the key mathematical ideas that I want to make important in this discussion?
- What intellectual resources do students bring as represented in their work that are related to the ideas that I am targeting?
- In what ways should I select and sequence the sharing of those ideas in order to ensure that all students have access to the discussion and that there is a coherent story line?

- In what ways during this discussion can I draw conceptual connections between different responses and to the key mathematical ideas that support student learning?

The use of formative assessment data can help teachers to structure the discussion of work on the task in productive ways that connect to the mathematical goal. The discussion is also likely to implicate additional data that the teacher might wish to collect to formatively assess what students took away from the discussion through the use of a carefully designed exit ticket. For example, for the Cycle Shop task, a teacher might ask students to describe the meaning of the intersection point in general and in the context of the Cycle Shop problem, or ask students to identify another contextual situation for which they could use a system of linear equations to investigate. Another option would be to give students a different number of seats and wheels, with larger numbers, and ask students which of the methods discussed they would use to solve the task and why. This question would press students to consider the strategies they had been exposed to in light of mathematical efficiency. A third option would be to ask students to identify another contextual situation for which they could use a system of linear equations to investigate. Exit tickets, with questions such as these, stand in sharp contrast with prototypical exit tickets that ask for a quick problem to be solved as evidence of the correct application of a mathematical procedure at play.

The task selection, setup, and implementation phases of the MTF provide teachers with opportunities to think about formative assessment and its relationship to the factors that support or inhibit the maintenance of cognitive demand as the lesson unfolds. The formative assessment strategies noted in this section connect with the factors that support the maintenance of cognitive demand, and provide teachers with information about student thinking that can guide their decision making within and across the MTF phases. For example, a teacher can set up or launch a task with a discussion designed to activate prior knowledge and prepare students to use a particular set of mathematical tools in their work on the task. By listening carefully and having clear formative assessment targets in mind for that discussion, a teacher can determine whether either students are ready to begin work on the task or more discussion is needed. For example, a teacher using the Cycle Shop task might want to ensure that students understand the basic relationships between bicycles, tricycles, seats, pedals, and wheels before starting small groups in their work. Similarly, the transitions from individual to small-group work and from small-group work to a whole-class discussion should be marked not by an arbitrary amount of time given to each activity, but by the teacher's collection of formative assessment data. For example, a teacher might want to ensure that all small groups can explain the meaning of the intersection point in the Cycle Shop task regardless of the strategy they are using before proceeding to a whole-class discussion across strategies. Teachers should have clear targets in mind for the understandings they wish to see during the small-group phase of a lesson that will be brought forward and built upon in the whole-group discussion of student solutions.

The Role of the MTF and Formative Assessment in Teacher Education

The MTF and its relationship to formative assessment can be a powerful organizing tool in the professional education of teachers. For teachers at all levels, the MTF can provide a common language for identifying the phases of lessons that can be directly connected to planning lessons and formatively assessing students. The MTF in combination with tools like the Task Analysis Guide and the Monitoring Tool supports the planning of meaningful instructional episodes, from the selection of tasks to the teacher moves and practices that are likely to support meaningful student engagement in the task as well as elicit important evidence of student thinking to guide instructional decisions. For a preservice teacher, the MTF and the notion of high-cognitive -demand tasks provides both a road map to plan a lesson and a clear set of criteria (fig. 7.5) to assess quality of instruction. These criteria can be used either to self-assess performance informally or as a part of a more formalized observation and evaluation system. Because the work of teaching for understanding revolves around supporting students as they work on a task by eliciting and using evidence of their thinking to move them toward the mathematical goals for the lesson, learning how to identify and enact tasks that elicit thinking and promote understanding can and should be considered a high-leverage practice. It is at the heart of a teacher's daily work and when done well, results in a great deal of formative assessment data teachers can use during and after a lesson.

For practicing teachers, professional development that focuses on the MTF gives teachers identifiable focal points for enhancing their teaching practice that meet a diverse set of needs. Teachers using curricular materials with few tasks that promote reasoning and problem solving can focus on identifying, adapting, or creating high-cognitive-demand tasks to use in their classrooms and how those tasks can provide better formative assessment information as they transform their practice. In districts that have already adopted curricula with many such tasks, teachers might choose to focus on the implementation of these tasks. Some teachers might focus on the launch or an aspect of the implementation phase of the lesson such as small-group work. Others might identify specific factors that support or inhibit cognitive demand as a means to strengthen their teaching practice, such as asking conceptual questions that yield formative assessment information that goes beyond the ability to apply a procedure. The activities in Table 7.1 provide some examples of teacher education experiences related to the MTF in which one might engage a group of teachers with an eye towards formative assessment. We have used the monitoring tool as an example throughout this chapter to show how it supports the implementation of cognitively demanding tasks and provides a systematic approach to collecting formative assessment data; we briefly describe a second tool (see Table 7.1).

Slices of Teaching: Launch. Teaching is a complex and multifaceted endeavor, and it can often be challenging for preservice teachers to reflect on a complete episode of instruction in ways that support growth. One activity that we have used in the context of a mathematics methods course is *Slices of Teaching*. This activity invites preservice teachers to zoom in on one aspect of the MTF—in this case, the setup or launch of the task. (We have also used a similar structure with slices such as assessing and advancing questions to support small group work, the summary phase of the lesson in which solutions are shared and connections are made, and the review of homework). In focusing on the launch, teachers are asked to select a high cognitive demand task, plan a lesson based on the task to implement in their classroom, and teach a lesson using that task, ideally recording the lesson on video. This process can also include rehearsing the launch in the context of a methods course or microteaching experience, with feedback from the instructor and peers about what they notice and what they wonder about. The analysis and reflection on that lesson centers only on the launch of the task. For the reflective assignment, teachers describe the task they used, their instructional goals for the task, the anticipated solutions they imagined students would make use of, and the prior knowledge and experiences that they thought would be useful for the task. Using their video records of the launch, they reflect on the ways in which what they chose to do and not do in launching the task influenced the opportunities students had to learn related to those components of the lesson. This detailed analysis allows teachers to make connections between their pedagogical moves and the ways in which those moves activate students as owners of their own knowledge, and the extent to which learning intentions and success criteria are made clear, two key formative assessment strategies.

Table 7.1. MTF professional development activities, goals, resources, and connection to formative assessment

Activity	Goals	Resources
Compare a high- and low-level task that focus on the same content.	To help teachers begin to see that not all tasks are created equal, some require application of known procedures and others require thinking, reasoning, and problem solving. FA CONNECTION: High-level tasks provide opportunities to collect data on students' thinking about concepts and practices; low-level tasks provide data about accuracy and procedural skills.	Martha's Carpeting Task and the Fencing Task in Smith, M. S. Stein, M. K., Arbaugh, F., Brown, C. A., & Mossgrove, J. (2004). Characterizing the cognitive demands of mathematical tasks: A sorting activity. *Professional Development Guidebook for Perspectives on the Teaching of Mathematics* (Companion to 2004 yearbook of the National Council of Teachers of Mathematics) (pp. 45–72). Reston, Va.: National Council of Teachers of Mathematics. Candy Jar Task and Find the Missing Value Task in SLIDE 16 in The Case of Mr. Donnelly and the Candy Jar Task in Principles to Action Professional Learning Toolkit. http://www.nctm.org/Conferences-and-Professional-Development/Principles-to-Actions-Toolkit/The-Case-of-Mr_-Donnelly-and-the-Candy-Jar-Task/ Pay it Forward Task and Petoskey Population in SLIDE 16 in The Case of Vanessa Culver and the Pay it Forward Task in Principles to Action Professional Learning Toolkit. http://www.nctm.org/Conferences-and-Professional-Development/Principles-to-Actions-Toolkit/The-Case-of-Ms_-Culver-and-the-Pay-it-Forward-Task/ See also the high-cognitive-demand tasks included in the Taking Action book series (Huinker & Bill, 2017; Smith, Steele, & Raith, 2017; Boston, Dillon, Smith & Miller, 2017). Boston, M.D., Dillon, F., Smith, M.S., & Miller, S. (2017). Taking Action: Implementing Effective Mathematics Teaching Practices in Grades 9-12. Reston, VA: National Council of Teachers of Mathematics. Huinker, D., & Bill, V. (2017). Taking Action: Implementing Effective Mathematics Teaching Practices in Grades K-5. Reston, VA: National Council of Teachers of Mathematics. Smith, M.S., Steele, M.D., & Raith, M.L. (2017) Taking Action: Implementing Effective Mathematics Teaching Practices in Grades 6-8. Reston, VA: National Council of Teachers of Mathematics.
Sort a set of tasks into two categories: high level and low level.	To help teachers develop the capacity to distinguish between high and low level tasks; develop criteria that are hallmarks of tasks at different levels; and ultimately understand the four levels of cognitive demand. FA CONNECTION: Only high-level tasks provide opportunities to uncover student thinking.	Elementary, Middle and High School sorts in Smith, M. S., Stein, M. K., Arbaugh, F., Brown, C. A., & Mossgrove, J. (2004). Characterizing the cognitive demands of mathematical tasks: A sorting activity. *Professional Development Guidebook for Perspectives on the Teaching of Mathematics* (Companion to 2004 yearbook of the National Council of Teachers of Mathematics) (pp. 45–72). Reston, VA: National Council of Teachers of Mathematics.

Table. 7.1. continues on the next page

Table. 7.1. continues on the next page

Table 7.1. Continued

Activity	Goals	Resources
Have teachers use the **Task Analysis Guide** to categorize tasks in their own curricula.	To support teachers' use of high-level tasks during instruction by ensuring that they know a good task when they see it. FA CONNECTION: Teachers can identify tasks that have particularly rich opportunities for formative assessment and consider how to effectively plan using those tasks.	Smith, M. S., & Stein, M. K. (1998). Selecting and creating mathematical tasks: From research to practice. *Mathematics Teaching in the Middle School, 3*(5), 344–350.
Compare two different enactments of the same task—one where the demands are maintained and one where the demands decline. (Use the factors of maintenance and decline to identify differences in implementation.)	To help teachers realize that selecting a high level task is the first step in providing students with opportunities to think, reason, and problem solve. Keeping the task at a high level during implementation requires that the teacher support students' productive struggle without taking over the thinking for them. FA CONNECTION: Keeping a task at a high level is critical in making students thinking public.	Multiplying Fractions with Pattern Blocks: The Cases of Fran Gorman and Kevin Cooper in Stein, M. K., Smith, M. S., Henningsen, M. A., & Silver, E. A. (2009). *Implementing Standards-Based Mathematics Instruction: A Casebook for Professional Development*, 2nd ed. New York: Teachers College Press. Examining Linear Growth Patters: The Case of Catherine Evans and David Young in Smith, M. S., Silver, E. A., Stein, M. K., Henningsen, M. A., Boston, M. & Hughes, E. K. (2005). *Improving instruction in algebra: Using cases to transform mathematics teaching and learning, Volume 2*. New York: Teachers College Press. The Case of Mr. Donnelly and the Candy Jar Task (Narrative Case and Sandral Pascal) in Principles to Action Professional Learning Toolkit. http://www.nctm.org/Conferences-and-Professional-Development/Principles-to-Actions-Toolkit/The-Case-of-Mr_-Donnelly-and-the-Candy-Jar-Task/ The Cases of Vanessa Culver (Chapter 1) and Steven Taylor (Chapter 3) in Boston, M. D., Dillon, F., Miller, S., & Smith, M. S. (2017). *Taking Action: Implementing Effective Mathematics Teaching Practices in Grades 9–12*. Reston, VA: National Council of Teachers of Mathematics. See also the high-cognitive-demand tasks included in the Taking Action book series (Boston, Dillon, Smith, & Miller, 2017; Huinker & Bill, 2017; Smith, Steele, & Raith, 2017)

Table. 7.1. continues on the next page

Table 7.1. Continued

Activity	Goals	Resources
Have teachers plan, enact, and analyze **Slices of Teaching** that focus on particular phases or sub-phases of the lesson as represented in the MTF.	To help teachers zoom in on particular aspects of a lesson with a focus on the ways in which each aspect of teaching might influence student learning, and what formative assessment opportunities might arise. For example, planning, enacting, and analyzing the **launch of a lesson** can support teachers in drawing strong connections between the moves made in the launch, how those moves may have influenced the thinking and learning that ensues. FA CONNECTION: Launching the lesson provides an opportunity to engage in the formative assessment practices of activating students as owners of their own learning and clarifying and sharing learning intentions and criteria for success.	Described in the section, Slices of Teaching - Launch.
Have teachers use the **Factors of Maintenance and Decline** to analyze an episode of their own teaching	To help teachers develop the capacity to critically reflect on and learn from their own teaching. FA CONNECTION: Keeping a task at a high level is critical in making students thinking public.	Stein, M. K., & Smith, M. S. (1998). Mathematical tasks as a framework for reflection: From research to practice. *Mathematics Teaching in the Middle School, 3*(4), 268–275.

Table. 7.1. continues on the next page

121

Table 7.1. Continued

Activity	Goals	Resources
Have teachers plan a lesson using the **Lesson Planning Template.**	To help teachers recognize that thorough and thoughtful lesson planning around cognitively demanding tasks can lead to more successful lessons—ones in which the level of the task is maintained during implementation and student thinking is central. FA CONNECTION: Student thinking and reasoning is reveled.	Smith, M. S., Steele, M. D., & Raith, M. L. (2017). Taking Action: Implementing Effective Mathematics Teaching Practices in Grades 6–8. Reston, VA: National Council of Teachers of Mathematics.
Have teachers teach the lesson they planned and collect data using the **monitoring tool.**	To help teachers recognize the ways in the data they collect can be used—to determine which solutions will be discussed during class, to keep track of students development over time, to determine if some students need additional help, to decide what direction to take instruction the following day. FA CONNECTION: The monitoring tool when fully implemented embodies the complete formative assessment process.	Information regarding monitoring and the use of the tool can be found in Smith, M. S., & Stein, M. K. (2011). 5 Practices for Orchestrating Productive Mathematics Discussions. Reston, VA: National Council of Teachers of Mathematics and in Smith, M. S., Steele, M. D., & Raith, M. L. (2017). Taking Action: Implementing Effective Mathematics Teaching Practices in Grades 6–8. Reston, VA: National Council of Teachers of Mathematics.

What's Next? Topics for Further Study

The MTF provides mathematics teachers and mathematics teacher educators with a common language for describing instructional practice and a structure for collecting and making use of formative assessment data. The Task Analysis Guide supports teachers in classifying instructional tasks by the cognitive demand required of students. The MTF framework itself provides identifiable markers within lessons that represent critical transition points where the cognitive demand of a task can be maintained or decline. The factors that support or inhibit cognitive demand relate to instructional practices that can be observed, discussed, and refined as teachers seek to analyze and change their instructional practice. The teacher moves that stem from the enactment of these factors can provide teachers with critical formative assessment information about the ways in which students are making sense of mathematical ideas and the implications for immediate and future instructional practice.

The MTF has spawned a series of tools that can be used across grade levels and mathematics content to support teacher planning, teaching, and reflecting, all of which have the potential to collect rich formative assessment data. The monitoring tool shown in figure 7.6 and lesson planning templates, such as the one included in Smith, Steele, and Raith (2017) provide teachers with scaffolding to support their thinking about the cognitive demands of tasks and teacher moves to help support those demands. Observation protocols (see Boston, Bostic, Lesseig, & Sherman, 2015) provide coaches and mentors with structures that support collecting data and providing feedback on lessons using the MTF (Rosenthal & Ampadu, 1999). Several questions that could be asked and answered through the use of the tools discussed herein include the following:

- In what ways do teachers make use of the formative assessment information that these tools can generate as they make instructional decisions during the enactment of a lesson?

- To what extent does the use of formative assessment information appear to support the ability to maintain the level of cognitive demand during instruction?

An area for future development would be the building of a database of tasks, planning tools, and cases of teaching related to specific mathematics content and specific grade levels. Such tasks, tools, and cases exist already in a number of collected volumes about the MTF (e.g., Stein, Smith, Henningsen, & Silver, 2000) and research-based effective mathematics teaching practices (e.g., Smith, Steele, & Raith, 2017). A next step in this development could be to create an online, open source database of tasks, plans, monitoring tools, and cases of implementation aligned to the MTF indexed by mathematics content and grade level. Formative assessment data could both inform the creation of this database and iteratively contribute to it. For example, the library could feature tasks and lessons that have been proven to be particularly useful in providing insights into student thinking and in surfacing key misconceptions in a domain. The library could also provide a venue for teachers to provide feedback on the strengths and limitations of particular tasks and lessons and to identify aspects of student thinking that were made public through work on a task.

Conclusion

The MTF provides mathematics teachers, instructional coaches, mathematics teacher educators, and mathematics education researchers with a common language to discuss tasks and classroom implementation. The MTF's efficacy is grounded in the relationships between the task implementation phases, the factors that support or inhibit cognitive demand, and student learning. Across the phases of the lesson, significant opportunities exist for teachers to collect formative assessment data that describes what students are learning and use that data to guide instructional decision-making. Continued development of teaching resources and tools that use the MTF components explicitly has the potential to collectively advance the quality of formative assessment and provide teachers with tools to collect and use those data in ways that will improve mathematics teaching and learning in pre-K–grade 12 mathematics classrooms.

Reflect on Your Practice

1. In what ways do the alignment between your task and your learning intentions and success criteria create opportunities for formative assessment?

2. What are you looking for and listening for as students work on a high-cognitive-demand task that tells you the class is ready to move to the next phase of instruction?

Connect Your Practice with Colleagues

1. How can your mathematics faculty increase the use of high-cognitive-demand tasks in the classroom?

2. How might teachers work together to plan for anticipated student thinking, assessing and advancing questions, and selecting, sequencing, and connecting solutions in a discussion?

3. How can teachers make use of the talk and work around high-cognitive-demand tasks to collect more robust formative assessment data?

References

Boston, M. D., Bostic, J., Lesseig, K., & Sherman, M. (2015). A Comparison of Mathematics Classroom Observation Protocols. *Mathematics Teacher Educator*, *3*(2), 154–175. https://doi.org/10.5951/mathtea, ceduc.3.2.0154

Boston, M. D., Dillon, F., Smith, M. S., & Miller, S. (2017). *Taking action: Implementing effective mathematics teaching practices in grades 9–12*. Reston, VA: National Council of Teachers of Mathematics.

Boston, M. D., & Wilhelm, A. G. (2015). Middle school mathematics instruction in instructionally focused urban districts. *Urban Education*, 1–33. https://doi.org/10.1177/0042085915574528

Hiebert, J., Carpenter, T. P., Fennema, E., Fuson, K., Human, P., Murray, H., . . . Wearne, D. (1996). Problem solving as a basis for reform in curriculum and instruction: The case of mathematics. *Educational Researcher*, *25*(4), 12–21. https://doi.org/10.3102/0013189X025004012

Hiebert, J., Gallimore, R., & Stigler, J. W. (2002). A knowledge base for the teaching profession: What would it look like and how can we get one? *Educational Researcher*, *31*(5), 3–15. Retrieved from http://www.jstor.org.proxy1.cl.msu.edu/stable/3594422

Huinker, D., & Bill, V. (2017). *Taking action: Implementing effective mathematics teaching practices in K–grade 5*. Reston, VA: National Council of Teachers of Mathematics.

Jackson, K. J., Shahan, E. C., Gibbons, L. K., & Cobb, P. A. (2012). Launching complex tasks. *Mathematics Teaching in the Middle School, 18*(1), 24. https://doi.org/10.5951/mathteacmiddscho.18.1.0024

Lappan, G., & Briars, D. (1995). How mathematics should be taught. In *Prospects for school mathematics: Seventy-five years of progress* (pp. 131–156). Reston, VA: National Council of Teachers of Mathematics.

Leahy, S., Lyon, C., Thompson, M., & Wiliam, D. (2005). Classroom assessment: minute by minute, day by day. *Educational Leadership, 63*(3), 18–24.

National Council of Teachers of Mathematics. (2000). *Principles and Standards for School Mathematics*. Reston, VA: National Council of Teachers of Mathematics.

National Council of Teachers of Mathematics. (2014). *Principles to actions: Ensuring mathematical success for all*. Reston, VA: National Council of Teachers of Mathematics.

National Governors Association Center for Best Practices, & Council of Chief State School Officers. (2010). *Common Core State Standards for Mathematics. National Governors Association Center for Best Practices, Council of Chief State School Officers*. Washington, DC.

Otten, S., & Soria, V. M. (2014). Relationships between students' learning and their participation during enactment of middle school algebra tasks. *ZDM, 46*(5), 815–827. https://doi.org/10.1007/s11858-014-0572-4

Rosenthal, M. M., & Ampadu, C. K. (1999). Making mathematics real: The Boston Math trail. *Mathematics Teaching in the Middle School, 5*(3), 140.

Smith, M. S., Steele, M. D., & Raith, M. L. (2017). *Taking action: Implementing effective mathematics teaching practices in middle school*. Reston, VA: National Council of Teachers of Mathematics.

Smith, M. S., & Stein, M. K. (1998). Selecting and creating mathematical tasks: From research to practice. *Mathematics Teaching in the Middle School, 3*(5), 344–350.

Smith, M. S., & Stein, M. K. (2011). *Five practices for orchestrating productive mathematics discussions*. Reston, VA: National Council of Teachers of Mathematics.

Stein, M. K., Grover, B. W., & Henningsen, M. (1996). Building student capacity for mathematical thinking and reasoning: An analysis of mathematical tasks used in reform classrooms. *American Educational Research Journal, 33*(2), 455–488.

Stein, M. K., Grover, B. W., & Henningsen, M. A. (1996). Building student capacity for mathematical thinking and reasoning: An analysis of mathematical tasks used in reform classrooms. *American Educational Research Journal, 33*, 455–488. https://doi.org/10.3102/00028312033002455

Stein, M. K., & Lane, S. (1996). Instructional tasks and the development of student capacity to think and reason: An analysis of the relationship between teaching and learning in a reform mathematics project. *Educational Research and Evaluation, 2*(1), 50–80.

Stein, M. K., & Smith, M. S. (1998). Mathematical tasks as a framework for reflection: From research to practice. *Mathematics Teaching in the Middle School, 3*, 268–275.

Stein, M. K., Smith, M. S., Henningsen, M., & Silver, E. A. (2000). *Implementing standards-based mathematics instruction: a casebook for professional development*. New York: Teachers College Press.

Wiliam, Dylan. Keeping learning on track: Classroom assessment and the regulation of learning. In F. K. Lester Jr. (Ed.), *Second Handbook of Research on Mathematics Teaching and Learning* (pp. 1053–1098). Greenwich, CT: Information Age Publishing, 2007.

Chapter 8

Using Formative Assessment to Guide the Effective Implementation of Response to Intervention (RTI)

Karen Karp and Beth Kobett

A large number of special education students spend the majority of the school day in general education classrooms (Heward, 2013). General education teachers are being asked to meet the needs of a more diverse student population, including those students with special needs. As a result of years of research that supports early intervention to address students' academic difficulties, many districts across the country are also adopting a multi-tiered system of support framework that focuses on the prevention of problem areas from developing in reading, mathematics, and behavior. This approach to support requires quick identification and immediate response to learning difficulties. The multi-tiered system uses the *formative assessment process* to identify students who are not meeting established benchmarks and subsequently provides intervention to meet the identified academic or behavioral need of students. The use of formative assessment methods in identifying and addressing the needs of students has reduced the number of students who have required more intensive services (Brown-Chidsey & Steege, 2005). As a result, schools have been able to identify students in need earlier and prevent many academic skills from worsening, thereby improving overall academic achievement.

Role of Response to Intervention

A multi-tiered system of support (MTSS) is commonly referred to as a Response to Intervention (RTI) model for all students. We will use the acronym RTI to reflect MTSS and RTI models throughout this chapter. This model has gained national prominence in the last decade and requires schools to focus on preventing students' academic failure in the general education classrooms like a medical model attempts to prevent illness, rather than wait for a dire situation. Commonly depicted as a triangle (fig. 8.1), the three-tiered framework includes a base called tier 1 or the universal level which represents the high-quality, grade-level, core-mathematics curriculum and evidence-based instruction received by all students. The next level, or tier 2, is supplemental instruction for students who have not made adequate progress in tier 1. This tier 2 instruction is not designed to help with homework or tutor students on the work presented in class that day. Instead it targets fundamental grade level content. The instruction in tier 2 is supplemental to the core mathematics instructional period (tier 1), not in lieu of the general education mathematics instruction. Interventions occurring in tier 2 may or may not be outside the general mathematics classroom. The top of the triangle, or tier 3, is the most intensive instruction for those students who have not been successful with tiers 1 and 2. This instruction usually is in a one-on-one or small group setting with a highly specialized mathematics interventionist or with a special education teacher. Importantly, promoters of RTI recognize that "the principles of RTI are met by using formative assessments" (Barnes & Harlacher, 2008, p. 424), while acknowledging that formative assessment is often "the missing link in response to intervention" (Reddy, Dudek, & Shernoff, 2016).

Formative assessment plays an essential role in the RTI system generally, and within each tier—especially in tier 1, where general education teachers take the lead. General-education teachers anticipate students' developing understanding and potential misconceptions, particularly for their struggling learners, adjust instruction, and provide in-time feedback to their students. This effort to design instructional opportunities that mindfully addresses students' mathematical needs is the hallmark of effective Tier 1 instruction. Therefore, general-education teachers in particular need to use the formative assessment process in order to notice and diagnose students' mathematical difficulties and design evidence-based interventions to address those learning needs.

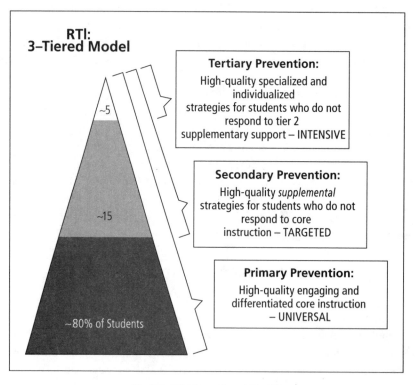

Fig. 8.1. RTI: Three-Tiered Model

Formative Assessment and RTI

Schools use many types of data to guide their decisions in determining which students may need supplemental or more intensive intervention. But many times these collected data are broad based and vague rather than being focused on the specific goals of the day's instruction. Therefore, these data cannot provide the teacher with enough timely information to identify the specific skills, concepts or mathematical practices that a student still needs to grasp on a given day that would allow for the design of an intervention to address the area(s) of difficulty. This chapter uses Heritage's (2013) focus on formative assessment through a process of both inquiry (assessing students' thinking on a mathematics concept or skill) and action (using the evidence gathered to design targeted interventions). As stated by Black, Harrison, Lee, Marshall, and William (2003), formative assessment "occurs when information about learning is evoked and then used to modify the teaching and learning activities in which teachers and students are engaged" (p. 122). Here, we suggest several strategies that are ideal for the inquiry stage of the formative assessment process. Each has the potential to be used as a more sensitive method to gather information on how students are thinking and to assess what strengths (including what they may have already mastered) and needs (essential learning that remains incomplete) they have as teachers monitor their progress. These strategies enable teachers to go to the underlying issues that may be causing students' knowledge gaps, gaps that, left unattended, can lead to "increased frustration, loss of motivation and interest in mathematics, and a vicious circle of low achievement that extends to the later years in school," (Heng & Sudarshan, 2013, p. 472). A carefully chosen tool or strategy to use in the process of formative assessment is followed by the design of targeted interventions that are research-based and teach explicit and structured strategies linked to what has been identified as a student's specific needs. This article describes these strategies for inquiring about students' thinking at each level of a multi-tiered system of support, gives examples of how to capture students' performance through these strategies, and details examples of how information from the formative assessment process can be put into action to guide intensive and explicit instructional interventions that lead to successful outcomes. We wish to note that explicit instruction is not "telling" but is instead systematically providing students with well-defined connections by linking previous knowledge to new knowledge via a distinct pathway. This pathway must be clear-cut and should be formed through the use of meaningful and relevant contexts, multiple representations, discussions of models of thought processes, and a strong feedback loop that captures students' depth of understanding using ongoing formative assessment strategies.

When you carry out the formative assessment process, one point that should be made clear, particularly in preservice mathematics methods courses and in in-service professional development, is whether the result will lead to an intervention that is a part of a multi-tiered system of support such as RTI or lesson differentiation. Differentiation occurs during tier 1 instruction when grade-level content is presented. Establishing a variety of activities that either ramp up to or ramp beyond current curriculum and instruction allows for different abilities in the same whole-class instructional session. So, if a formative assessment strategy reveals minor issues within a lesson—or if students demonstrate they can handle further challenge—this model of individualization hides the fact that students are working on different tasks on the same topic. On the other hand, if the data gathered suggests missing foundational concepts from prior grades, then an intervention to occur during tier 2 instruction is planned. The intervention develops specific skills and concepts for a targeted group of students to address areas of identified weakness by building on those students' strengths and current understandings. Unlike differentiation, it provides intentional support addressing content that is likely not within grade level standards or curriculum.

As noted in the first chapter of this volume, students in classrooms in which the formative assessment process is regularly and systematically used experience learning gains (Black & Wiliam, 1998). Some research suggests that students experience increases of one-half to one standard deviation (Black & Wiliam, 1998). In fact, Black and Wiliam report effect sizes between 0.4 and 0.7 in classrooms where the formative assessment process was conducted. Remarkably, these gains occur across grade levels, content, and for above-, on-, and below-grade level students (Wiliam, Lee, Harrison, & Black, 2004). In addition, Black and Wiliam (1998) stated that "while formative assessment can help all pupils, it yields particularly good results with low achievers by concentrating on specific problems with their work and giving them a clear understanding of what is wrong and how to put it right" (p. 14). The research indicates the positive academic response students may experience when engaging in a targeted formative assessment process within an RTI model. Therefore, to be most effective, the design, purpose, and implementation of the formative assessment process needs to be strategically addressed across the three tiers.

Using Evidence of Student Learning to Inform Instructional Decisions

Simply collecting evidence of student learning is not enough to make instructional decisions about student understanding. Teachers must be able to modify and adapt instruction continually to address diverse students' learning needs (Leahy, Lyon, Thompson, & Wiliam, 2005). The evidence collected about students' mathematical understanding must be robust and in enough depth to provide teachers with critical information to design subsequent instructional learning opportunities that will move learning forward (NCTM, 2014). Teachers must be curious, investigative, and willing to employ an inquiry stance (NCTE, 2013) about their students' mathematical understanding. Much like detectives, the teacher investigates students' strengths, developing understandings, and misconceptions to select instructional tasks that target individual student's prior knowledge and gaps in foundational understanding. Two asset-based techniques that naturally align with each tier of the RTI model and are respectful of students' strengths include Interviews and Show Me strategies (Fennell, Kobett, & Wray, 2017).

In the following examples, there is a discussion of the strategies chosen for use in the formative assessment process across various tiers, the information gleaned from the feedback from the student, the identification of strengths and weaknesses, and most important the decisions and actions taken by the teacher as to how next instructional steps will be presented. Although not discussed in detail in this chapter, the final step after the revised instruction is another effort to collect evidence of student understanding to monitor student progress fully and evaluate the success of the chosen intervention. Students described in the following scenarios are all performing below grade level, in some cases performing more than two grade levels below their peers.

Emphasizing Students' Mathematical Assets

Before we unpack the examples of the two strategies used in the formative assessment process— Interviews and Show Me—we begin by describing an approach to instruction (data collection and analysis) that focuses on evidence of students' mathematical strengths or assets rather than on what they do not know. *Asset-based instruction* is a recent movement that is informed by research in the health and psychology literature. Wasiak and Cramer (2006) describe asset-based thinking as a "cognitive process aimed at identifying the assets (e.g., strengths, talents, synergies, and possibilities) that are immediately available in yourself, other people and any situation" (p. 14). An asset-based instructional approach recognizes the academic, socio-emotional, and dispositional strengths that students exhibit while learning. Both teachers and students focus on what is working well to bridge learning to new content and accommodate content, processes, and concepts that challenge the learner (Paek, 2008). From this knowledge, asset-based accommodations and differentiation strategies can be anticipated and applied as formative assessment data are collected and applied at different points in the formative assessment process. In a typical scenario, student weaknesses are identified and given extra instructional attention in interventions, often in the very area that represents the student's greatest weakness. Within an asset-based thinking paradigm, student strengths and weaknesses are considered collectively to develop, design, and implement particular tier 2 instruction.

Let's look at a classroom implementing this process.

Ms. Weyforth is a sixth-grade teacher who is careful to incorporate a variety of components of the formative assessment process into the tier 1 core instruction in her classroom. One of her students, Joseph, is in her on-grade level mathematics class and receives an additional mathematics intervention session twice a week with other struggling learners. Joseph's academic team decided to individually collect data about his strengths, using classroom-based evidence. Ms. Weyforth conducted a diagnostic interview with Joseph on multi-step word problems and the other tier 2 instructor gathered observation evidence. Using this evidence, the team identified and recorded the following as his learning strengths and challenges. (see Table 8.1).

Table 8.1. Joseph's strengths and challenges

Joseph	
Strengths	**Challenges**
Mathematical drawings/representations	Retention of material just learned.
Storytelling (Can tell a personal story from start to finish)	Following multi-step directions.
	Deconstructing word problems.

Targeting Joseph's strengths, Ms. Weyforth incorporates multiple opportunities for Joseph and other students to create visual representations of their mathematical thinking as a way to share their thinking during tier I and tier 2 instruction. She also designs lessons that incorporate requests for both concrete and visual representations. For example, for a recent ratio lesson, students created equivalent ratios using cubes, graph paper, and drawings. Students made posters of their representations, which she then hung around the room as models for equivalent ratios. Although Ms. Weyforth cannot display everyone's poster, this will likely create an opportunity to feature Joseph's group's poster, given that they typically offer clear visual representations of the mathematics with logical organization of the information. Joseph's tier 2 instruction uses strengths-based accommodations to help him deconstruct word problems. Ms. Weyforth asks Joseph to create a story around the procedures being discussed using text boxes (comic strip speech bubbles) and connect the word problem to a visual model he created (see fig. 8.2). Using Joseph's strengths in visualizing mathematical ideas, Mrs. Weyforth and the tier 2 instructors are able to create opportunities for him to develop conceptual understanding and retain the mathematics taught in what Dougherty (2008) calls mental residue. Joseph's teachers gathered data through the formative assessment cycle, designed instruction capitalizing on his strengths, and addressed his challenge around the structure of word problems.

Fig. 8.2. Joseph's ratio story

Note the various ways in which Ms. Weyforth continues to facilitate the formative assessment process at multiple points during the lesson by making strategic instructional decisions, gathering student evidence, and scaffolding the ways in which students may share their mathematical understanding.

Strategy I: The Diagnostic Interview

The diagnostic interview is an effective strategy in the formative assessment process across all RTI tiers. Piaget (1970) first introduced the notion of interviewing as a means for understanding a child's thinking around a chosen task. The goal of a Piagetian interview is to understand the child's perspective and viewpoint by observing the student during the task, asking initial questions, and probing particular thinking and understanding as a reaction to observed behaviors and responses—all key components of the formative assessment process. While the task was pre-designed, Piaget recommended that the interviewer respond to the student's thinking individually to develop an in-depth and complete picture of the student's understanding. This level of analysis might require developing an on-the-spot question as a reaction to a unique student response. The interviewer must make interpretations and follow up with appropriate questions to probe mathematical thinking. Clinical interviews can provide unique insight into student mathematical thinking that cannot be known by merely examining paper and pencil student solutions (Ginsburg, 1997, 2009). The ultimate beauty of the diagnostic interview is that the teacher never wonders what the child is thinking or doing as they can always pose another question to find out. These interviews may reveal evidence about how students use everyday knowledge to create meaning about the mathematics they are learning or how they apply prior learning in mathematics to solve new real-world problems, also called mathematizing (Ginsburg, 1997; Ginsburg & Seo, 1999). Diagnostic interviews might also be used to understand better how students apply mathematical "rules" (Karp, Bush, & Dougherty, 2014) that may create cognitive conflict (Ginsburg, 2009; Piaget, 1985) and naïve misconceptions that can prevent full conceptual understanding and long-term retention.

A diagnostic interview is a brief one-on-one analysis of students' thinking used in the inquiry stage of the formative assessment process. It involves the presentation of a task for individual students to solve followed by probing questions. Students then verbalize their thinking. An analysis of multiple research studies on instructional practices revealed that one of the most effective approaches in improving students' learning is getting feedback from students as to what they know and do not know (Hattie, 2009). To reinforce the full understanding of the range of the student's conceptual grasp of the content, a diagnostic interview can be used to ask the student to show with manipulative materials or drawings, the same idea he or she may have shared through a procedural response. But in an effort to collect the most in-depth data about students' strengths and weaknesses, the teacher should avoid providing hints or teaching students.

During this time, the teacher can notice how flexibly students are using multiple representations and most importantly observe the "visible" or overt reasoning presented by the student. The teacher's role is to select an appropriate task based on a student's prior performance and commonly known misconceptions, ask probing questions that explore the student's thinking, offer the student a variety of materials to demonstrate the ideas, or ask him or her to display the knowledge in a different way. This connects to the formative assessment process by pinpointing learning needs that guide instructional decision-making.

Koellner, Colsman, and Risley (2011) recommend using multiple interviews that encompass varying mathematical perspectives of the learner to form a multi-dimensional perspective of the student's understanding. By assessing mathematical understanding from multiple perspectives, interventionists can develop mathematics lessons that target underdeveloped or immature understanding and promote mathematical connections. For example, in a multi-dimensional diagnostic interview, Alexandra revealed that when joining two parts (adding two numbers), she needed to re-count the joined quantities over and over again before determining the total. Another interview revealed that Alexandra did not need to count for values below six and simply could "see" or subitize the addends. In yet another interview, Alexandra could subitize all values consistently up to ten using a ten frame. Using knowledge of her mathematical strengths and her mathematical goal to join sets with totals greater than six, the teacher designed a lesson for Alexandra to use blank double ten-frames to add using a counting on strategy. This new lesson design built specifically on Alexandra's current mathematical understanding to target new learning. While some might perceive multiple interviews as time consuming, knowledge gained from these interviews significantly reduced actual instructional time. As this example illustrates, moving student understanding forward can only be achieved by developing a crystal clear understanding of student's current mathematical strengths, understandings, and misconceptions.

In another example of a multi-dimensional diagnostic interview that occurred over one week, Ray revealed his depth of understanding of adding and subtracting integers. In the first interview, Ray used integer chips to add and subtract integers. He confidently explained how to compare negative and positive values and began generating some conclusions about adding and subtracting integers. During the next interview, his teacher asked Ray to model addition and subtraction using a number line. This time, Ray understood the magnitude of the numbers but faltered as he struggled to explain the direction of the operation, particularly for adding two negative numbers. Using the data gathered from the two brief diagnostic interviews and her knowledge about Ray's love for football, his teacher designed a lesson using the football field as a real-world representation of a number line. In addition, she had Ray model integer problems using both integer counters and the number line, capitalizing on his strengths with the counters to bridge his mathematical learning across both representations.

Typical questions that we might ask to determine student understanding must be unpacked or adapted when interviewing students with disabilities. In particular, questions that can help students reconstruct their solution process are often helpful in eliciting useful formative assessment data. Asking students to link their explanations to drawings and procedures and particular parts of the problem can be helpful in gathering explicit data about student mathematical understanding. Table 8.2 provides both general questions that may be used formatively and adapted versions that may be more useful with struggling students.

Table 8.2. Probing questions adapted for students who struggle

General Questions	Questions for Students Who Struggle
What steps did you use to get your answer?	Where did you begin as you started to think about this problem?
Can you explain your thinking?	Can you talk about your drawing? What were your ideas as you made that model?
How did you solve this problem?	How does the drawing you made match the problem? Can you show me each part?
Explain your partner's thinking.	What did you think about doing first?
How do you know your answer makes sense?	What makes sense to you about _____?
What did you do here?	I notice that you erased (scratched out) something here. Can you tell me what you were thinking and why you changed your mind?

These questions can be asked at every tier because they guide the next instructional steps, which will vary by tier. For example, Ms. Frazier, a tier 1 teacher, stops to assist a first grade struggling learner, and asks the student to describe how her drawing matches a number sentence. Ms. Frazier notes that the first grader is struggling to count sequentially, and promptly requests that the tier 2 instructor to design specific instructional activities to target counting, conservation, and one-to-one correspondence. Ms. Frazier quickly adjusts her instruction and designs opportunities for the students to estimate and count items in a counting jar during the morning number routine. During tier 2 intervention, the intervention teacher designs an instructional activity where the students match number sentences to pictorial representations. All these instructional activities are informed by evidence collected through questioning and observation as part of the formative assessment cycle.

Strategy II: Show Me Strategy

Another formative assessment strategy that is particularly useful for struggling learners is the Show Me strategy. This strategy can provide additional information about student thinking and can inform teachers' "on-the-spot" instructional decision-making at any Tier. Fennell, Kobett, and Wray (2017) define the Show Me strategy as a "performance response by a student or group of students that extends and often deepens what was observed and what might have been asked within an interview" (p. 63). As teachers pose questions, they use their keen observation skills to survey student responses to identify advanced understanding or potential naïve conceptions and follow up with additional questions to reveal or demonstrate student's current thinking. Let's look at a situation to explore how that process plays out.

Mr. Camper taught multiplication of fractions using an array model, then connected the procedure to the array, and finally moved students to just using the algorithm. He asked the students to use white boards to show $\frac{2}{3} \times \frac{3}{9} = \_\_\_$. As he looked around the room at the students' white boards, he noted Sam, Kia, Alli, and Maria all wrote:

$$\text{Student writing: } \frac{2}{3} \times \frac{3}{9} = \frac{6}{9}$$

He then prompted the class to complete another problem and **show** a visual representation to match what was happening in the procedure. He followed up this request by asking students, to "Show me how your visual representation matches your algorithm." As the students drew the multiplication arrays, all but Sam discovered the error. Through the Show Me technique, Mr. Camper was able to diagnose student understanding and develop a new instructional plan for Sam.

Teachers may also design probes based on anticipated students' developing understandings and misconceptions about particular mathematics concepts. Tobey and Brodesky (2016) define these probes as "a short, highly focused, quick-to-administer diagnostic assessment designed to pinpoint key foundational ideas that students understand as well as any specific misunderstandings they may have regarding a particular mathematics concept" (p. 148). Using the language of formative assessment, this use of Show Me questions as described in the vignette above allowed the teacher to collect data that could be used to adjust instruction during instruction, *and* as an instructional strategy to help students make sense of algorithms by connecting them to models that highlight underling mathematical concepts.

A translation task is another activity that falls in the "Show Me" category. A translation task puts students in the position of "showing" their ability to use different representations for the same mathematical idea. Using this translation task approach (Van de Walle, Karp, & Bay Williams, 2016), data can be collected on a student's ability to solve problems, represent problems (i.e., writing equations that match a word problem), produce models of mathematical ideas using materials or illustrations, and describe the connections between the various representations.

Students with learning disabilities frequently find word problems challenging, partially due to some students having concomitant weak reading skills but more often due to a lack of cognitive structures for reasoning (Geary, 2004; Vukovic & Siegel, 2010). An older elementary student with disabilities was still trying to respond successfully to additive multi-digit word problems. So, the following "translation task" activity was conducted to see how the student thought about situations with smaller whole numbers as a means to explore any misconceptions as well as to seek out strengths. Using an adaptation of a template for assessing concept mastery from Frayer, Frederick, and Klausmeier [1969 (see fig. 8.3)] the student was given a teacher-authored word problem about children with amounts of pennies. Then the student was asked to write the corresponding equation, model the problem with materials, and write (or in this case orally state) an explanation of how to solve this problem with each of the four components placed in one of the quadrants on the template.

Equation	Word Problem
$7 + 12 = 19$	Jack had ⑦ pennies. Caroline gave him some more pennies. Now Jack has ⑫ pennies. How many did Caroline give him?

Model	Explanation
o o o o o o o o o o o o o o o o o o o	I look for the numbers and circle them. Then I look for important words — all together total take away lost Then I added the numbers

Fig. 8.3. Concept template with a student's incorrect responses
(Note: the explanation section was scribed by the teacher)

Evidence from the explanations the student gave in this Show Me activity revealed the student had previously been taught a "key word" strategy. Therefore, when he was unable to locate key words (from the collection he was able to remember) in the problem he immediately became frustrated. When his initial approach did not work, he did not have a strategy with which to proceed and basically resorted to adding the numbers in the problems. Even in the model developed (see fig. 8.3), the student took out counters to represent both numbers. Instead of comparing the amounts to find the difference, he combined them.

Moving this student, and others targeted as needing support, away from the use of a key word strategy, Ms. Fregoso decided that explicitly examining additive situations with concrete models was the way to begin and over several days incorporated the following supplemental instruction. Using the book *10 Little Hot Dogs* (Himmelman, 2014) as a context, students were given problems to act out using small photos of dachshund puppies and an activity sheet that had an upholstered chair. After several problems, Ms. Fregoso moved to using a graphic organizer (see fig. 8.4), not only to help structure the guinea pig problems, but also to introduce the variety of additive problems that the student would encounter. This included not only the common problem structure of "add to with result unknown" word problem (e.g., The chair in the kitchen had three little dogs. The chair in the living room has six more little dogs. How many little dogs are on the two chairs?) but also the "add to with change unknown" (e.g., Eight little dogs were on the chair. Ginger put on some more. Now there are 13 little dogs on the chair. How many did Ginger put on the chair?), and "add to with start unknown" problems (e.g., The family had some little hot dogs on a chair. When Sarah put 5 more on the chair, now they have 11 little hot dogs. How many little dogs were on the chair in the beginning?). (Problem types are from Carpenter, Fennema, Franke, & Empson, 1999; CCSSO, 2010.)

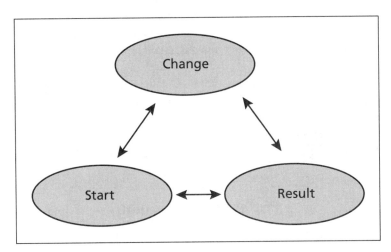

Fig. 8.4. Additive problem structures graphic organizer for problems involving a change

As the word problems were presented, the student was then asked to model the now familiar situation using the graphic organizer. After acting out several problems Ms. Fregoso segued to modeling problems on a part-part whole graphic organizer to expand students' understanding of the additive structure (see fig. 8.5) and the student stated, after multiple examples, "I see, if I am missing a part then I must subtract." Then Ms. Fregoso and the student revisited the more challenging problems that generated the original concern, this time with the student able to use a more effective thinking model than the search for "key words" that he previously used to signal an operation. Here we see that the student was able to make sense of the problem through physical actions with counters and mental actions with linking the situation to the graphic organizer—in this case used as a mental schema. In addition, Ms. Fregoso capitalized on the student's strength, using manipulatives to develop understandin, rather than relying on a shortcut that could not be sustained over time.

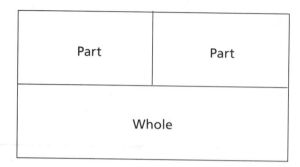

Fig. 8.5. Graphic organizer for part-part whole problem

Reflecting at the end of this teaching sequence, Ms. Fregoso stated that the "key word approach is not useful" for students generally, and particularly not useful for students with disabilities. Although taught with good intentions, general education students and students with disabilities can learn "rules" and then collapse into confusion or frustration when those instructions are partially remembered or rigidly adhered to regardless of the situation. This is especially true as students encounter word problems that do not contain key words, contain key words used in other contexts, and when they eventually find multi-step problems that are impossible to solve when relying on this strategy alone (Karp, Bush, & Dougherty, 2014). In addition, the switch to an approach that highlights the problem structure builds the network of connections and "dense structures" (Fosnot & Jacob, 2010) that will allow the approach to be used for other additive situations with fractions, decimals, money and so on. This is an example of an instructional design that supports mathematics learning for all students across all tiers, general education and special education, by anticipating their needs, current concept development, and potential misconceptions.

Professional Learning

As educators seek to reach all learners and "hold themselves and their colleagues accountable for the mathematical success of every student" (NCTM, p. 4), specific development in how to use the formative assessment process to target learning needs, design instructional tasks, and adjust for students with disabilities is critical. Professional development for preservice and in-service teachers must incorporate multiple opportunities for professional learning communities to create and implement a formative assessment process including techniques that provide effective ways to gather evidence of student strengths, current understandings, and misunderstandings. The professional development may include courses, formal sessions with a lead speaker, and facilitated professional learning communities. Certainly, these learning communities often target lesson design and implementation, but strategic development and selection of formative assessment strategies that are specifically intended to move learning forward for tier 1, 2, and 3 learners during teaching may be left to chance. Most preservice teachers complete a general assessment course, but they may not receive specific instruction about how formative assessment may be applied to mathematics classrooms or about mathematics classrooms that are responsive to students with disabilities. Similarly, in-service teachers may receive targeted professional learning for mathematics instruction. But often the main instructional strategies used in the formative assessment process may be relegated to broad strategies such as collecting student exit tickets that may or may not be used to adjust ongoing instruction, and cannot provide in-time evidence to make on-the-spot instructional decisions targeted to each and every child.

Mathematics professional learning for both groups needs to focus on anticipating, how and what evidence will be collected, for whom it will be collected, and the instructional decision-making resulting from these decisions. These course assignments or professional learning activities must include the full spectrum of the formative assessment cycle, including planning an appropriate task, anticipating student responses, implementing formative assessment strategies, and evaluating how the formative assessment activity revealed student mathematical thinking. Preservice and in-service teachers will benefit from designing lessons that include Interview and Show Me formative assessment strategies for instruction at all Tiers. Ample opportunities should be given for preservice and in-service teachers to bring evidence of student thinking to analyze and reflect upon. For example, preservice teachers watched a brief interview used to gather evidence of student thinking as part of the formative assessment process and then analyzed the student's strengths, current concept understanding, and misconceptions and determined next instructional steps. The interviewer asked the student to place 29 on an open number line (see fig. 8.6). On the first number line, the student drew "frog hops" to place 29. When asked whether 29 was closer to 0 or 100, the student explained that his "frog hops" were not correct. He then decided to make bigger "frog hops" on the next number line. He realized his second attempt was not working and he would need to make smaller "frog hops" on the third number line. After completing the third number line, the interviewer asked him to determine if 29 is either closer to 0 or 100. This time, the student incorrectly responded that his frog hops show that 29 is either closer to 100.

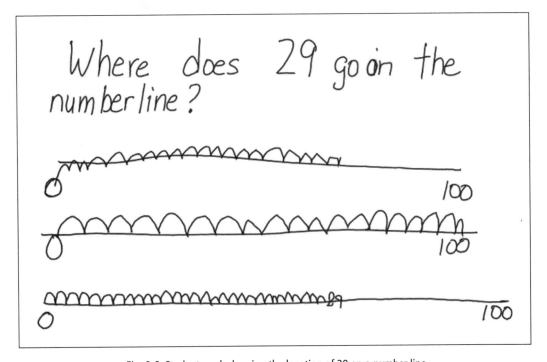

Fig. 8.6. Student work showing the location of 29 on a number line

Preservice teachers worked collaboratively to determine the student's strengths, developing understanding, misconceptions, and next instructional steps (see fig. 8.7). Note in the example how the preservice teachers pose inquiry *questions* about the misconceptions rather than statements about student understanding. Inquiry questions about student mathematical misconceptions invite further inquiry, develop anticipation skills for lesson planning, and help the preservice teachers develop diagnostic skills. As the teachers plan next steps, they use their inquiry questions to guide lesson planning and instructional accommodations across all tiers making the instruction visible and purposeful. By participating in the formative assessment process in the university classroom, preservice teachers experience the complexity of the interaction between teaching, learning, and assessment.

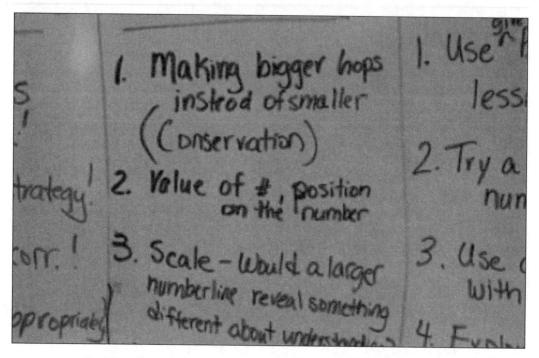

Fig. 8.7. Analyzing student interviews as part of the formative assessment process

Whole School Agreement

One practical approach that all schools can do to support the success of the formative assessment process with struggling learners is to agree to the same rules, mathematical models, vocabulary, and notation. This is called the "Whole School Agreement" (Karp, Bush, & Dougherty, 2016). To participate fully all teachers (special education and general education), paraprofessionals, interventionists, and regular school volunteers such as parents and grandparents must be consistent and in agreement about direction. This enhances the process of formative assessment when all models from the various grades are shared and integrated and a single vocabulary and notation are used to communicate mathematical ideas. All stakeholders can engage more effectively in the formative assessment process when the strategies (e.g., diagnostic interviews and show me) are agreed upon.

Summary

Research consistently reveals that showing students with disabilities structured and explicit thinking strategies is essential in supporting their successful learning of mathematical concepts (Gersten et al., 2009; Swanson & Jerman, 2006). Yet, these targeted strategies cannot be effectively presented without the informed knowledge of students' thinking—including their learning gaps, misconceptions, immature understandings and strengths. Show Me Strategies and Diagnostic Interviews are promising ways for teachers to collect data that can fine-tune teaching so that the emphasis is on explicitly supporting students with disabilities by collecting their feedback and avoiding generalized instruction.

When we attempt to teach concepts to students with disabilities without carefully assessing their assets and proficiencies as well as their confusions, we are moving students farther away from being able to independently structure and model their world of mathematical ideas. We know that merely "covering" material is probably going to be least successful with students with disabilities. As Daro et al. (2011, p. 48) state when "teachers move on without the students, students accumulate debts of knowledge (knowledge owed to them)." These authors also suggest that the starting point for instruction should be the mathematical content and the thinking the student already has about that topic—precisely the direction taken by the formative assessment process.

As more evidence emerges regarding research-informed learning trajectories and progressions of concepts in mathematical domains, the use of the two approaches described here has the potential to assess how students with disabilities are developing competence along a route of logically linked instructional tasks. Their path may differ from the trajectory of students in the general education population by either initial prior knowledge, approaches that are most successful or just the length of time involved in reaching mastery. What we do know is as Fennell (2011, p. 1) states: "All Means All," and in our commitment to reducing the debts of knowledge owed to all students, we must invest in approaches that are successful for assessing and instructing students with disabilities. Using Diagnostic Interviews and Show Me activities as strategies to uncover students' understandings and misconceptions, and applying an explicit instructional model using a variety of sensory input allows students to use personal resources and develop independence as they encounter problem solving situations.

Reflect on Your Practice

1. What role does RTI play in your practice? How is it incorporated into the instructional profiles of all students?

2. How does Heritage's (2013) thinking about inquiry and action play out in your classroom instruction?

3. How do you alter your questions for students who struggle?

Your Practice: Connect with Colleagues

1. Discuss ways of gathering evidence of students' thinking that have you found most informative in tailoring your instruction.

2. Make a chart, such as Table 8.1, for a student in your class. Bring it to the next PLC to brainstorm ways to teach a particular topic to the student.

3. Work with colleagues to develop and use the same diagnostic interview with several students, then share what you learned about each child and discuss next instructional steps.

Resources for Diagnostic Interviews

Burns, M. (2008–2011). *Do the math* (series includes topics such as addition and subtraction, fractions, multiplication, division). New York: Scholastic Books.

Richardson, K. (2003). *Assessing math concepts* (series includes topics such as counting, comparing, addition and subtraction, place value). Bellingham, WA: Mathematical Perspectives.

Tobey, C. R., & Arline, C. B. (2013). *Uncovering student thinking about mathematics in the common core.* Thousand Oaks, CA: Corwin.

Keeley, P. D., & Tobey, C. R. (2001). *Mathematics formative assessment, vol. 1: 75 practical strategies for linking assessment, instruction, and learning.* Thousand Oaks, CA: Corwin.

References

Association of Mathematics Teacher Educators, & National Council of Supervisors of Mathematics (n.d.). *Improving student achievement in mathematics through formative assessment in instruction.* Joint position paper, http://amte.net/sites/default/files/overview_amte_ncsm_position_paper_formative _assessment.pdf.

Barnes, A. C., & Harlacher, J. E. (2008). Clearing the confusion: Response-to-Intervention as a set of principles. *Education and Treatment of Children, 31*(3), 417–31.

Black, P., Harrison, C., Lee, C., Marshall, B., & Wiliam, D. (2003). *Assessment for learning: Putting it into practice.* Maidenhead, UK: Open University Press.

Black, P. J., & Wiliam, D. (1998). Assessment and classroom learning. *Assessment in Education, 5*, 7–74.

Black, P., & Wiliam, D. (1998). Inside the black box: Raising standards through classroom assessment. *Phi Delta Kappan*, 139–148.

Brown-Chidsey, R., & Steege, M. W. (2005). *Response to intervention: Principles and strategies for effective practice.* New York: Guilford Press.

Carpenter, T., Fennema, E., Franke, M. L., Levi, L., & Empson, S. (1999). *Children's mathematics: Cognitively guided instruction.* Portsmouth, NH: Heinemann.

CCSSO/NGA. (2010). *Common Core State Standards: Mathematics.* Washington, DC: Council of Chief State School Officers and the National Governors Association Center for Best Practices. Retrieved from http://corestandards.org

Daro, P., Mosher, F., & Corcoran, T. (2011). *Learning trajectories in mathematics: A foundation for standards, curriculum assessment and instruction.* Philadelphia, PA: Consortium for Policy Research in Education.

Dougherty, B. J. (2008). Measure up: A quantitative view of early algebra. In J. J. Kaput, D. W. Carraher, & M. L. Blanton (Eds.), *Algebra in the early grades* (pp. 389–412). Mahwah, NJ: Erlbaum.

Fagan, E. R., Tobey, C. R., & Brodesky, A. R. (2016). Targeting instruction with formative assessment probes. *Teaching Children Mathematics, 23*(3), 146–157.

Fennell, F. (2011). All means all. In F. Fennell (Ed.), *Achieving fluency in special education and mathematics* (pp. 1–14). Reston, VA: National Council of Teachers of Mathematics (NCTM).

Fennell, F., Kobett, B. M., & Wray, J. (2017). *Formative 5: Everyday assessment techniques for every classroom.* Thousand Oaks, CA: Corwin.

Fosnot, C. T., & Jacob, B. (2010). *Young mathematicians at work: Constructing algebra.* Portsmouth, NH: Heinemann.

Frayer, D. A., Fredrick, W. C., & Klausmeier, H. J. (April 1969). *A schema for testing the level of concept mastery (Working Paper No. 16)*, University of Wisconsin Center for Educational Research.

Geary, D. C. (2004). Mathematics and learning disabilities. *Journal of Learning Disabilities, 37*(1), 4–15.

Gersten, R., Beckmann, S., Clarke, B., Foegen, A., Marsh, L., Star, J. R., & Witzel, B. (2009). *Assisting students struggling with mathematics: Response to Intervention (RtI) for elementary and middle schools* (NCEE 2009-4060). Washington, DC: National Center for Education Evaluation and Regional Assistance, Institute of Education Sciences, U.S. Department of Education. Retrieved from http://ies.ed.gov/ncee/wwc/publications/practiceguides/.

Ginsburg, H. (1997). *Entering the child's mind: The clinical interview in psychological research and practice.* Cambridge, MA: Cambridge University Press.

Ginsburg, H. P. (2009). The challenge of formative assessment in mathematics education: Children's minds, teachers' minds. *Human Development, 52*(2), 109–128.

Ginsburg, H. P., & Seo, K. H. (1999). Mathematics in children's thinking. *Mathematical Thinking and Learning, 1*(2), 113–129.

Hattie, J. (2009). *Visible learning: A synthesis of over 800 meta-analyses relating to achievement.* New York: Routledge.

Heng, M. A., & Sudarshan, A. (2013). "Bigger number means you plus!"—Teachers learning to use clinical interview to understand students' mathematical thinking. *Educational Studies in Mathematics, 83*, 471–485.

Heritage, M. (2013). *Formative assessment in practice: A process of inquiry and action.* Cambridge, MA: Harvard Education Press.

Heward, W. L., (2013). *Exceptional children: An introduction to special education.* Boston: Pearson.

Himmelman, J. (2014). *10 Little Hot Dogs.* Las Vegas, NV: Amazon Children's Publishing.

Karp, K., Bush, S., & Dougherty, B. (2016). Establishing a mathematics whole-school agreement. *Teaching Children Mathematics, 23*(2), 69–71.

Karp, K., Bush, S., & Dougherty, B. (2014). 13 rules that expire. *Teaching Children Mathematics, 21*(1) 18–25.

Koellner, K., Colsman, M., & Risley, R. (2011). Multidimensional assessment: Guiding response to intervention in mathematics. *Teaching Exceptional Children, 44*(2), 48.

Leahy, S., Lyon, C., Thompson, M., & Wiliam, D. (2005). Classroom assessment minute by minute, day by day. *Educational Leadership, 63,* 18–24.

National Center for Education Statistics. (2007). *The nation's report card mathematics 2007 (National Assessment of Educational Progress at grades 4 and 8).* Washington, DC: Institute for Education Sciences.

National Council of Teachers of English. (2013). *Formative assessment that truly informs instruction.* Retrieved from http://www.ncte.org/library/NCTEFiles/Resources/Positions/formative -assessment_single.pdf

National Council of Teachers of Mathematics. (2000). *Principles and standards for school mathematics.* Reston, VA: NCTM.

National Council of Teachers of Mathematics. (2006). *Curriculum focal points for prekindergarten through grade 8 mathematics: A quest for coherence.* Reston, VA: NCTM.

National Council of Teachers of Mathematics. (2014). *Principles and actions: Ensuring mathematical success for all.* Reston, VA: NCTM.

National Mathematics Advisory Panel. (2008). *Foundations for success.* Jessup, MD: U.S. Department of Education.

Paek, P. L. (2008). *Asset-based instruction: Boston Public Schools [Case study from Practices worthy of attention: Local innovations in strengthening secondary mathematics].* University of Texas: Charles A. Dana Center.

Phelan, J., Choi, K., Vendlinski, T., Baker, E., & Herman, J. (2011). Differential improvement in student understanding of mathematical principles following formative assessment intervention. *The Journal of Educational Research, 104*(5), 330–339.

Piaget, J. (1970). Piaget's theory. In P. Mussen (Ed.), *Carmichael's manual of child psychology* (3rd ed., Vol. 1, pp. 703–732). New York: Wiley.

Piaget, J. (1985). *The equilibration of cognitive structures: The central problem of intellectual development.* Chicago: University of Chicago Press.

Reddy, L. A., Dudek, C. M., & Shernoff, E. S. (2016). Teacher formative assessment: The missing link in response to intervention. In S. R. Jimmerson, M. K. Burns, & A. M. VanDerHeyden (Eds.), *Handbook of response to intervention: The science and practice of multi-tiered systems of support.* (2nd Ed.) 607–626, New York: Springer.

Swanson, H. L., & Jerman, O. (2006). Math disabilities: A selective meta-analysis of the literature. *Review of Educational Research, 76*(2), 249–274.

Van de Walle, J., Karp, K., & Bay-Williams, J. (2016). *Elementary and middle school mathematics: teaching developmentally.* New York: Pearson.

Vukovic, R. K., & Siegel, L. S. (2010). Academic and cognitive characteristics of persistent mathematics difficulty from first through fourth grade. *Learning Disabilities Research and Practice, 25*(1), 25–38.

Wasiak, H., & Cramer, K. D. (2006). *Change the way you see everything through asset-based thinking.* Philadelphia, PA: Running Press.

Wiliam, D., Lee, C., Harrison, C., & Black, P. (2004). Teachers developing assessment for learning: Impact on student achievement. *Assessment in Education, 11*, 49–65.

 # Section 3

Using the Power of Formative Assessment

The four chapters contained in Section 3 consider major crosscutting themes and lessons drawn from the earlier chapters. Chapter 9 examines the connections between formative assessment and the Effective Mathematics Teaching Practices identified in NCTM's *Principles to Actions*. Chapter 10 looks carefully at educational equity and its linkages to formative assessment, drawing connections to other work in the field on equity and to the chapters in Section 2 of this book. Chapter 11 considers the proposition that an explicit and intentional focus on formative assessment might afford greater coherence across teachers' professional learning experiences and thereby improve the effectiveness of the professional learning experiences of teachers. The final chapter in this section and the book summarizes the major arguments developed and proposes a few topics that might constitute useful next steps in efforts to promote formative assessment in mathematics classrooms.

Chapter 9

Focusing on Formative Assessment to Improve Mathematics Teaching and Learning

Megan Burton and Wanda Audrict

Introduction

Formative Assessment is an integral part of instruction, because when evidence about student learning is effectively gathered and used, it informs and moves learning forward. It is assessment *for* learning (Broadfoot, 2008), unlike summative assessment which is the assessment *of* learning (Black et al., 2004). It occurs at all phases in the instructional cycle. Lessons and goals are established based on evidence of student thinking. During instruction, teachers and students make adjustments in the moment based on formative assessment to further learning. After instruction, evidence is used to determine the next steps of instruction. To implement each of the teaching practices described in *Principles to Action* (NCTM, 2014) successfully elements of formative assessment must be used. Practice Eight: elicit and use evidence of student thinking, explicitly notes this need for using formative assessment throughout the instructional cycle. In order to maximize student learning potential, teachers need to identify what students know and adjust instruction based on this information to further learning.

In addition to Mathematics Teaching Practice Eight, which directly connects to common definitions of formative assessment, formative assessment positively informs and supports the remaining seven Mathematics Teaching Practices (NCTM, 2014). The eight practices are:

1. Establish mathematics goals to focus learning.
2. Implement tasks that promote reasoning and problem solving.
3. Use and connect mathematical representations.
4. Facilitate meaningful mathematical discourse.
5. Pose purposeful questions.
6. Build procedural fluency from conceptual understanding.
7. Support productive struggle in learning mathematics.
8. Elicit and use evidence of student thinking.

This chapter explores these eight mathematics teaching practices in relation to the formative assessment process. The frameworks, tools and approaches described in this book provide illustrations of how formative assessment is integral to effective instruction.

Mathematics Teaching Practices and Formative Assessment Establish Clear Learning Goals

Learning goals are connected to where students currently are in their development of mathematical understanding and procedural fluency of concepts related to the standards. Formative assessment involves monitoring student progress toward meeting learning goals, and also using evidence about student thinking to inform which learning goals are selected. Learning goals need to be specific enough to support teachers' abilities to formatively assess where students are in meeting these goals. This helps teachers determine what scaffolds or adjustments might be needed to meet these goals. Learning goals can be communicated differently, depending on the task and classroom environment. For example, chapter 4 notes that, while Cognitively Guided Instruction (CGI) classrooms have general learning goals, they also have specific individual learning goals for students, but both goals are determined by formatively assessing the class and student needs. Similar to CGI, chapter 6 focuses on using learning trajectories in formative assessment to inform learning goals of students. If formative assessment information from previous lessons is examined during the planning phase, then learning goals that are appropriate can be determined more accurately. Real-time instructional decisions can be more appropriately made when clear learning goals, based on formative assessment, are established in the planning phase (Stein & Merkle, 2017).

As mentioned in Chapter 7, clarifying learning goals and criteria for success are important elements in the set-up stage of the mathematical task framework. Teachers must maintain a focus on the ultimate learning goals when determining how much to make visible without jeopardizing the challenge of the task for students. Criteria for success must be clear to students, but solutions to complex problems should not be immediately clear.

Implement Tasks That Promote Reasoning

A complex mathematical problem, or set of problems, that centers around one or more specific mathematical idea(s) is often considered a mathematical task (Stein, Grover, & Henningsen, 1996). We see many connections between the selection and implementation of tasks that promote reasoning and the formative assessment process.

First, student learning opportunities and the information learned about student thinking are both impacted by the type of tasks selected for instruction. Tasks that promote reasoning and problem solving facilitate understanding *and* are a central element of effective classrooms (Boston, Madler, & Cutone, 2017). The Mathematical Tasks Framework (Stein, Grover, & Henningsen, 1996) number and kind of representations, and communication requirements facilitates the careful analysis of tasks and introduces the construct of *cognitive demand of mathematical tasks* as a means to identify the learning opportunities that a task provides for students (Stein, Smith, Henningson, & Silver, 2009). In addition, the cognitive demand of the task impacts the amount and type of evidence of student thinking that can be demonstrated and a teachers' ability to further learning based on this thinking. Cognitively demanding tasks are often more open-ended, involving complex thinking and decision-making. They promote reasoning and problem solving, as described in the second teaching practice, and they allow both student and teacher more insight into student understanding and thinking.

The importance of student connections to the task, are a second connection between the selection and use of reasoning tasks for instructional purposes and formative assessment. Effective formative assessment and teaching involves selecting and implementing tasks that connect to and value student experiences, culture, and perspectives in the mathematics classroom. As noted in Chapter 5, in order for the tasks to engage students meaningfully, they need to build authentically upon students' funds of knowledge, which includes seeing a connection to self in the curriculum, as advocated by Culturally Responsive Pedagogy (CRP). For example, implementing a task that involves purchasing subway tokens might require prior knowledge of and experiences with a subway system. For young children in rural areas, this may not be part of their funds of knowledge and the context of the problem might impede the ability to delve into the mathematics, thus limiting the problem's use both for instructional and formative assessment purposes. However, with knowledge of the their experiences, the teacher could introduce students to different forms of transportation and connect these with their own experiences prior to using this task. The context of the problem could also be changed to a topic more relevant to the students' experiences. Allowing students to share how their experiences influence the way in which they connect to and approach tasks can provide both instructional and formative assessment information.

Finally, task selection and formative assessment are connected ,because implementing tasks that are instructionally appropriate for students at their current level of understanding is critical. Formative assessment involves identifying the current level of understanding of students. CGI instructional frameworks and other learning progressions can help identify this level of understanding, as well as aid in selecting and implementing the most appropriate task to promote problem solving and reasoning.

The mathematics tasks that a teacher chooses will frame both the learning opportunities and student beliefs about the nature of mathematics (Lappan & Briars, 1995). Likewise, tasks are a critical factor in the efficacy of the formative assessment process. The design of the task determines the level of thinking in which students can potentially engage, as well as the opportunities to reveal students' thinking. If appropriate tasks are selected, then those tasks should elicit actionable evidence of student thinking that teachers can use during the lesson or to inform future instruction to push learning forward.

Use and Connect Mathematical Representations

Representations can be anything that stands for a particular object, concept, image, or process, or some combination of these (Hodges & Johnson, 2017). Representations in mathematics can be used to explore, share, and justify ideas (Goldin & Shteingold, 2001). *Principles to Action* (NCTM, 2014) describes the importance of using and connecting contextual, verbal, visual, physical, and symbolic representations. This teaching practice intertwines with formative assessment at the planning, instructional and reflection phases of the instructional cycle. Representations can facilitate understanding and communication about mathematical thinking (Hodges & Johnson, 2017).

Using evidence from the formative assessment process to inform planning can impact which representations teachers use during instruction and how they plan to use these representations. For example, documentation can be used during the planning phase to understand what representations students gravitate to currently and to make decisions regarding ways to advance learning and deepen mathematical connections. CRP and learning progressions are examples of frameworks and tools that recognize that different representations resonate with different students based on their respective funds of knowledge, current understanding of content, and experiences. Therefore, experiences and classroom discussions that make visible and value the various ways mathematics can be seen in the work is important. For example, if evidence has shown that students are comfortable using base-ten blocks to represent three-digit numbers, but they still struggle with understanding the zero in the tens place, a teacher can design questions and tasks that use base-ten blocks to help address this confusion.

Representations can provide windows into student thinking during instruction. For example, if a first-grade student is using tally marks in single digit addition, the teacher can identify, where they might be on the learning progression of addition for this problem. Evidence of student thinking can impact how teachers use representations during instruction to move each student's learning forward. For example, if a student is struggling to understand how $22 - 9 = 23 - 10$, a teacher could ask the student to use base-ten blocks or a number line to explore the relationship between these problems. fig. 6.1 in Chapter 6 illustrates different solutions for a single problem. This example illustrates how the analysis of the representations in student solutions creates opportunities to make connections across representations to inform the next instructional steps guided by learning trajectories.

Formative assessment information can provide insight into the ways students struggle to use and connect mathematical representations in whole group settings. This evidence can inform the small group and one-on-one instruction provided in tiers 2 and 3 Response to Intervention groups. For example, if a student is able to use concrete manipulatives and pictorial representations to add single digit numbers, but they struggle to add numbers with abstract symbols, tTier 2 representation might involve a task where students are challenged to directly connect these three types of representations in a real world context.

Connecting formative assessment and the teaching practice of using and connecting representations throughout the instructional cycle is another example of how formative assessment intertwines with these teaching practices. Mathematics teachers can formatively assess student thinking by examining the representations students use, and they can use this information to select experiences students might need with other representations to advance learning strategically.

Facilitate Meaningful Mathematical Discourse

Meaningful mathematical discourse and formative assessment influence each other in an effective classroom. Discourse includes gestures, diagrams, illustrations, and any other form of communication that conveys our thinking and meaning to others (Staples & King, 2017). Each form of communication can be used within the process of formative assessment.

In order to facilitate meaningful mathematical discourse, teachers should have clear goals and success criteria in mind. This step in the formative assessment process is guided by knowledge of student understanding and needs, as well as the pedagogical content knowledge related to the subject. These goals and success criteria guide the lesson and communication that occurs.

A second part of the formative assessment process is gathering evidence of learning. Teachers can gather evidence that informs how the discourse unfolds; they can also gather evidence from the discourse itself. Staples and King (2017) note that one key role of the teacher, in regard to mathematical discourse, is to elicit student thinking, which allows both the teacher and student to gather evidence of learning.

The formative assessment process also includes adjusting instruction to advance learning, which is a natural part of effective discourse. The formative assessment evidence gathered during discussions or prior activities may influence examples a teacher chooses to share during the discussion or questions that he or she asks. Meaningful mathematics discourse allows teachers and peers to ask clarifying and extending questions about student thinking that advance learning for all. Discussions are an important way for student thinking to be made visible and for teachers to move the thinking forward by using the strengths and comments shared by others. It also provides an opportunity to see what connections across various strategies students make.

One of the tools explored in this book, Classroom Discourse and Discussion Tools (Chapter 3), focuses on the learning and formative assessment that can occur from meaningful discourse that is purposeful, productive, and powerful. This chapter reminds the reader that effective discourse not only allows students to clarify and express their thinking, but allows teachers to gather important formative assessment documentation that might be missed without these opportunities. In addition, students are able to take ownership of their own learning as they receive feedback from the teacher or their peers through meaningful mathematical discourse. Students are able to make use of the feedback to either revise or clarify their thinking. Therefore, formative assessment is an important element in facilitating meaningful mathematics discourse.

Pose Purposeful Questions

Posing purposeful questions is an excellent way to elicit student thinking. In addition, using evidence of student thinking to design questions is an effective way to advance student understanding. Four main question types are described in *Principles to Action* (NCTM, 2014) and each can support the formative assessment process. Question types include those that gather information, probe thinking, make mathematics visible, and those that push students to justify and reflect. All four types are connected to the basic tenets of formative assessment. Each of the frameworks, tools, and approaches discussed in this book focuses in some way on the importance of posing questions that provide evidence of student thinking that can be acted upon by both teachers and students.

Gathering information questions are used to probe for facts, definitions, procedures, and context. These are important baseline questions to understand what students know. While these tend to be more surface-level questions, *Principles to Action* (NCTM, 2014) notes that they do have a place in the classroom. However, they should be balanced by the other types of questions. When asking a gathering information question, such as, "What is the formula for finding the volume of a rectangular prism?," it is important to ask follow-up questions or provide experiences that allow teachers and students to gain deeper understanding of student thinking. For example, asking why it is important information or how it could connect to previous questions could build upon the initial information-gathering question. The follow-up questions should focus the learning by probing, supporting mathematical connections, or encouraging reflection and justification without funneling students to a desired procedure or track. This provides more complete evidence of student thinking to support instructional decisions.

Probing questions push students deeper in the content. They ask students to articulate or expand on their thinking. This could take the form of explaining steps or strategies used in a problem or clarifying a previous response. These questions can be designed from the formative assessment information gained from prior lessons, discussions or questions. These questions allow students to begin to clarify their thinking and to communicate effectively with peers about their understandings. As they communicate responses to probing questions, teachers are able to gain valuable information about student thinking.

When students are asked to make mathematical connections across situations or strategies, they are being asked questions that make mathematics visible. For example, asking students how a broader topic relates to the specific situation they just explored or asking students to connect representations support making mathematical connections. Learning trajectories can be informative to teachers as they design questions, because identifying where student responses are on a learning trajectory can allow teachers to determine what types of mathematical connections could be made to move along a learning continuum. These types of questions can be designed based on prior evidence about student thinking and strategies. The responses provide great insight into the larger picture and conceptual understanding students may have.

Questions can encourage students to support or reflect more deeply on their reasoning, thus allowing them to reveal their true understanding of a mathematical situation. This supports students developing an awareness and ability to formatively assess their thinking and the thinking of others when questions are a typical part of classroom discussions. Asking questions that challenge students to reflect and justify their strategies and solutions provokes students to think deeper or differently about the mathematics they are experiencing.

When balanced and based on prior formative assessment evidence, these types of questions can facilitate and deepen student understanding while also providing formative assessment information about current student thinking. Moving beyond the initial question and carefully sequencing questions to focus, rather than funnel learning can be challenging (NCTM, 2014), but is critical in effective instruction and the formative assessment cycle. This type of balanced, focused questioning is informed by formative assessment and also provides additional formative assessment evidence.

Build Procedural Fluency from Conceptual Understanding

Principles to Action (NCTM, 2014) emphasizes the importance of conceptual understanding facilitating procedural fluency to solve mathematical tasks. This involves being able to think flexibly about concepts in an efficient, accurate manner, while also maintaining understanding. Martin (2009) noted the detrimental effects of blindly using procedures without deeper conceptual understanding of why these procedures are the most effective in that situation. One example would be using the formula to calculate surface area of a cube, without understanding what these numbers mean. This could lead students to accidentally multiply by eight, rather than six, without realizing why this would not work. With conceptual understanding, they would realize that the shape would need eight sides for this to be accurate. In order to support students building fluency from conceptual understanding, teachers need to assess not only the procedures used and solutions obtained, but also to examine the thinking and reasoning behind the procedures and strategies selected by students. Experiences where students are pushed to use their own reasoning strategies provides formative assessment evidence and also supports the development of that conceptual understanding. Learning trajectories can identify the path building from conceptual understanding towards procedural fluency. It can support the connections that should be made between various student strategies in the move towards efficiency. By identifying research based frameworks, such as CGI, or learning trajectories, one is better able to identify where students are in their current thinking, understand common errors and misconceptions, and determine what the appropriate next steps might be to move them towards procedural fluency that is solidly undergirded by conceptual understanding.

Support Productive Struggle in Learning Mathematics

Effective teaching of mathematics consistently provides students, individually and collectively, with opportunities and supports to engage in productive struggle as they grapple with mathematical ideas and relationships. (NCTM, 2014, p. 48)

Interacting with students while they are working on a cognitively demanding task provides teachers with opportunities to gather evidence of student thinking in the moment and to provide students with feedback that helps them make continued progress. Designing and implementing appropriate tasks that promote productive struggle and providing feedback that advances the learning process without removing student ownership or problem solving is an instructional balance, but also a balance related to formative assessment.

Formative assessment allows teachers to design appropriate tasks based on evidence of student thinking. It also makes it feasible for teachers to make immediate adjustments to instruction when productive struggle is absent. This is important, because there is often a fine line between students engaged in productive struggle and students who have reached the point of frustration and desperation. At the same time, some tasks need scaffolding to increase the complexity, so as to create an environment that produces productive struggle. Hiebert and Wearne (2003) noted that effective mathematical tasks should be within students' capabilities, but the answer should not be immediately apparent. Students need opportunities to grapple with the content and to develop their own strategies and ways of communicating their thinking. Therefore, teachers need to know where their students are when making the decision as to whether struggle is productive.

The teacher's role is to find ways to support students in persevering when faced with a high-level task, without detracting from student thinking and reasoning opportunities. Formative assessment during a lesson can guide the teacher in determining when scaffolds are needed and what type of scaffolds will maximize the student decision making and ownership in the experience. Students, however, may experience frustration when faced with a task they cannot immediately solve. In such situations, they may press the teacher to provide assistance which inadvertently takes away from the meaning-making processes and removes the teacher's ability to determine what the student could do without that support. Studies have shown that the most effective teacher feedback offers information about areas needing improvement and also gives suggestions about how to improve, while not providing the solution or promoting one strategy over others (Butler, 1987; Kluger & DeNisi, 1996). This type of formative feedback not only supports student learning, but also allows the teacher to continue to gather formative assessment data as the student moves forward on the task.

Teachers and students need to see the importance of challenge and struggle in mathematics, while also believing in students' abilities to make sense of the mathematical situations they encounter (NCTM, 2014). Giving students the opportunity to explain and justify their strategies and also discuss the strategies of their peers allows for further growth and connections between formative assessment and productive struggle in a task.

Elicit and Use Evidence of Student Thinking

This teaching practice is the heart of formative assessment. Therefore, this section simply elaborates on the meaning of this teaching practice. According to Black and Wiliam (2009), "practice in a classroom is formative to the extent that evidence about student achievement is elicited, interpreted, and used by teachers, learners, or their peers, to make decisions about the next steps in instruction that are likely to be better, or better founded, than the decisions they would have taken in the absence of the evidence that was elicited" (p. 9). There are numerous effective ways to elicit evidence of student thinking and context is an important part in the decision-making process of which way would be most effective. In most lessons, a variety of strategies should be used to gain a full body of evidence about student thinking. In this section, some of these ways are described as observing, with observing being used in a broad sense. It can be listening to peer conversations, listening to students in conversation with the teacher, questioning, observing students' processes in problem solving, and analyzing student work.

Listening to conversations between students and engaging in conversations with students are two ways to gather evidence about student thinking. Davis (1997) noted the importance of "listening to" students, as active participants in mathematical meaning making, rather than "listening for" the mathematics students share as they acquire it from the teacher. However, Cox, Meicenheimer, and Hickey (2017) take this a step further by synthesizing the ideas into one of "listening for students' mathematics" (p. 90). This requires taking the stance that students bring funds of knowledge from which to build their own mathematical understandings, similar to the ideas expressed through culturally responsive teaching. Therefore, eliciting and using evidence of student thinking should be done in a way that values multiple perspectives and entry points into problems. Student thinking can be used to further learning as classrooms provide opportunities for this thinking to be made public and to guide instructional discourse. Student thinking is a part of the entire instructional cycle. It should guide the planning, implementation, and analysis of learning after the lesson is complete.

Conclusion

Leahy, Lyon, Thompson, and Wiliam (2005) explained five aspects of instruction that are informed by formative assessment:

1. Sharing clear learning goals and benchmarks for success;
2. Designing lessons that involve successful classroom discussions, questions, and instructional tasks;
3. Enhancing and progressing learning through feedback;
4. Fostering student ownership of learning and;
5. Creating an environment where students serve as resources for one another.

The Mathematics Teaching Practices and formative assessment are intertwined; one set of strategies cannot happen without the other and both lead to effective instruction and student growth. Ramaprasad (1983) described three key processes in effective teaching and learning: analyzing where the learner is, determining where the learner is going, and identifying how to get the learner to this goal. These same three processes were the foundational ideas Wiliam and Thompson (2007) used to create a formative assessment framework. This is one example that illustrates the intricate, close connection between formative assessment and effective teaching and learning. Through this text, we hope that the connection between the frameworks, tools, and approaches described in the text and formative assessment is made visible. This chapter specifically connects formative assessment to the Mathematics Teaching Practices to illustrate how ideas about teaching and learning are all interrelated.

References

Black, P., Harrison, C., Lee, C., Marshall, B., & Wiliam, D. (2004). *Assessment for learning: Putting it into practice.* New York, NY: Open University Press.

Black, P., & Dylan, W. (2009). Developing the theory of formative assessment. *Educational Assessment, Evaluation and Accountability, 21*(1), 5–3.

Boston, M. D., Madler, K., & Cutone, C. (2017). Implementing tasks that promote reasoning and problem solving. In D. A. Spangler & J. J. Wanko (Eds.), *Enhancing classroom practice with research behind Principles to Action* (pp. 13–26). Reston, VA: National Council of Teachers of Mathematics.

Broadfoot, P. (2008). *An introduction to assessment.* London, England: Continuum.

Butler, R. (1987). Task-involving and ego-involving properties of evaluation: Effects of different feedback conditions on motivational perceptions, interest, and performance. *Journal of Educational Psychology, 79*(4), 474–482.

Cox, D. C., Meicenheimer, J., & Hickey, D. (2017). Eliciting and using evidence of student thinking: Giving students voice. In D. A. Spangler & J. J. Wanko (Eds.), *Enhancing classroom practice with research behind Principles to Action* (pp. 89–97). Reston, VA: National Council of Teachers of Mathematics.

Davis, B. (1997). Listening for differences: An evolving conception of mathematics teaching. *Journal for Research in Mathematics Education, 28*(3). 355–376.

Goldin, G., & Shteingold, N. (2001). Systems of representations and the development of mathematical concepts. In A. A. Cuoco & F. R. Curcio (Eds.), *The roles of representation in school mathematics: 63rd Yearbook of the National Council of Teachers of Mathematics* (pp. 1–23). Reston, VA: National Council of Teachers of Mathematics.

Hiebert, J., & Wearne, D. (2003). Developing understanding through Problem Solving. In H. L. Schoen & R. I. Charles (Eds.), *Teaching mathematics through problem solving: Grades 6–12* (pp. 3–13). Reston, VA: National Council of Teachers of Mathematics.

Hodges, T. E., & Johnson, M. (2017). Representations as tools for mathematical understanding. In D. A. Spangler & J. J. Wanko (Eds.), *Enhancing classroom practice with research behind Principles to Action* (pp. 27–36). Reston, VA: NCTM.

Lappan, G., & Briars, D. (1995). How should mathematics be taught? In I. M. Carl (Ed.), *Prospects for school mathematics* (pp. 131–156). Reston, VA: National Council of Teachers of Mathematics.

Leahy, S., Lyon, C., Thompson, M., & Wiliam, D. (2005). Classroom assessment: Minute by minute, day by day. *Educational Leadership, 63*(3), 19–24.

Kluger, A. N., & DeNisi, A. (1996). The effects of feedback interventions on performance: A historical review, a meta-analysis, and a preliminary feed-back intervention theory. *Psychological Bulletin, 119*(2), 254–284.

Martin, W. G. (2009). The NCTM high school curriculum project: Why it matters to you. *Mathematics Teacher, 103*(3), 164–166.

National Council of Teachers of Mathematics (NCTM). (2014). *Principles to Action: Ensuring mathematics success for all.* Reston, VA: Author.

Ramaprasad, A. (1983). On the definition of feedback. *Behavioral Science, 28*, 4–13.

Reddy, L. A., Dudek, C. M., & Shernoff, E. S. (2016). Teacher formative assessment: The missing link in response to intervention. In S. R. Jimmerson, M. K. Burns, & A. M. VanDerHeyden (Eds.), *Handbook of response to intervention: The science and practice of multi-tiered systems of support* (2nd Ed.) (pp. 607–626). New York: Springer.

Staples, M., & King, S. (2017). Eliciting, supporting, and guiding the math: Three key functions of the teacher's role in facilitating mathematical discourse. In D. A. Spangler & J. J. Wanko (Eds.), *Enhancing classroom practice with research behind Principles to Action* (pp. 37–48). Reston, VA: National Council of Teachers of Mathematics.

Stein, M. K., Grover, B. W., & Henningsen, M. (1996). Building student capacity for mathematical thinking and reasoning: An analysis of mathematical tasks used in reform classrooms. *American Educational Research Journal, 33*(2), 455–88.

Stein, M. K., & Merkle, E. (2017). The nature and role of goals in and for mathematics instruction. In D. A. Spangler & J. J. Wanko (Eds.), *Enhancing classroom practice with research behind Principles to Action* (pp. 1–12). Reston, VA: National Council of Teachers of Mathematics.

Stein. M. K., Smith, M. S., Henningsen, M., & Silver, E. A. (2009). *Implementing standards-based mathematics instruction: A casebook for professional development.* 2nd ed. New York: Teachers College Press.

Wiliam, D., & Thompson, M. (2007). Integrating assessment with instruction: What will it take to make it work? In C. A. Dwyer (Ed.), *The future of assessment: Shaping teaching and learning* (pp. 53–82). Mahwah, NJ: Erlbaum.

Chapter 10

Formative Assessment and Equitable Mathematics Classrooms: Probing the Intersection

Marilyn E. Strutchens and Edward A. Silver

In recent years, many conceptions of educational equity have been proposed and considered. Some focus on achievement disparities, others on differential access to human and material resources, and others on systemic linkages to issues of race, language, culture, socioeconomic status or gender. Yet, at the core of these disparate views, we find a deep concern for the nature and the quality of the experience that schools and teachers offer students as opportunities to learn. In this regard, we find the writings of Pauline Lipman and colleagues (Lipman, 2002, 2004; Lipman & Gutstein, 2000) to be particularly compelling. For example, consider Lipman's assertion—

> All students need an education that is intellectually rich and rigorous, and that instills a sense of personal, cultural, and social agency—an education that helps students to think critically about the inequalities enveloping our lives while it prepares them for a wide range of academic and vocational choices . . . a commitment to educate all students requires the deployment of significant material and intellectual resources. (Lipman 2002, p. 411)

Applying this view of educational equity to school mathematics, we argue that equity can be realized in the mathematics classroom if and when teachers ensure that every student has regular opportunities to (1) encounter challenging mathematics tasks that call for reasoning and sense making; (2) learn worthwhile mathematics within contexts that are relevant and meaningful, and that reveal how mathematics can be used as a tool to examine and challenge inequality and injustice; and (3) develop proficiency in working collaboratively with peers to solve challenging problems along with a strong sense of personal agency and identity as a competent and confident doer of mathematics.

In the remainder of this chapter, we elaborate these core notions of educational equity in mathematics classrooms. We conclude by discussing some of the ways we see formative assessment practices being inextricably bound up in this vision of equitable mathematics classroom instruction. Along the way, we draw connections to the instructional approaches discussed in chapters 3–8 of this volume.

Unpacking Components of Equity in Mathematics Classrooms

Encounter Mathematics Tasks Calling for Reasoning and Sense Making

In an equitable classroom, a teacher should ensure that every student has opportunities to encounter mathematics tasks that call for reasoning about and making sense of mathematics and applying mathematical knowledge to solve complex problems. Reasoning is the process of drawing conclusions on the basis of evidence or stated assumptions (National Council of Teachers of Mathematics [NCTM] 2009, p. 4). Mathematical reasoning can range from informal explanations and justifications to formal deductions or inductive observations (NCTM, 2009, p. 4). Sense making is "developing understanding of a situation, context, or concept by connecting it with existing knowledge" (NCTM, 2009, p. 4). Reasoning and sense making often happen simultaneously.

The mathematics education community's interest in promoting reasoning and sense making in mathematics classrooms as a regular feature of instruction has deep roots in mathematics education (e.g., Fawcett, 1938; Pólya, 1945), but the level of interest has varied over time. After intense attention in the 1970s, community interest waned somewhat in the 1980s (Lester, 1994; Schoenfeld, 2007). Renewed attention was stimulated when NCTM published its standards for school mathematics programs (NCTM, 1989, 2000). One component of the Standards became known as "Process Standards," which complemented the more familiar Content Standards (i.e., mathematics topics to be taught and learned) and included the mathematical processes of problem solving, reasoning and proof, connections, communication, and representation.

Interest in developing students' proficiency with mathematical reasoning, problem solving, and sense making has continued with the advent of the Common Core State Standards for Mathematics (National Governor's Association [NGA] and the Council of Chief State School Officers [CCSSO] 2010), which include a set of Standards for Mathematical Practice that are similar in many ways to the earlier NCTM Process Standards. Among the standards for mathematical practice are the following: develop the ability to make sense of problems and persevere in solving them, reason abstractly and quantitatively, construct viable arguments and critique the reasoning of others, model with mathematics, look for and make use of structure, and look for and express regularity in repeated reasoning (NGA & CCSSO, 2010).

Any effort to promote reasoning and sense making as a regular feature of mathematics classroom instruction must attend to the central role that mathematics instructional tasks play in daily lessons in providing opportunities for students to learn mathematics. For example, the *Professional Standards for Teaching Mathematics* (NCTM, 1991) claimed that students' learning of worthwhile mathematics depends to a great extent on teachers using "mathematical tasks that engage students' interests and intellect" (p. 1). Such tasks, when implemented well in the classroom, can help develop students' understanding, maintain their curiosity, and invite them to communicate with others about mathematical ideas. Unfortunately, research on instructional practice has found both that such teaching does not occur regularly in U.S. mathematics classrooms (Porter, 1989; Stake & Easley, 1978; Stigler & Hiebert, 1999; Stodolsky, 1988), even when teachers display what they regard as their best practice (Silver, Mesa, Morris, Star, & Benken, 2009),

Mathematics tasks that encourage or require students to engage in reasoning and sense making are often called cognitively complex (Stein, Smith, Henningsen, & Silver, 2000). Promoting the successful use of such tasks in mathematics classrooms is challenging for teachers (Stein, Grover, & Henningsen, 1996), but research has demonstrated that the regular use of cognitively demanding tasks in ways that maintain high levels of cognitive demand can lead to increased student understanding and the development of problem solving and reasoning (Stein & Lane, 1997) and greater overall student achievement (Hiebert et al., 2005). It is these ideas that lie at the heart of the MTF, which is discussed extensively in chapter 7 (Smith & Steele), and the "five practices" (Smith & Stein, 2011), which are discussed in chapter 3 (Cirillo & Langer-Osuna). Interestingly, those instructional improvement suggestions emerged from the QUASAR project (Silver, Smith, & Nelson, 1995; Silver & Stein, 1996), an initiative driven by a commitment to promote educational equity in mathematics classrooms in schools serving low income communities that some scholars have argued "broadened the imagination of the field for national reform for marginalized children" (Gholson & Wilkes, 2017, p. 237).

Examples of cognitively demanding mathematics tasks appear often in chapters 3–7 in this book. Consider, for example, the task below (Task D; fig 10.1) that is discussed by Smith and Steele in chapter 7.

Task D (Doing mathematics)

You work for a small business that sells bicycles and tricycles. Bicycles have one seat, two pedals and two wheels. Tricycles have one seat, two pedals and three wheels.

On Monday, there are a total of 24 seats and 61 wheels in the shop. How many bicycles and how many tricycles are in the shop? Show all your work using any method you choose and explain your thinking.

Fig. 10.1. A cognitively demanding mathematics task

Smith and Steele (see chapter 7) discuss how a teacher might use Task D with students in a way that maintains the cognitive demand as students attempt to solve it. In so doing, Smith and Steele demonstrate how a teacher can help students to reason and make sense of mathematics and how a teacher may support productive struggle and increase students' confidence in their ability to solve such problems.

Levi and Ambrose (see chapter 4) illustrate that even very young children can be appropriately and productively engaged with tasks that call for them to reason about and make sense of mathematics problems. Cognitively Guided Instruction (CGI) is a problem-based approach to promote mathematics learning in the primary grades.

CGI is based on the premise that teachers can make productive use of research findings regarding how children think about problem situations and use mathematical ideas to make sense of the problems (Carpenter et al., 1996).

Research with young children has shown that—even before receiving formal instruction on basic addition, subtraction, multiplication, or division—children are able to solve many situational problems by modeling, counting, or inventing solutions that are not tied to traditional arithmetic computation. Knowing this corpus of research on children's reasoning and sense making invites teachers to think differently about how to design and enact their classroom lessons.

Levi and Ambrose (see chapter 4) describe the work of Ms. Harris, a second-grade teacher, as she plans her instruction, sets goals for individual students, selects an appropriate problem to engage her students and help them reach her instructional goals, orchestrates student-to-student discourse to move students to higher levels of thinking, and reflects on her lesson during and after the lesson. The authors use Ms. Harris to illustrate hallmarks of CGI encouraging teachers to—

- author their own problems based not only on their students' mathematical development but also on their interests and activities;
- assess students by closely observing and listening during individual interactions with children;
- convey high expectations for children by prompting them to attempt more sophisticated strategies when the time is right; and
- facilitate collaborative learning.

The vignette of Ms. Harris's teaching, along with many other examples of teaching provided in chapters 3–7, vividly illustrates the critical importance of basing mathematics lessons on cognitively demanding tasks that invite students to engage in reasoning and sense making.

It is also worth noting, in relation to formative assessment, that the use of cognitively demanding tasks in the mathematics classroom can create opportunities for students to make their mathematical thinking visible to themselves, other students, and the teacher. In this way, students allow teachers to gather evidence of their understanding that can guide instructional decision making.

Learn Mathematics in Contexts That Are Relevant and Meaningful

Closely related to the notion that cognitively demanding tasks are essential to mathematics classroom instruction, and consistent with a longstanding interest in helping students understand the application of mathematics to solve important problems, there has been a renewed interest in application contexts spurred by the CCSS emphasis on the mathematical practice of modeling. In addition, and with particular relevance to our vision of equity in mathematics classrooms, is the notion that relevant problem contexts can be found in the examination of social inequality, local community issues, or students' cultural backgrounds, and interests. The intention of this work is to help students to see that mathematics is used and developed by all people and to help motivate students to learn mathematics.

A number of scholars and educators have noted either the potential value of linking classroom instructional activity to students' culture and interests or the difficulties that arise when students do not see school mathematics as connected in any way to their lives. Though there are many seemingly different perspectives taken on this issue—such as culture and cognition (e.g., Saxe, 1991), inclusive mathematics (e.g., Strutchens, 1995, 2002), culturally responsive pedagogy (e.g., Ladson-Billings, 1995; Leonard, 2008; Bonner & Adams, 2012; Rubel & Chu, 2012; Tate, 1995; Wager, 2012), funds of knowledge (e.g., González, Andrade, Civil, & Moll 2001; Civil, 2008), social justice (e.g., Gutstein, 2003, 2012) and ethnomathematics (e.g., D'Ambrosio, 1985, 2001; Furuto, 2014)—there is large-scale agreement on the likely value of making explicit connections to students' lived experience for their engagement with and learning of mathematics in school. In this section, we discuss a few of these ideas as they pertain to our vision of equity in the mathematics classroom.

As Adams and Bonner discuss (see chapter 5) culturally responsive pedagogy incorporates tasks and situations that link explicitly to students lived experiences or topics that allow students to develop a sense of personal agency with respect to learning and using mathematics. Ford (2005) describes a culturally responsive classroom as one where—

1. Diversity is recognized and honored—a color-blind and culture-blind philosophy is avoided;

2. Cultural mismatches are minimal, not only among students, but also between teachers and students;

3. Teachers take the time to get to know students for the unique individuals they are—students feel physically and emotionally safe to be themselves;

4. Formal and informal, standardized and non-standardized assessments are fair and equitable;

5. Materials are culturally relevant and meaningful—students' backgrounds and experiences are central to teaching and learning;

6. Lesson plans and activities are infused with multicultural content that is respectful; and

7. Teachers display cultural sensitivity and competence (p. 30).

Adams and Bonner (see chapter 5) assert that culturally responsive pedagogy requires that teachers know their students in ways that support them to facilitate their students having meaningful interactions with mathematics through tasks and other learning experiences that are authentic. In chapter 5, Adams and Bonner describe how Ms. Pace used culturally relevant pedagogy.

See figure 10.2 for an excerpt from the vignette.

It is a typical day in Ms. Pace's class. Her sixth grade students are sitting in groups of three to four students working on a warm-up in preparation for a mathematics lesson. When the students have completed the warm-up, Ms. Pace says, "Recently, I have asked you to think about problems that we see in your community, and how we might be able to use mathematics to solve them. In your groups, I want you to write down two such problems and share them with the class."

After two minutes, student groups take turns discussing what they are seeing in their community. There is a lot of discussion around City Park located just one block from the school. The students really enjoy playing there, but would like to build a short fence around the playground area because of the high number of unleashed dogs in the area. After some initial discussion about this, the teacher launches the following task:

You are a city planner, and you want to know how much it will cost to build a short fence around the playground area at City Park. What information do you need to solve this problem? What is a good estimate of the cost of building a fence?

Fig. 10.2. A task used in a culturally responsive mathematics lesson

Through this vignette, Adams and Bonner illustrate how a teacher can use a cognitively demanding mathematics task in conjunction with culturally responsive pedagogy to orchestrate student engagement with and discourse about worthwhile mathematics, as students work in groups to solve the problem and then share solution strategies with their classmates.

In addition to the use of mathematics tasks that connect to students' lives, our vision of equitable mathematics classrooms also suggested the possibility that tasks could create opportunities for students to see how mathematics might be used as a tool to examine and challenge inequality and injustice. This idea is closely related to culturally responsive pedagogy and is often referred to as teaching for social justice. According to Gutstein (2007) teaching mathematics for social justice builds on students' culture and experiences and engages students in using mathematics to think about, and act on, the world, especially in relation to inequity and injustice.

Teaching for social justice entails engaging students in critical mathematics through a pedagogy of questioning, incorporating students' life experiences directly into the curriculum, helping students to develop sociopolitical consciousness, facilitating student's development of mathematical power (NCTM, 2000), using problems that motivate students to study and use mathematics, and cultivating students' sense of personal, cultural and social agency (Gutstein, 2006, 2012).

Gutstein (2006) described a lesson that he taught to middle school students entitled "Driving While Black or Brown. " Students were given the following information to ponder:

This is a sample of Illinois data based on police reports from 1987–1997. In an area of about 1,000,000 motorists, approximately 28,000 were Latinos/as.

Over a certain period of time, state police made 14,750 discretionary traffic stops (e.g., if a driver changes lanes without signaling, or drives 1 to 5 mph over the speed limit, police may stop her or him but do not have to). Of these stops 3,100 were of Latino/a drivers.

Fig. 10.3. A task used in mathematics for social justice lesson

Students were asked to determine whether racial profiling occurred through developing a mathematical simulation of the event. They were also asked to reflect on their findings and the lesson in general. During a lesson such as this, the teacher monitors students' mathematical processes, as well as their thinking about the social justice issue. This type of lesson affords students with the opportunity to determine how just an occurrence in society is through the use of mathematics in multiple ways. They can use theoretical and experimental probability to determine if the discretionary stops were influenced by a person's race. During the lesson, the teacher raises questions to the students, and the students respond to the teacher and to each other based on their mathematical findings and their beliefs about the situation. In this lesson, a social justice issue provided a context within which one or more cognitively demanding mathematics tasks were embedded. As students engaged with this situation and associated tasks, the teacher could both assess their mathematical reasoning and sense making and cultivate in students a disposition to use mathematics as a tool to address complex socio-political issues. Moreover, we think it likely that students would want to hold themselves accountable to a higher standard of argumentation on such issues because they know that the issues are likely to be controversial and evidence is likely to be viewed skeptically. A teacher could certainly make a compelling case to students for the need to produce a clear, concise, mathematically sound argument in order to have a chance of persuading and convincing skeptics.

Learn Collaboratively and Develop Mathematical Agency and Identity

The ideas discussed in relation to the first two principles of equitable mathematics classrooms have already highlighted the importance of cognitively demanding tasks as a basis for students to develop a positive mathematical identity—as mathematical thinkers who solve challenging problems, reason about relationships, and make sense of ideas. Experience with cognitively demanding tasks can also assist students in developing a sense of personal, cultural, and social agency in relation to their lived experience and to sociopolitical challenges they and their families may face in their communities. In addition to the use of tasks that can build a strong sense of agency, there are instructional practices that can also play an important role. Among the most important of these is the use of collaborative work to support individual student growth and to promote discourse among students about mathematical ideas.

The notions of agency, autonomy and identity are intertwined, but all refer at least in part to: beliefs about oneself as a mathematics learner and doer of mathematics, one's perceptions of how others perceive him or her as a mathematics learner, one's beliefs about the nature of mathematics and mathematical activity, and one's self-perception as a potential participant in mathematical activity (Solomon, 2009; Aguirre, Mayfield-Ingram, & Martin, 2013). In equitable mathematics classrooms, teachers and students not only capitalize on the knowledge and strengths that students bring with them to affirm them as learners, but also provide opportunity for every student to develop a sense of personal agency and confidence as a doer of mathematics.

The development of individual identity, agency and autonomy can often be supported through collaborative classroom work. Working with peer support, students not only learn to work productively with others but also to make visible ways that they can contribute to the learning and success of their peers. Critically important to the development of agency, identity and autonomy is the role of classroom discourse as discussed by Cirillo and Langer-Osuna (see chapter 3), especially in classrooms where collaborative learning is also used to support individuals as they solve cognitively demanding mathematics tasks and to encourage student-to-student discourse and discussion.

Teachers often use collaborative learning or cooperative group work to teach at a high academic level in diverse classrooms. In such settings, cognitively demanding tasks, including open-ended, interdependent group tasks, can be assigned, and the classrooms are organized to maximize student interaction. One pioneering version of this approach to support mathematics learning in classrooms with diverse student populations is called *complex instruction* (Cohen et al., 1994). One important feature of complex instruction is that teachers paid particular attention to unequal participation of students, and they employ strategies to address such status problems (Cohen, Lotan, Scarloss, & Arellano, 1999). Status perception is closely linked to how competent a student feels about himself or herself, as well as the extent to which a student is perceived as competent by his or her classroom peers (Horn, 2012). The use of cognitively demanding tasks and collaborative group work is intended to convey a sense of challenge and accomplishment, within a setting that supports each student to contribute to completing the task, and conveys the value of each student's contribution to success.

Boaler (2006) used *relational equity* to refer to what occurs when students learn both to appreciate the contributions of students from different cultural groups, social classes, genders, and attainment levels and to develop positive intellectual relations. Boaler (2006) has argued that students can develop these relationships through a collaborative problem-solving approach in which students work together and learn to appreciate the variety of insights, methods, and perspectives that different students can generate when solving problems together. Relational equity can develop both through experience with culturally relevant or historical situations and also through the collaborative solution of worthwhile mathematical tasks. To illustrate this point further, consider figure 10.4, which shows a mathematics task and some student comments about their experience in solving it collaboratively (Boaler, 2011).

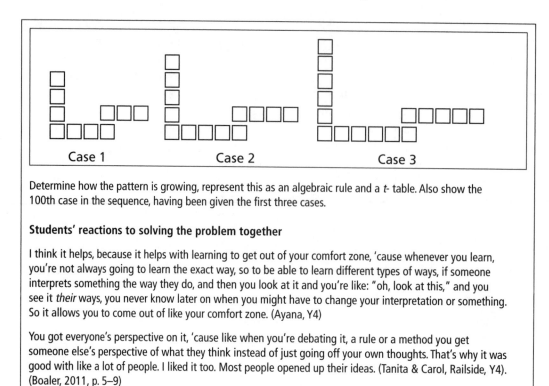

Determine how the pattern is growing, represent this as an algebraic rule and a *t-* table. Also show the 100th case in the sequence, having been given the first three cases.

Students' reactions to solving the problem together

I think it helps, because it helps with learning to get out of your comfort zone, 'cause whenever you learn, you're not always going to learn the exact way, so to be able to learn different types of ways, if someone interprets something the way they do, and then you look at it and you're like: "oh, look at this," and you see it *their* ways, you never know later on when you might have to change your interpretation or something. So it allows you to come out of like your comfort zone. (Ayana, Y4)

You got everyone's perspective on it, 'cause like when you're debating it, a rule or a method you get someone else's perspective of what they think instead of just going off your own thoughts. That's why it was good with like a lot of people. I liked it too. Most people opened up their ideas. (Tanita & Carol, Railside, Y4). (Boaler, 2011, p. 5–9)

Fig. 10.4. A mathematics task and students' responses to it

In complex instruction, such as CGI, the teacher is key to insuring that all students have an opportunity to participate and contribute, that multiple voices are heard in the classroom and that all students are respected and valued for their contributions to the collective reasoning and sense making about mathematics. In this regard, the role of classroom discourse and discussion, as discussed by Cirillo and Langer-Osuna (see chapter 3) is critically important. As the student quotes above suggest, it is through classroom discourse and discussion that students become aware of their own contributions, as well as those of peers, and the perceptions of value that peers convey when a student contributes to a group effort to solve a challenging problem. In addition, of course, the student-to-student discourse allows teachers to access evidence of students' reasoning and sense making. This information then informs not only teachers' short-term decisions about if and how to assist a student or collaborative group in their quest to solve a problem but also longer-term planning of future lessons or decisions about whether to reteach a topic about which students appear to be uncertain. The use of evidence of student thinking to make such instructional decisions is the heart of formative assessment. Moreover, collaborative experiences in the classroom can facilitate peer assessment and self-assessment, which in turn support the development of agency and identity.

Linking Instruction, Formative Assessment, and Equity

The vision of equitable mathematics classrooms discussed in this chapter suggests the importance of a problem-based approach to mathematics instruction. Students work individually and collaboratively on cognitively demanding mathematics tasks, which are often connected in important ways to students' lives. Teachers monitor student work on the tasks, probing students' reasoning and sense making and eliciting evidence of students' mathematical thinking and learning. Teachers then use the evidence of students' thinking to plan and enact next steps that will increase students' understanding of and proficiency with worthwhile mathematical concepts and skills. Students are treated as agents of their own mathematical activity and also as seen as intellectual resources for each other.

This characterization aligns well not only with our vision of equitable mathematics classrooms but also with Leahy et al.'s (2005) five strategies for effectively implementing formative assessment. Table 10.1 summarizes the core components of our proposed vision of the equitable mathematics classroom, the key features of classroom practice highlighted in our earlier discussion as being consistent with our vision and Leahy et al.'s (2005) five strategies.

Table 10.1. Summary of key features of equity, instruction and formative assessment

Equity in Mathematics Classrooms Equity is reached in the mathematics classroom when each and every student has the opportunity to:	Features of Equitable Mathematics Classrooms	Leahy et al.'s Five Formative Assessment Strategies
1. Encounter challenging mathematics tasks that call for reasoning and sense making;	1. Lessons use cognitively demanding mathematics tasks.	1. Clarifying and sharing learning intentions and criteria for success.
2. Learn worthwhile mathematics within contexts that are relevant and meaningful, and that reveal how mathematics can be used as a tool to examine and challenge inequality and injustice; and	2. Teachers monitor and probe student thinking about the mathematics or issue addressed in the problem, or both.	2. Engineering effective classroom discussions, questions, and learning tasks.
3. Develop proficiency in working collaboratively with peers to solve challenging problems along with a strong sense of personal agency and identity as a competent and confident doer of mathematics.	3. Teachers use this evidence of student thinking to make short- and long-term instructional decisions to support student learning.	3. Providing feedback that moves learners forward. 4. Activating students as the owners of their own learning. 5. Activating students as instructional resources for one another.
	4. Students are seen as agentic and as intellectual resources for each other.	

In our presentation in this chapter, we have tried to underscore several points made in other chapters in this book:

1. The centrality of using cognitively demanding tasks that are linked to worthwhile mathematical ideas that correspond to a teacher's curricular goals;

2. The key role of classroom discourse to promote students' learning and identity formation;

3. The importance of gathering evidence of student thinking, reasoning and sense making to gauge student progress and to inform teachers' instructional decision making; and

4. The value of multiple methods of supporting all students to learn important mathematical concepts and skills, including collaborative group work and scaffolded, individually tailored learning opportunities.

However, our intent was not simply to summarize these key points; rather we sought to emphasize the ways in which these instructional ideas are central to efforts to promote equitable mathematics classrooms.

We would assert that formative assessment is not only effective in promoting students' mathematics achievement in general but also essential to promoting our vision of the equitable mathematics classroom. In this regard, the ideas expressed by A. Wade Boykin (2014) resonate with us:

> Educational assessments should be coupled with a schooling purpose that emphasizes more human capacity building rather than sorting and selecting. The thrust here is that it is a societal good to foster extensive, high-level knowledge, skills, and abilities in intellectual, technical, and civic participation domains, for successive cohorts of the American population. And in turn, assessments should function principally to help actualize such human capital production. (p. 499)

The impact on student learning of the intentional and systematic use of formative assessment to improve student learning has been well documented. For example, an oft-cited study by Ehrenberg et al. (2001) estimated that the impact of formative assessment on student achievement was four to five times greater than the impact of reducing class size. Furthermore, Black and Wiliam (1998) reported that "improved [student-involved] formative assessment helps low achievers more than other students and so reduces the range of achievement while raising achievement overall" (p. 141).

Formative assessment is not just a nice thing to do if one has time, it is an essential component of our professional obligation to promote excellence and equity in mathematics education.

References

Aguirre, J. M., Mayfield-Ingram, & Martin, D. B. (2013). *The impact of identity in K–8 mathematics: Rethinking equity-based practices.* Reston, VA: National Council of Teachers of Mathematics.

Black, P., & Wiliam, D. (1998). Inside the back box: Raising standards through classroom assessment. *Phi Delta Kappan, 80*(2), 139–148.

Boaler, J. (2006). How a detracked mathematics approach promoted respect, responsibility, and high achievement. *Theory into Practice, 45*(1), 40–46.

Boaler, J. (2011). Stories of success: Changing students' lives through sense making and reasoning. In M. E. Strutchens & J. R. Quander (Eds.), *Focus in high school mathematics: Fostering reasoning and sense making for all students* (pp. 1–16). Reston, VA: National Council of Teachers of Mathematics.

Bonner, E., & Adams, T. (2012). Culturally responsive teaching in the context of mathematics: a grounded theory case study. *Journal of Mathematics Teacher Education, 15*(1), 25–38.

Boykin, A. W. (2014). Human diversity, assessment in education, and the achievement of excellence and equity. *The Journal of Negro Education, 83*(4), 499–521.

Carpenter, T. P., Fennema, E., & Franke, M. L. (1996). Cognitively guided instruction: A knowledge base for reform in primary mathematics instruction. *The Elementary School Journal, 97*(1), 3–20.

Civil, M. (2007). Building on community knowledge: An avenue to equity in mathematics education. In N. Nasir & P. Cobb (Eds.), *Improving access to mathematics: Diversity and equity in the classroom* (pp. 105–117). New York, NY: Teachers College Press.

Cohen, E. G., Lotan, R. A., Scarloss, B. A., & Arellano, A. R. (1999). Complex instruction: Equity in cooperative learning classrooms. *Theory into Practice, 38*(2), 80–86.

Cohen, E. G., Lotan, R. A., Whitcomb, J. A., Balderrama, M. V., Cossey, R., & Swanson, P. E. (1994). Complex instruction: Higher-order thinking in heterogeneous classrooms. In S. Sharan (Ed.), *Handbook of cooperative learning methods* (pp. 82–96). Westport, CT: Greenwood Press.

D'Ambrosio, U. (1985). Ethnomathematics and its place in the history and pedagogy of mathematics. For the *Learning of Mathematics, 5*(1), 44–48.

D'Ambrosio, U. (2001). What is ethnomathematics and how can it help children in schools? *Teaching Children Mathematics, 7*(6), 308–310.

Ehrenberg, R. G., Brewer, D. J., Gamoran, A., & Williams, J. D. (2001). Class size and student achievement. *Psychological Science in the Public Interest, 2*(1), 1–30.

Fawcett, H. P. (1938). The nature of proof. *Thirteenth yearbook of the National Council of Teachers of Mathematics.* New York: Teachers College.

Ford, D. Y. (2005). Welcoming all students to room 202: Creating culturally responsive classrooms. *Gifted Child Today, 28*, 28–30, 65.

Furuto, L. (2014). Pacific ethnomathematics: Pedagogy and practices in mathematics education *Teaching Mathematics and its Applications: International Journal of the IMA*, Oxford University Press.

Gholson, M. L., & Wilkes, C. E. (2017). (Mis) Taken identities: Reclaiming identities of the "collective black" in mathematics education research through an exercise in black specificity. *Review of Research in Education, 41*, 228–252.

González, N., Andrade, R., Civil, M., & Moll, L. (2001). Bridging funds of distributed knowledge: Creating zones of practices in mathematics. *Journal of Education for Students Placed at Risk, 6*(1/2), 115–132.

Gutstein, E. (2006). Driving while Black or Brown: The mathematics of racial profiling. In D. Mewborn (Series Ed.), J. Masingila (Vol. Ed.), *Teachers engaged in research: Inquiry in mathematics classrooms, grades 6–8. Vol.3* (pp. 99–118). Charlotte, NC: Information Age Publishing.

Gutstein, E. (May 2007). Possibilities and challenges in teaching mathematics for social justice. *Working Paper prepared for the Third Annual Symposium of the Maryland Institute for Minority Achievement and Urban Education*, College Park, MD.

Gutstein, E. (2012). Reflections on teaching and learning mathematics for social justice in urban schools. In A. A. Wager & D. W. Stinson (Eds.), *Teaching mathematics for social justice: Conversations with educators* (pp. 63–78). Reston, VA: National Council of Teachers of Mathematics.

Gutstein, E. (2003). Teaching and learning mathematics for social justice in an urban, Latino school. *Journal for Research in Mathematics Education, 34*, 37–73.

Hiebert, J., Stigler, J., Jacobs, J., Givvin, K., Garnier, H., Smith, M., et al. (2005). Mathematics teaching in the United States today (and tomorrow): Results from the TIMSS 1999 video study. *Educational Evaluation and Policy Analysis, 27*, 111–132.

Horn, I. S. (2013). *Strength in numbers: Collaborative learning in secondary mathematics.* Reston, VA: National Council of Teachers of Mathematics.

Ladson-Billings, G. (1995). But that's just good teaching! The case for culturally relevant pedagogy. *Theory into Practice, 34*(3), 159–165.

Leahy, S., Lyon, C., Thompson, M., & Wiliam, D. (2005). Classroom assessment: Minute by minute, day by day. *Educational Leadership, 63*(3), 19–24.

Leonard, J. (2008). *Culturally specific pedagogy in the mathematics classroom: Strategies for teachers and students.* New York: Routledge.

Lester, F. (1994). Musings about mathematical problem-solving research: The first 25 years in *JRME*. *Journal for Research in Mathematics Education, 25*(6), 660–675.

Lipman, P. (2002). Making the global city, making inequality: The political economy and cultural politics of Chicago school policy. *American Educational Research Journal, 39*(2), 379–419.

Lipman, P. (2004, April). *Regionalization of urban education: The political economy and racial politics of Chicago-metro region schools.* Paper presented at the annual meeting of the American Educational Research Association, San Diego, CA.

Lipman, P., & Gutstein, E. (2001). Undermining the struggle for equity: A case study of Chicago school policy in a Latino/a school June 1, 2000. *Race, Gender and Class*, 57–80.

National Council of Teachers of Mathematics. (1980). *An agenda for action.* Reston, VA: Author.

National Council of Teachers of Mathematics. (1989). *Curriculum and evaluation standards for school mathematics.* Reston, VA: Author.

National Council of Teachers of Mathematics. (1991). *Professional standards for teaching mathematics.* Reston, VA: Author.

National Council of Teachers of Mathematics. (1995). *Assessment standards for school mathematics.* Reston, VA: Author.

National Council of Teachers of Mathematics. (2000). *Principles and standards for school mathematics.* Reston, VA: Author.

National Council of Teachers of Mathematics. (2006). *Curriculum focal points for prekindergarten through grade 8 mathematics: A quest for coherence.* Reston, VA: Author.

National Council of Teachers of Mathematics. (2009). *Focus in high school mathematics: Reasoning and sense making.* Reston, VA: Author.

National Council of Teachers of Mathematics. (2014). *Principles to actions: Ensuring mathematical success for all.* Reston, VA: Author.

National Governors Association Center for Best Practices and Council of Chief State School Officers. (2010). *Common core state standards for mathematics.* Washington, DC: Authors.

Pólya, G. (1945). *How to solve it (2nd edition, 1957).* Princeton: Princeton University Press.

Porter, A. (1989). A curriculum out of balance: The case of elementary school mathematics. *Educational Researcher, 18*(5), 9–15.

Rubel, L., & Chu, H. (2012). Reinscribing urban: teaching high school mathematics in low income, urban communities of color. *Journal of Mathematics Teacher Education, 15*(1), 39–52.

Saxe, G. B. (1991). *Culture and cognitive development: Studies in mathematics understanding.* Hillsdale, NJ: Lawrence Erlbaum.

Schoenfeld, A. H. (2007). Problem solving in the United States, 1970–2008: Research and theory, practice and politics. *ZDM, 39*(5–6), 537–551.

Silver, E. A., Mesa, V., Morris, K. A., Star, J. R., & Benken, B. M. (2009). Teaching mathematics for understanding: An analysis of lessons submitted by teachers seeking NBPTS certification. *American Educational Research Journal, 46*(2), 501–531.

Silver, E. A., Smith, M. S., & Nelson, B. S. (1995). The QUASAR project: Equity concerns meet mathematics education reform in the middle school. In W. Secada, E. Fennema, & L. Byrd Adajian (Eds.), *New directions in equity in mathematics education* (pp. 9–56). New York: Cambridge University Press.

Silver, E. A., & Stein, M. K. (1996). The QUASAR project: The "revolution of the possible" in mathematics instructional reform in urban middle schools. *Urban Education, 30*(4), 476–521.

Solomon, Y. (2009). *Mathematical literacy. Developing identities of inclusion.* New York: Routledge.

Stake, R. E., & Easley, J. (1978). *Case studies in science education.* Urbana, IL: University of Illinois.

Stein, M. K., Grover, B. W., & Henningsen, M. (1996). Building capacity for mathematical thinking and reasoning: An analysis of mathematical tasks used in reform classrooms. *American Educational Research Journal, 33*, 455–488.

Stein, M. K., & Lane, S. (1996). Instructional tasks and the development of student capacity to think and reason: An analysis of the relationship between teaching and learning in a reform mathematics project. *Educational Research and Evaluation, 2*(1), 50–80.

Stein, M. K., Smith, M. S., Henningsen, M., & Silver, E. A. (2000). *Implementing standards-based mathematics instruction.* New York: Teachers College Press.

Stigler, J. W., & Hiebert, J. (1999). *The teaching gap.* New York: The Free Press.

Stigler, J. W., Gonzalez, P., Kawanaka, T., Knoll, S., & Serrano, A. (1999). *The TIMSS videotape classroom study: Methods and findings from an exploratory research project on eighth-grade mathematics instruction in Germany, Japan, and the United States.* (NCES 1999-074). Washington, DC: U.S. Department of Education: National Center for Education Statistics.

Stodolsky, S. S. (1988). *The subject matters: Classroom activities in math and social sciences.* Chicago: University of Chicago.

Strutchens, M. (1995). Multicultural mathematics: A more inclusive mathematics. *Eric Digest, Clearinghouse for Science, Mathematics, and Environmental Education*, EDO-SE-95-3, March.

Strutchens, M. (2002). Multicultural literature as a context for mathematical problem solving: Children and parents learning together. *Teaching Children Mathematics, 8*(8), 448–454.

Strutchens, M. E., & Martin, W. G. (2017). Transforming preservice secondary mathematics teachers' practices: Promoting mathematical problem solving and sense making. In T. Brush & J. Saye (Eds.), *Developing and Supporting PBL Practice: Research in K–12 and Teacher Education Settings.* Purdue Press.

Tate, W. (1995). Mathematics communication: Creating opportunities to learn. *Arithmetic Teacher, 1*(6), 344–349, 369.

Wager, A. (2012). Incorporating out-of-school mathematics: from cultural context to embedded practice. *Journal of Mathematics Teacher Education, 15*(1), 9–23.

Chapter 11

A Vision for Professional Learning Design that Repositions and Reinforces Formative Assessment Practices

Valerie L. Mills and Marjorie Petit

Implications for Professional Learning Design: A New Approach in Support of Formative Assessment Understanding and Use

At this point in the book, readers will have begun to understand the powerful relationship between formative assessment and many effective mathematics teaching practices. Clearly, when formative assessment is understood to be a process of setting expectations, gathering evidence, and adjusting instruction to advance learning, recognizing key elements of this process within other instructional designs become straightforward. Whether it is a *framework* such as the Mathematical Tasks Framework, a *tool,* such as OGAP that defines a learning progression, or an *approach,* such as Culturally Responsive Pedagogy, the formative assessment process is frequently found at the heart of effective instruction. These explicit examples help us to understand more deeply what Paul Black and Dylan Wiliam (1998) meant when they wrote 20 years ago, "Indeed, it is clear that instruction and formative assessment are *indivisible.*"

The first chapter of this volume reminded us that there is broad agreement among the research and practice communities, regarding formative assessment's power to advance learning outcomes for all students. It also reminded us that U.S. educators have been challenged to understand the indivisible nature of instruction and formative assessment and therefore have been slow to adopt these practices as intended. We wonder then, what might the leadership community do differently with both preservice and in-service teachers to change this reality? Would a different approach to teaching the formative assessment process and accompanying strategies help educators make these needed connections and motivate adoption more swiftly and effectively? Finally, we ask, what would such a different approach look like?

Let's begin by considering how professional learning activities for formative assessment are typically presented to educators today. The illustration below for model 1 (fig. 11.1) is intended to suggest that the approach currently used with both preservice and in-service teachers addresses formative assessment as one of several distinctly different and separate topics to be understood and adopted for use in classrooms individually.

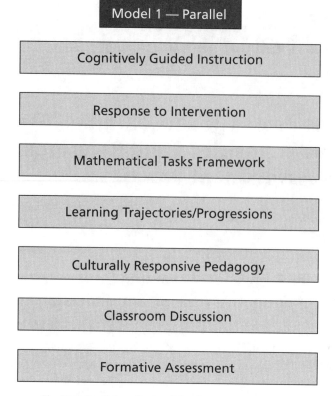

Fig. 11.1. Parallel professional development experiences

In this model, multiple parallel professional learning efforts are developed and implemented for different groups of educators, or in some cases the same educators, over time. Each effort is a separate professional learning experience, focused on a different set of topics, including the professional learning activities for formative assessment. Data from the 2014 NCSM/AMTE survey of professional learning practices suggests that many educational leaders offer two to four separate strands of professional learning for teachers each year. It also indicated that relatively few of these leaders make use of formative assessment connections within other professional learning activities. As model 1 suggests, the ideas explored in various professional learning experiences are treated as *unique* to a particular topic. However, understanding that formative assessment is not distinct from other important instructional topics positions us to wonder if this stand-alone professional learning model is optimal. Put another way, how might formative assessment connections be leveraged to improve our current professional learning model?

One possibility would be to organize the professional learning activities in a way that makes formative assessment connections *visible within* professional learning activities for the other related instructional topics. Consider a second approach represented by model 2, an integrated model (see fig. 11.2).

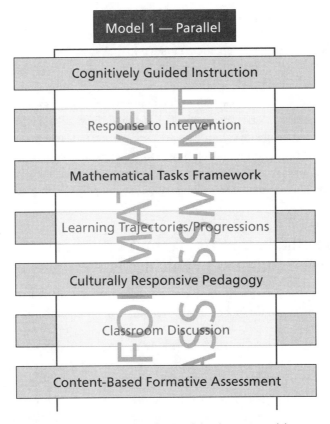

Fig. 11.2. Integrated professional development model

Here the process of formative assessment remains available as a focus for study *and* is woven into discussions for each of the other frameworks, tools, and approaches. With an integrated model, formative assessment becomes a thread that is visible within many instructional topics. From a teacher's perspective, they experience multiple opportunities to learn about formative assessment in ways that are clearly *connected* to instruction. An integrated model means that a teacher does not have to stop learning about formative assessment each time they explore something new. Rather this model allows the teacher's focus to remain connected to the process of employing strategies to elicit and act on evidence of student learning *while* they consider other important instructional ideas. It is interesting to notice that different frameworks, tools, and approaches naturally draw attention to different elements of the formative assessment process. With an integrated model professional learning activities would allow for a periodic deep dive into individual elements of the formative assessment process without losing track of the process as a whole. For example, during a study of the OGAP framework and its use in daily instruction, one of the foci would be on using learning progressions to analyze learning evidence found in student work. This focus affords teachers the opportunity to think carefully and deeply about the last phase in a formative assessment cycle: how to move learners from where they currently are to the appropriate next step in the learning progression. Other frameworks, tools, and approaches naturally offer opportunities to look carefully at different formative assessment elements. Other examples include a professional learning series on classroom discourse that offers a close examination of questioning to gather evidence of learning and a study of CGI focusing on the use of clinical

173

interviews to gather evidence of student learning associated with arithmetic operations. Both of these additional examples allow the learners to dig into a challenging aspect of the formative assessment process while exploring another framework, tool, or approach to effective instruction.

In addition to allowing for the close examination of formative assessment elements from different points of view, an integrated approach to professional learning design honors what we know about the time needed for teachers to understand fully new strategies and to translate them into the particulars of their practice. Professional learning designs, like the Integrated Model, intentionally plan for recurring opportunities to examine formative assessment. This approach both acknowledges the need for multiple learning experiences and supports the implementation of new pedagogies over time. An integrated approach to formative assessment professional learning design has the potential to develop deeper understanding and perhaps, more effective use of the process in classrooms.

Extrapolating the Power of Coherent Curriculum and Instruction for Student Learning to Enhance Professional Learning

The possibility of deepening teachers' understanding of the formative assessment process is by itself a powerful reason to embed the topic across multiple instructional conversations. However, there is a second opportunity that is both more subtle and simultaneously transformative for professional learning design. The second opportunity that the Integrated Model affords us is the opportunity to broadly cohere professional learning experiences for educators across topics and over time. It is a shift that moves our thinking about the knowledge needed for teaching from a collection of disparate skills and topics toward an understanding of *related* instructional competencies. In this mindset, effective teaching requires a constellation of competencies that reinforce, connect, and strengthen one another. Together, they form a connected coherent vision of instructional knowledge that is capable of advancing learning for each and every student. For professional learning design, this vision suggests a move toward creating experiences that introduce new ideas in ways that make connections to previous understanding visible and explicit. Effective professional learning would be designed to continuously broaden and deepen previously acquired knowledge and instructional efficacy over time. It is interesting to notice that there was a parallel shift in thinking about teaching and learning for students during mathematics education's "standards-based movement" of the 1980s and 90s. This foundational shift sought to develop an understanding of mathematics as a connected coherent set of concepts, representations, and skills to be developed over time with increasing complexity and sophistication. The move toward a more coherent vision of mathematics curricula and instruction was understood to be beneficial to students for a number of reasons, each of which was connected to what we have come to understand about instruction that supports learning for a diverse range of learners. An examination of these ideas as applied to adult learning offers us insights into both *why* and *how* greater coherence in professional learning might be beneficial. The arguments for greater coherence in school mathematics include—

- enabling learners to connect prior knowledge of practice to new teaching and learning insights;
- developing deeper learning that persists; and
- making visible the utility of new learning.

What follows is an examination of these three affordances for student learning to understand why and how establishing greater coherence in professional learning could be productive for educators as well.

Instructional Coherence Enabling Learners to Connect Prior Knowledge of Practice to New Teaching and Learning Insights

The opening section of *Principles and Standards for School Mathematics* (NCTM, 2000) names six fundamental principles that describe high quality mathematics education and includes the Curriculum Principle. It reads, "A coherent curriculum effectively organizes and integrates important mathematical ideas so that students can see how the ideas build on, or connect with, other ideas, thus enabling them to develop new understandings and skills" (NCTM, 2000, pp. 14–15). Extending this rationale into the context of learning for educators, we consider professional learning design. Parallel to a coherent curriculum for students learning mathematics, a coherent approach to professional learning would effectively organize, sequence, and integrate important instructional practices. Such an approach would enable teachers to see the connections among various strategies and frameworks. Further, it would encourage teachers to improve their practice by connecting to and building on prior knowledge of how students learn and the skills needed to advance learning. Imagine the advantage we create for teachers who already understand the formative assessment process when we position new learning around CGI as an instructional framework that uses a process they already understand. Turning the order around, consider teachers who have learned to recognize and use formative assessment as an embedded element in CGI. For these teachers, the formative assessment process is a useable tool not only when teaching early number and operations, but also for teaching other mathematical topics such as geometry or measurement. In both cases, a teacher's thinking about growing their practice shifts from the work needed to acquire an entirely new single-purpose skill to an elaboration of ideas already understood that are now usable for new purposes. This approach to professional learning design encourages the learner to bring all of their past classroom experiences to bear on understanding and implementing new learning. It is useful not only because it is likely to support more efficient flexible learning over time, but also because it encourages the development of reflective habits of mind for practitioners. Professional learning activities that ask practitioners to build new ideas from prior knowledge and experience offers learners' evidence that a reflective stance toward practice is a critical element of continuous professional growth.

Instructional Coherence Develops Deeper Learning That Persists

There is a second rationale for a coherent approach to teaching and learning mathematics that we can take from *Principles and Standards for School Mathematics* and apply to professional learning. "When students can connect mathematical ideas, their understanding is deeper and more lasting" (NCTM, 2000, p. 64). This quote is a reminder that while coherence is about taking up new ideas more effectively as described above, it is also about supporting a learner's ability to hold onto a set of competencies. When considering learning for students and teachers alike, bringing past understanding and experiences to bear on the challenges of learning new ideas is important. It allows the learner to leverage prior knowledge in the service of learning new applications or new related concepts in a way that reinforces prior knowledge and sustains learning. Building on prior knowledge is a powerful tool for developing depth *and* sustaining learning for students and teachers. Whether it is a *student* learning to use the distributive property with variables in a way that is connected to their understanding of multiplying whole numbers or a *teacher* learning to select tasks for formative assessment purposes by drawing on her experience selecting and using high-demand tasks. While not every slice of the teaching and learning universe intersects with formative assessment, it makes sense for us to exploit the opportunities where they do exist.

Instructional Coherence Makes Visible the Utility of New Learning

The third and final argument in support of a more coherent approach to professional learning builds on our understanding that real-world contexts employed to teach mathematics can suggest to students that mathematics is a powerful, useful tool. *Principles and Standards for School Mathematics* notes this connection in the section that describes the Connections Standard, "Through instruction that emphasizes the interrelatedness of mathematical ideas, students not only learn mathematics, they also learn about the utility of mathematics" (NCTM, 2000, p. 64). For teachers, positioning formative assessment as a process with a vital role in a variety of research-based frameworks, tools and approaches can also suggest to teachers that the *utility* of formative assessment in their practice is far greater than that of an early warning system for student learning. Our understanding of its usefulness is illuminated and extended when we notice that formative assessment strategies intersect with effective classroom discourse strategies. Its utility is enhanced when one identifies the formative assessment engine operating inside RTI and CGI. Noticing the presence of formative assessment in so many research-based frameworks, tools, and approaches may also suggest that this process occupies a place of foundational importance in effective teaching and learning. For this reason, understanding the import of formative assessment is likely to heighten teachers' need to fully understand and more effectively incorporate the process into their daily practice. In this way formative assessment becomes the generative locus of teacher reflection guiding practice and prompting further exploration. When professional learning emphasizes the interrelatedness of formative assessment as a connector across professional learning sessions, topics, and even years, teachers are afforded the opportunity to develop an awareness of formative assessment's utility that can motivate and support the ongoing development of one's practice.

Moving Toward an Integrated Model for Professional Learning

Understanding the power and possibility of a more coherent integrated approach to professional learning design leads one naturally to wonder how preservice and in-service leaders might go about designing activities for more coherent professional learning experiences. Further, one wonders where and how leaders might insert this through-line across professional learning experiences. To do this, facilitators will need to identify opportunities to connect formative assessment to the goals associated with other important professional learning topics. As with instruction for students, it will be important for facilitators to plan in advance for the best ways and times to make these connections to formative assessment visible. Preservice and in-service leaders will be able to consider opportunities to connect formative assessment to other instructional learning in at least two different ways. First, facilitators can look for connections that can be made to one or more of the components in the formative assessment process:

- Establishing learning goals;
- Gathering evidence of student's current thinking; and
- Making instructional decisions based on evidence to advance learning toward the goals.

Second, facilitators can look for opportunities to make connection to *instructional strategies* typically associated with formative assessment; consider, for example, the strategies described by Leahy et al. (2005)—

- clarifying and sharing learning intentions and criteria for success;
- engineering effective classroom discussions, questions, and learning tasks;
- providing feedback that moves learners forward;
- activating students as the owners of their learning; and
- activating students as instructional resources for one another.

An example of connecting to the formative assessment *process* might involve intentionally planning to reference the ways teachers can collect evidence of student thinking during a workshop on the use of learning progressions for secondary function concepts. Thinking about connections to formative assessment *strategies*, facilitators may plan to connect teachers' prior experiences engineering effective classroom discussions to support new work on improving student engagement and sense of agency with regards to learning mathematics. Notice that the equity context of this last example is outside the six frameworks, tools, and approaches highlighted in the pages of this book. It should be noted that while the six in this book are well-known subjects for professional learning programs, they are not the only productive subjects in which formative assessment's process and strategies can be used to cohere and strengthen learning. Leaders are encouraged to look for and exploit connections between formative assessment and other instructional approaches wherever they exist.

Formative assessment's *process* and *strategies* are two avenues for embedding planned connections during professional learning. In addition, it is also likely that formative assessment may be useful in responding to "unplanned openings" that occur during professional learning. Remillard and Geist describe "unplanned openings" as unanticipated questions, challenges, observations, or actions from participating teachers that require facilitators to make on-the-spot judgments about how to guide the discourse (Remillard & Geist, 2002). Their analysis of difficult situations faced by facilitators in supporting teachers' learning through an inquiry process suggested that navigating these "unplanned openings" was the central challenge of this work (Remillard & Geist, 2002). Because formative assessment is tied to many aspects of effective instruction, facilitators who are aware of this relationship may be able to respond productively to such openings by exploiting connections between the question or dilemma raised by a participant, and formative assessment strategies that are already familiar to participants. For example, consider a professional learning session designed to support the implementation of a new textbook with cognitively demanding tasks. In this setting, participants may raise the dilemma of deciding how to facilitate the summary discussion of a task that has multiple valid solution strategies— Where do you start? Do you share all of the strategies with the class, some of the strategies, or only one? One possible facilitator response to this "unplanned opening" is to ask participants to recall and consider applying strategies previously used to collect evidence of student thinking while students are working on the task. Could these familiar formative assessment strategies be deployed now to support decisions of sorting and selecting strategies for the summary discussion? What data would you need to collect? How might a mapping of the data you collect to your learning goals help you think about orchestrating a summary discussion? Understanding the highly connected nature of the formative assessment process and its associated strategies provides leaders with a powerful toolbox of options for unplanned professional learning moments. Particularly in contexts that honor a stance of inquiry for teacher learning, facilitators will surely find these tools indispensable for navigating the challenging but inevitable "unplanned openings."

Summary

An acknowledgment that formative assessment practices are challenging for educators and that there is an intersecting relationship between formative assessment and many of the popular research-based mathematics education frameworks, tools, and approaches leads one almost directly to reconsider professional learning designs typically employed for formative assessment practices. In contrast to a traditional model that addresses mathematics education topics as separate professional learning experiences, an Integrated Model, that weaves formative assessment conversations throughout professional learning activities on other topics, seems to be a more productive approach. This model addresses the demands of becoming proficient with the formative assessment process and offers additional affordances for teachers. Building on what we know about the importance of a coherent presentation of mathematics for student learning, there is reason to suspect that the coherence of an integrated professional learning model may also be useful. Coherence across professional learning topics has the potential to support a more reflective, generative disposition toward growing teacher practice and a deeper understanding of formative assessment that is more likely to persist. Finally, this model is likely to make visible the utility and centrality of formative assessment in effective teaching and learning.

In the twenty years since the mathematics education community was made aware of the potential of formative assessment to support higher achievement for our students, our understanding of the challenges associated with widespread implementation of this process have evolved. In addition, we now recognize the intersecting relationship of formative assessment with many of the other research-based frameworks, tools and approaches. Moving forward, we have an opportunity to use these connections to adapt our professional learning practices in ways that can address the implementation difficulties we better understand today. Leaders are now positioned to leverage the connections between formative assessment and other key instructional resources in the service of deeper understanding and more effective applications of formative assessment. An Integrated Model for professional learning offers real promise for advancing practice and moving the profession closer to realizing formative assessment's full potential for improving student achievement.

References

Black, P., & Wiliam, D. (1998). Inside the back box: Raising standards through classroom assessment. *Phi Delta Kappan, 80*(2), 139–148.

Leahy, S., Lyon, C., Thompson, M., & Wiliam, D. (2005). Classroom assessment: Minute by minute, day by day. *Educational Leadership, 63*(3), 19–24.

National Council of Teachers of Mathematics. (2000). *Principles and standards for school mathematics.* Reston, VA: Author.

Remillard, J. T., & Kaye Geist, P. (2002). Supporting teachers' professional learning by navigating openings in the curriculum. *Journal of Mathematics Teacher Education, 5*(1) 7–34.

Chapter 12

Putting It All Together and Moving Forward: Concluding Thoughts

Valerie L. Mills and Edward A. Silver

We close this volume with a few reflections on what has been offered in the previous chapters and some thoughts regarding the need for additional shifts in our evolving understanding of formative assessment and the design of professional learning to support its use.

First, we want to underscore the valuable contribution that the authors of chapters 3 through 8 have made in explicating the connections that were anticipated and speculated about in chapters 1 and 2 between formative assessment and other powerful instructional frameworks that have been important to teachers of mathematics. These chapters help us understand how members of the mathematics education community who are engaged in working with preservice and in-service teachers of mathematics might be able to capitalize on prior work done in our field regarding cognitively guided instruction, learning trajectories, classroom mathematical discourse, cognitively demanding mathematics tasks, and culturally responsive pedagogy to leverage even greater improvements in mathematics teaching and learning through explicit attention to closely related formative assessment practices. Further, the chapter on RtI illustrates a possible convergence of mainstream mathematics education with the dominant instructional approach to accommodating learners with special needs.

Each of these chapters has appropriately focused on the work of teachers, and the role that formative assessment practices play in effective mathematics teaching viewed through the lenses of different instructional frameworks. In particular, the focus was on the work of teachers as they establish learning goals, as they gather evidence of student thinking, and as they use work to adjust instructional plans to advance the learning. In each chapter, the authors examined *instruction* with attention to the critical work of *teachers* in planning, implementing, and reflecting for formative assessment. In this way, they have positioned formative assessment as a process *central* to effective mathematics instruction, rather than an additional set of practices to be *added* to instruction.

Focusing on the teacher and the work of teaching is a valuable perspective. But we think there might be much to gain by also focusing on formative assessment as a process of facilitating the *work of learning.* Doing so draws our attention to the fact that there is another important actor in the classroom, namely, the student.

One might say that the student is portrayed as a "silent partner" in much of the formative assessment literature within the domain of mathematics education. Of course, it is clear that students are present as producers of the work that teachers analyze in order to make informed instructional decisions, and in the chapters of this volume we find students playing that role. But we think there may be additional ways in which students can be positively engaged in and influenced by formative assessment practices.

In line with this point of view, we see evidence of educators beginning to focus more and more on the role of students in formative assessment. For example, the new FAST SCASS definition (see fig. 1.1) brings greater attention to students by listing them before teachers and by replacing the word *instruction* with *teaching and learning*. Other examples can be found throughout Chapter 10. Here the authors explore formative assessment's contributions to equitable achievement by illustrating how the formative assessment process can promote a more active, self-aware role for students, which enhances the development of self-efficacy and positive identity with respect to mathematics.

This analysis of the process focuses on the positive effects of students' beliefs about themselves when they are given tools to monitor and direct their own learning. Outside this volume, British researcher Sue Swaffield (2011) notes, "All the practices identified by Black and William in their review shared a common feature—active involvement of students. Pupils are cast as partners in the learning process, rather than as passive recipients of knowledge transmitted or delivered by the teacher." From her perspective, students can also be seen as engaged in self-assessment, monitoring their understanding and proficiency in relation to the instructional goals and ready to solicit additional assistance as needed to promote their attainment of the goals.

Though foregrounding the role of teachers in the formative assessment process is critical for its effective use, it is important that we not ignore or minimize the role of students. In formative assessment, one important lesson that we derive from studies of mathematics teaching and learning in so-called high-performing countries is the observation that the intellectually demanding work of learning mathematics requires the active participation of teachers and students. Teachers on their own cannot make students learn mathematics; students must become partners in their own learning in order for effective teaching and learning to occur.

Going forward we think that both research on and the practical application of formative assessment in mathematics classrooms will benefit from a more balanced attention to the student's role and the teacher's role. Following the lead of FAST SCASS, shifting our thinking about formative assessment from an instructional process to a process embedded in both *learning* and *teaching* would be a productive first step.

Another aspect that was not prominently displayed and discussed in this volume, but that we see as important for future research and practice in this area is the use of technology. By this we refer not so much to the technology-based monitoring, testing, and grading systems that abound in the educational marketplace. Rather, we are thinking about creative uses of technology to support what we understand to be good instructional practice such as digital systems that provide scaffolding of student learning through tailored, graduated assistance (Noss & Hoyles, 1996). Other examples are based in the use of graphing calculator technologies. Both handheld tools, such as the TI-Nspire, and online applications, such as Desmos, will allow a teacher to efficiently review each student's work displayed simultaneously on a single computer screen.

Teachers can easily use these systems to collect real-time evidence of student thinking and to inform next instructional decisions. Decisions might include a teacher selecting a few or all of the calculator displays to share with the whole class as the context for a whole group discussion comparing differing strategies or as an opportunity for students to engage first in peer and then self-assessment prior to a whole group discussion. In line with our comments above about paying more attention to the active role of students in the formative assessment process, we note that some recent work has explored the possibility of using student-activated, learner-controlled scaffolding in digital learning environments (Edson, 2017).

Recognizing the ubiquity of technology both inside and outside contemporary mathematics classrooms, we think it is important for us to examine rigorously the affordances provided by digital tools and systems to enhance all aspects of mathematics teaching and learning, including the formative assessment practices of teachers and their students. Innovative uses of technology to support mathematics teaching and learning with an emphasis on supporting students' reasoning and sense making have been introduced in recent years (e.g., Dick & Hollebrands, 2011) suggest many ways that digital tools can support formative assessment that go well beyond the limited use of technology merely to deploy interim assessments or to keep detailed records of student progress along some hypothesized continuum. In addition to the innovative technology work in the United States., we think the work of teachers and researchers in Italy offers one useful example of how collaborations might be formed to examine the uses of technological tools and systems in relation to formative assessment practices in mathematics teaching and learning (Aldon, Cusi, Morselli, Panero, & Sabena, 2017; Cusi, Morselli, & Sabena, 2017).

Finally, another shift we would propose in the evolution of our thinking about formative assessment regards the design of professional learning to support its use. For many in the field, formative assessment, with its process steps and strategies, is an approach that is independent of the content area in which it is being employed. Such thinking leads to "content neutral" treatment of formative assessment practices in professional development for teachers.

Though there are certainly features of formative assessment practice that apply across multiple domains, the discussions and examples provided in this volume demonstrate not only the value and importance of attending closely to specific content issues in order to engage in formative assessment successfully but also the ways in which formative assessment done well can lead to enhanced teaching and learning of subject matter. In our view, every step of the formative assessment process requires deep disciplinary knowledge to implement effectively.

It is no coincidence that the authors of the chapters associated with each of the frameworks, tools, and approaches found in this book discuss the connections to formative assessment though a disciplinary lens. Knowledge of teaching and learning in each discipline is at the heart of every instructional decision in the formative assessment process. Effectively setting student learning goals and revising instruction based on evidence of learning requires grappling with the constellation of learning goals in a unit of study and the particular teaching and learning progression for each topic. Selecting a task to be used within the formative assessment process requires careful thought about the potential a task has to reveal what students do and do not understand. Further, it requires attention to how the task discussion will be facilitated so that it allows teachers and students to gather evidence of student learning around specific goals.

The effective use of formative assessment requires minute-by-minute instructional decisions that are not separate from the particulars of the subject being taught; rather, they are integral to the particulars of the subject being taught. The role of content knowledge and pedagogical content knowledge in formative assessment decision-making suggests users will need learning experiences that marry process and discipline. Leaders in both preservice and in-service educational communities need to ensure that formative assessment professional learning activities are positioned within the contexts of the disciplines in which teachers will be using the process. We believe that embedding professional learning about formative assessment within a specific disciplinary framework can create opportunities for teachers to grapple with and learn about the specific instructional decisions they need to make to assist their students in learning the intended mathematical content.

We hope this volume will be both a useful source for mathematics educators seeking to foreground the importance of formative assessment in their work with teachers of mathematics and a stimulus for further research and development in this territory. By emphasizing formative assessment as an integral part of effective mathematics teaching, linked in important ways to a host of other ideas we recognize as central to effective mathematics teaching, we can make greater progress toward our collective goal of equity and excellence in mathematics teaching and learning.

References

Aldon, G., Cusi, A., Morselli, F., Panero, M., & Sabena, C. (2017). Formative assessment and technology: Reflections developed through the collaboration between teachers and researchers. In G. Aldon, F. Hitt, L. Bazzini, & U. Gellert (Eds.), *Mathematics and technology: A CIEAEM source book* (pp. 551–578). Dordrecht: Springer.

Cusi, A., Morselli, F., & Sabena, C. (2017). Promoting formative assessment in a connected classroom environment: Design and implementation of digital resources. *ZDM Mathematics Education, 49*, 755–767.

Dick, T. P., & Hollebrands, K. F. (2011). *Focus in high school mathematics: Technology to support reasoning and sense making.* Reston, VA: National Council of Teachers of Mathematics.

Edson, A. J. (2017). Learner-controlled scaffolding linked to open-ended problems in a digital learning environment. *ZDM Mathematics Education, 49*, 735–753.

Noss, R., & Hoyles, C. (1996). *Windows on mathematical meanings: Learning cultures and computers.* Dordrecht: Springer.

Swaffield, S. (2011). Getting to the heart of authentic assessment for learning. *Assessment in Education: Principles, Policy and Practice, 18*(4), 441–443.